Dr Ashley's Pleasure Yacht

Robrulln
with good mkin

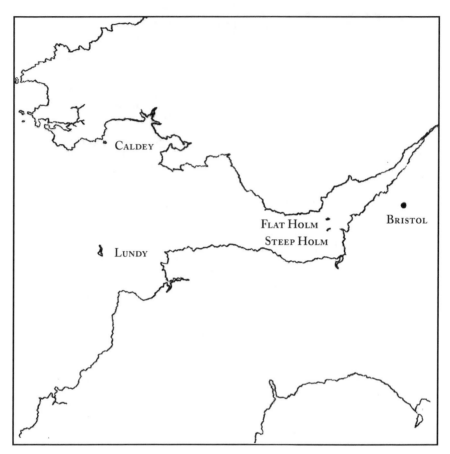

A Map of the Bristol Channel

Dr Ashley's Pleasure Yacht

John Ashley,
the Bristol Channel Mission
and all that Followed

R.W.H. Miller

The Lutterworth Press

The Lutterworth Press
P.O. Box 60
Cambridge
CB1 2NT
United Kingdom

www.lutterworth.com
publishing@lutterworth.com

ISBN: 978 0 7188 9450 4

British Library Cataloguing in Publication Data
A record is available from the British Library

First published in the United Kingdom, 2017

Contents

Illustrations   vii

Abbreviations   viii

Acknowledgements   ix

Preface   xi

Foreword by Martin Foley   xv

Chapter One   Who was John Ashley? | **1**

His Parents   1
His Early Years   3
After School   4
Indefatigable Curate   7
With Qualifications   14

Chapter Two   John Ashley Discovers a Need | **17**

A Pleasure Yacht for Dr Ashley   18

Chapter Three   John Ashley and his Committee | **29**

John Ashley States his Case   37

Chapter Four   The Bristol Channel Mission:
Lame Duck or Phoenix? | **43**

Chapter Five   John Ashley and The Missions to Seamen | **51**

Negotiations with the Bristol Channel Mission   53

Chapter Six   John Ashley's Later Years | **63**

John Ashley in Court Again?   74
John Ashley Leaving the Church of England?   79

Chapter Seven   John Ashley in Context:
Early Modern Seamen's Missions | **84**

The Bible and Tract Societies   86
G.C. Smith   92
And what of Bristol?   97
London Episcopal Floating Church Society   100
Liverpool Mariners' Church Society   102

Conclusion   What has been Achieved? | **103**

John Ashley's Faith   104
The Contradictions   105

Appendix One   John Ashley: An Inspiration   109
Appendix Two   John Ashley: An Indirect Inspiration   120
Appendix Three   John Ashley's Siblings   135
Appendix Four   John Ashley, his Wife and Children   138

Bibliography   142
Index   145

Illustrations

Frontispiece: A Map of the Bristol Channel   ii

1. John Ashley from *Flying Angel: The Story of the Missions to Seamen,*
   L.A.G Strong, 1956 (Methuen & Co. Ltd, England)   xiv

2. Downton Church, 1833   10

3. Croscombe Church   11

4. *The Bristol Channel Mission Cutter,* Eirene, 1843   20

5. Ashley's flag system   24

6. W.H.G. Kingston from M.R. Kingsford, *Mersey Mission to*
   Seamen, 1957   54

7. 'The Mission Ship *Eirene* Bristol Channel 1843'   56

8. Somersham Church, 1844   59

9. Title page of *The Church of the Period or the Church of England in*
   my own time, (reprint, 1879)   70

10. Ashley's grave at Holy Trinity East Finchley   81

Abbreviations

BFBS	British and Foreign Bible Society
DNB	Oxford Dictionary of National Biography
IJMH	*International Journal of Maritime History*
LEFCS	London Episcopal Floating Church Society
MSABS	Merchant Seamen's Auxiliary Bible Society
NMBS	Naval and Military Bible Society
PBHS	Prayer Book and Homily Society
SAWCM	St Andrew's Waterside Church Mission
SPCK	Society for the Promotion of Christian Knowledge
SPG	Society for the Propagation of the Gospel
TCD	Trinity College Dublin
TCM	Thames Church Mission

Acknowledgements

For pictures I thank the incumbents and church wardens variously of the parishes of Downton, Croscombe and Somersham; Suffolk Record Office (Bury St Edmund's), The Mission to Seafarers; Daisy Maryon.

For particular advice I am grateful to Ian Bateman of St George, Nympton; the incumbents of Kilburn St Mary and East Finchley; the Nadder Clergy Team; Dr Alston Kennerley of Plymouth University; the Archivists of Winchester College, Trinity College, Dublin and Balliol College, Oxford; and Christopher von Patzelt.

Three anonymous referees of the Bristol and Gloucestershire Archaeological Society made helpful comments.

The Legacies of British Slavery database of University College London and the Jamaican Family Search website (www.jamaicanfamilysearch.com) have been indispensable in discovering information regarding Jamaican estates and British owners.

The staff of Lambeth Palace Library, the British Library, Suffolk Records Office (Bury St Edmund's), Wiltshire Records Office, Somerset Heritage Centre, Hampshire Records Office, Essex Records Office, Bristol Records Office, Bath Records Office, Bristol Reference Library, Bath Reference Library, Lewisham Reference Library, London Metropolitan Archives, and Hull History Centre have, without exception, been extraordinarily kind and patient.

For sourcing newspaper references, the British Newspaper Archive online has proved invaluable. Bristol Reference Library holds those Bristol newspapers lacking online. The General Register Office makes ordering copies of marriage and death certificates easy. Ashley's ordination papers can be found among the appropriate diocesan records in the Somerset Heritage Centre and Wiltshire Records Office.

I thank Alan MacDermot, Alex Romano and Robert Vaux for technical assistance, Mark MacDermot for assistance with translation, and Fr Clive Lee for accommodation and general assistance.

Dr Jan Setterington gave the first draft a very necessary brutal vetting, picked up many infelicities, and contributed greatly to the present structure of the book. Catherine Vaux has helped with proof reading. I am deeply indebted to the sensitive pen of my editor, Bethany Churchard.

A note on style

Some may wonder at 'Catholic' receiving an upper case initial while 'Protestant' is not always capitalised. I use Catholic as part of a proper church name. Protestant is given an upper case initial where it is used as a noun; as an adjective, lower case. Where Evangelical indicates membership of the movement which rose in the earlier part of the nineteenth century, the upper case initial is used.

Preface

In 1964, I went to work for the The Missions to Seamen (now renamed Mission to Seafarers) as a student helper, a very junior pastoral assistant, as a prelude to training for the Anglican ministry. I was told about the possibility of placements in Hong Kong, Mombasa, Capetown and other exciting ports, but sent to London's East End, where The Missions to Seamen had a multi-storey mission, offering chapel, bar, restaurant, dance hall, cinema, and many bedrooms, by the busy Royal Docks. On the River Thames, The Missions to Seamen had a motor vessel named *John Ashley*. The crew comprised a remarkable skipper/ chaplain, Padre Freddy Laight, his accent clearly identifying him as coming from the North East, with his young engineer, Douglas. I got to know both better in 1966, when I was sent down-river to Tilbury. Though a Thames trip on the *John Ashley* was popular with parish groups visiting in the summer to discover the work of The Missions to Seamen, the vessel's primary function was to serve the colliers from the North East. These colliers were usually tied up in parts of the river difficult of access, their crews valuing the visits of this floating chapel, library and its chaplain. But, who was John Ashley?

The Missions to Seamen had a network of people publicising the work to raise the funds necessary for its support from parishes around the country. It was quite common for congregations to be told that the society owed its origins to The Rev. John Ashley, a point made with a touching story. The preacher – on occasions it was me – conveyed the received version, one perpetuated in the various histories of the Society, and later included in my book, *One Firm Anchor: The Church and the Merchant Seafarer, An Introductory History*:

> In 1835, The Rev. John Ashley and his small son, on holiday at Clevedon, near Bristol, were looking out at the islands of Flat Holm and Steep Holm in the Bristol Channel. His son asked how the islanders went to church.

This short section on Ashley's work continued:

> Ashley, having no answer, went to see for himself and, finding fishermen and light-house keepers untended by any church, used the remaining three months of his holiday to continue his visits, holding services for them. From the islands he could see large fleets of wind-bound ships

waiting in the Bristol Channel. On his farewell visit to the islanders, preparatory to taking up a benefice, he asked how the crews of these vessels lived and what were the conditions of their ship-board life; the number of vessels and their neglect revealed in his question's answer determined Ashley to turn down the proffered living and instead try to do something for these men.[1]

A charming picture: picturesque islands, caring father, holiday by the sea, but one, as this book will show, at best, misleading.

My time with The Missions to Seamen prompted the spending of many years researching the history of the Church and the seafarer. Early in 1970, I was encouraged in my study by meeting the distinguished maritime missiologist and Lutheran minister, Roald Kverndal, and subsequently interested to see, unsourced but there, a little of my earliest research in his *Seamen's Missions*. Around 1973, Dr Alston Kennerley made contact and has been a wonderful guide to matters maritime ever since. At the same time, I was recruited by Peter Anson, the first popular maritime missiologist of modern times, who based much of his writing on the original work of Fr Goldie SJ, to help with what was intended to be Anson's final book, *Church Maritime*, which was never published. I was shown many years later a typescript of *Church Maritime* in Rome, and in it, duly credited, some of the material I had then sent its author.

One Firm Anchor attracted an email from The Rev. Andrew Huckett, a long-time chaplain of The Missions to Seamen with a distinguished record of service, who questioned the historicity of the story of Ashley's son prompting his father's interest in those islanders in the Bristol Channel. I realised, when I examined his evidence, that I was guilty of academic laziness, having relied on a received version rather than primary documents.

Andrew's path had crossed mine many years before. In 1966, I went to study for the Anglican ministry. The incumbent of the parish where my mother lived, knowing of my time with The Missions to Seamen, contacted me to say that a young man in the parish was hoping to train for ordination, and asking if my experience of The Missions to Seamen would lead me to recommend it to this young man, who also had to spend time gaining experience before going to theological college. The young man was Andrew Huckett. At the time, I thought it a fine organisation; Andrew duly went to work for the society.

Andrew's email revealed that he had been researching the life of John Ashley. By his calculation, if the received story was true, Ashley's son would have been two years old and unlikely to have been able to question his father in the way traditionally told, something with which it is difficult to disagree.[2]

---

1. R.W.H. Miller, *One Firm Anchor*, Cambridge 2012, 135-8.
2. Mary Walrond, *Launching out into the Deep*, 1904, 21f seems to have been the source of this story, and my original source. Her vague dating could allow son John to be aged four or five. Her father had been Secretary of the Missions to Seamen almost from its inception, so it is possible that she was the vector of an early tradition.

The received version was in need of revision. Following an exchange of emails, Andrew generously offered to make his material available to me, and I agreed to reciprocate; hence this book. The extent of my debt to Andrew for his series of key dates in Ashley's life is immediately obvious (see Appendices three and four). This book is my response to his challenge that I try to produce a *Life* of Ashley.

Ashley's influence extended beyond the foundation of the Bristol Channel Mission, with which his name is always connected, to the Thames Church Mission and the ensuing offspring, the (Royal National) Mission to Deep Sea Fishermen, and thence to the French Catholic *Œuvres de Mer*; also to the St Andrew's Waterside Church Mission. The link with the *Œuvres de Mer* places him in the ancestry of the (Catholic) Apostleship of the Sea, a connection not without irony, given Ashley's views on Catholicism, clearly stated in his tract of 1874 explaining why he was leaving the Church of England; his reason relating to ritualism and the Catholic revival in the Church of England. I shall consider further whether Ashley did leave the Church of England.

Lack of sources makes Ashley difficult to study. Andrew Huckett's initial outline of Ashley and his children (Appendix Four) was most useful as a starting point, though at a few points in need of adjustment. His brother, David, generously shared census and similar details. Andrew further provided, again with the help of David, a detailed list of Ashley's siblings (Appendix Three).

There is some autobiographical material in Ashley's published pamphlets, themselves not easy to obtain, and in newspaper reports of his public appearances on behalf of the Bristol Channel Mission. A subject is not always his own best witness; on occasions Ashley's version of events is at variance with reliable information sourced elsewhere. I had access many years ago to what seem to have been the only two surviving of Ashley's logs for his years on the *Eirene*. The logs were kept at The Missions to Seamen's Headquarters. When the society's records were transferred to the Hull History Centre, Ashley's logs were not among them – their whereabouts remains unknown. The Mission to Seafarers' helpful Press and Digital Media Officer provided two pictures of the *Eirene*.

Bristol Records Office holds a Minute book for the Bristol Channel Mission Committee. The Bristol Reference Library has a Bristol Channel Mission Report, Ashley's published account of his disagreement with his Committee, and microfilm of *Felix Farley's Bristol Journal* (1742-7) which contains the letter behind that disagreement. Unfortunately, silence obtrudes just at that point at which Ashley and his committee were at loggerheads; he first and then his committee members resigning for opposing reasons. The Reports of the

M.R. Kingsford, *The Mersey Mission to Seamen*, 1957, (139) implies that The Rev. C.D. Strong was responsible for the story of Ashley's son, but gave no indication of his source; he was aware (140) of its doubtful authenticity: 'it is unlikely that . . . the Missions to Seamen will ever sacrifice to accuracy . . . Dr Ashley's little son.' The story is perpetuated in G.A. Gollock, *At the Sign of the Flying Angel*, 1930, 56; L.A.G. Strong, *Flying Angel*, 1956, 20; Michael Jacob, *The Flying Angel Story*, 1973, 19; Roald Kverndal, *Seamen's Missions*, 1986, 382.

Bristol Channel Seamen's Mission (which rose from the ashes of the Bristol Channel Mission), and Ashley's 1870s pamphlets, are in the British Library. The Winchester College archivist was particularly helpful on his education there. As the various pieces of the jigsaw began to connect, a picture of Ashley emerged. Strangely, it was easier to discover material about Ashley's early life than anything referring to his later years.

The inscription on Ashley's grave stone, reproduced here, is an interesting testament to what somebody, probably his widow, believed of him at the time of his burial.[1] Useful as it is, the inscription raises a number of questions. These I try to answer in this book.

IN LOVING MEMORY

OF

REV. JOHN ASHLEY LLD

WHO DIED 30TH MARCH 1886

AGED 85 YEARS

FOUNDER OF MISSIONS TO SEAMEN 1835

WHICH HE CONDUCTED FOR 21 YEARS

ON BOARD THE '*EIRENE*' IN THE

BRISTOL CHANNEL.

I have mentioned that my first experience of The Missions to Seamen in 1964 was at its Victoria Dock Road Mission, London E16. As a student helper, I served under The Rev. George Thexton Morphet (Agnes, his wife, his great support). He had been a chaplain to the Australian Forces, then to The Missions to Seamen in Townsville. In 1962, he was appointed its Senior Chaplain in the Port of London for a five-year stint, before returning to Australia. The London mission was probably the Society's most difficult assignment, and its various problems required a tough man to resolve them; chaplains before and after Morphet rarely stayed 5 years. The mission then comprised the large 150-bed Victoria Dock Road hostel, a Chinese chaplaincy, the MV *John Ashley*, and at Tilbury a 30-bed hostel and a day centre in Tilbury's West Africa House. Morphet's team included assistant chaplains, stipendiary lay readers, a full hotel staff, and always 1 or 2 student helpers, the latter often, like me, straight from school. Ship-visiting was conducted throughout London's docks. I shall always be in his debt, which this book allows me to acknowledge.

---

1. Ashley's grave is in Holy Trinity Cemetery, East Finchley, London. It lies a few paces to the right as the visitor enters the main church gate. A copy of the Holy Trinity burial register is held by the London Metropolitan Archive.

Foreword

Why would the UK National Director of the Apostleship of the Sea, a Catholic organisation, be invited to write the foreword to a book about an early pioneer of nineteenth-century Church of England work among merchant seafarers who in his later years was virulently anti-Catholic?

There is a simple answer. The subject, John Ashley, whose influence has featured prominently in most published versions of the foundation of the Anglican Missions to Seamen (now Mission to Seafarers) also features in the distant ancestry of the modern work of the Catholic Church among seafarers via the Thames Church Mission, the (Royal) National Mission to Deep Sea Fishermen and thence to the *Œuvres de Mer* and the inspiration of Peter Anson and the present form of the Apostleship of the Sea.

This foreword allows me to attest the great progress that has been made away from Christian disunity, to the point at which today's several church societies work among seafarers with a great measure of harmony and goodwill, something for which I thank God.

Martin Foley,
National Director, Apostleship of the Sea

THE REV. JOHN ASHLEY, D.D.
Pioneer Chaplain in the Bristol Channel

1. John Ashley from *Flying Angel: The Story of the Missions to Seamen*,
L.A.G Strong, 1956 (Methuen & Co. Ltd, England)

Chapter One

Who was John Ashley?

His Parents

The story of John Ashley begins on the Caribbean island of Jamaica, where his father had various estates. Estates in Jamaica, following the British acquisition of the island from Spain in 1655, were granted to settlers by the British Crown 'by Letters Patent, fee simple estate being conferred on the grantee. The only requirement was payment to the Crown of an annual quitrent'.[1] Many of the estate owners were absentees. The principal crop was sugar cane, followed by coffee; there were also cattle. The name of Ashley appears frequently in Jamaican records as part of an Irish diaspora long established in the West Indies. In 1670, a John Ashley is recorded as having 156 acres in Clarendon parish. In 1699, a John Ashley, son of John and Mary Ashley, appears in the Church of England baptismal register of St Catherine's.

'Our' John's father is listed in a long run of the *Jamaica Almanack*, consistently as the owner of the Ashley Hall estate, in Vere, employing there some 200 slaves (in 1838, their status changed to that of apprentices, under the Abolition Act), and variously of the smaller Manningsfield and Exeter estates. His cattle numbers fluctuated and sugar was his major source of income. By 1844, the Ashley Hall estate encompassed 1,733 acres.[2] Nowhere on the island's 4,230 square miles is further than 25 miles from the sea. Vere is in the centre of the southern part of the island. According to a statement made under oath by his father, which has been included in the papers necessary before his son's ordination as a deacon by the Bishop of Salisbury, his son, John, had been born on 29 December, 1800, and baptised by the Rector of Vere, Edward Ledwich, on 23 March, 1801.[3]

---

1. B.W. Higman, *Jamaica Surveyed etc.*, University of the West Indies Press, 2001, *passim*.
2. These details derive from University College London's Legacies of British Slave-ownership site, www.jamaicanfamilysearch.com, and the *Jamaica Almanack*. Volumes of the *Almanack* are conveniently summarised on-line; some hard copies are available in the British Library (for 1800) and The National Archive.
3. Martin Crossley Evans, 'Nonconformist Missionary Work among the Seamen of Bristol', 165 gave 1799 as the birth date of Ashley. He seems to be following L.A.G. Strong, *Flying Angel: The Story of the Missions to Seamen*, 1966. Huckett deduced 1801 as the date of birth from the date of baptism. Ledwich (income £420) is listed in the *Jamaica Almanack* of 1800.

Over the next nineteen years, the Ashleys had six more children (Appendix Three). 'Our' John nowhere refers to his time in Jamaica in any published speech but, as his sister Elizabeth and their brother Jephson were born in Jamaica in 1803 and 1805 respectively, it is probable that some or all the family were together there at least until 1805, for their sister, Martha, was born (c.1806) in Clifton, Bristol. The birth of the next sister, Olive, in Jamaica in 1808, confirms a return of their parents, at least for a period, perhaps to attend to estate matters, possibly accompanied by the children. By Post Office packet from Falmouth (the expensive option) Jamaica could be reached in some two weeks, with the return taking slightly longer – but there were less expensive slower options. The next birth, of son Francis in 1811, was in Clifton. The remaining children were born in England. Ashley (senior) was listed as one of Vere's magistrates in 1817, an indication of his status in the island community, but asterisked to indicate his absence at the time of publication – presumably he had returned to Clifton.

'Our' John's siblings find little mention in his public story. A rare newspaper notice has him officiating in 1845 at the marriage of his youngest sister Ellen.[1] The family home in Clifton was in a desirable part of Bristol, many residents were enriched by estates in the West Indies. Clifton clergy had links with the evangelical movement in Cambridge, the university having produced a number of significant figures in the growing movement to abolish slavery. One example of a Cambridge abolitionist visiting Bristol to campaign for abolition in the late eighteenth century was Thomas Clarkson (1760-1846); Bristol's dependence on sugar, tobacco and similar products for its wealth ensured that Ashley was not the only one. From these imports, the income of Bristol's charities was derived; the Merchant Venturers were the wealthiest, allowing the building of local schools and churches, ensuring that campaigners had no easy task.

A little information about the income of the Ashleys from the family estate in Jamaica appears in the Bristol Channel Mission Minutes, which refer to the estate becoming a victim of cheaper imports of sugar from Cuba. The latter was able to sell sugar at a lower price because it was still farmed by slaves; a change in British government policy (1846) permitted its import into the United Kingdom. Few details about Ashley senior's income have survived, some of it surely responsible for the school fees of at least one son at Winchester and more to allow the family to live in a very 'good' part of Bristol. That drop in 'our' John's income, caused by the availability of cheap Cuban sugar, suggests that young John received from his father either an allowance or a share in the family estate.[2]

---

1. *Bristol Mercury*, 16 August 1845. The newspaper notice gives her father's address as York Crescent, Clifton and Ashley Hall, Jamaica, implying that in 1845 the family still had property in Jamaica. By 1850, his father had become 'late of Ashley Hall'.
2. I have checked the National Debt Office records in The National Archive at Kew, which list the people compensated after the 1833 Abolition Act but failed to find Ashley among the thousands of names listed. See TNA NDO 4/2 and NDO 4/18 (Kingston & Vere). University College London's Legacies of British Slave-ownership site reveals Ashley senior's compensation as nearly £10,000; in today's equivalent not a small sum.

John's mother, Elizabeth (*née* Busteed) born in Dublin about 1779, had married his, then twenty-five-year-old, father John in Bristol on 16 September 1799.[1] Little is known of either parent. The deaths column in a Bristol newspaper announced in 1850: 'at the Manor House, Little Marlow, Bucks, aged 75, John Ashley Esq. of York Crescent, Clifton, late of Ashley-hall, in the parish of Vere, Jamaica.' Elizabeth Ashley died in Buckinghamshire in April 1854.

His Early Years

Ashley Junior's use of the pen name 'A WYKEHAMIST' in his 1870s pamphlets suggested that he might have been educated at Winchester College, and, if a Wykehamist, that the College loomed large and perhaps happily enough in his memory for it to allow his choice of pseudonym. It could equally have been chosen to attract the attention of fellow Wykehamists.

College records reveal a boy with the surname 'Ashley' listed as a Commoner in the school between 1813 and 1817 – the right dates for 'our' John Ashley. The college archivist wrote:

Commoners were the fee-payers and we know very little about them until the 1830s. A former archivist has suggested that this Ashley was called John, but I have no means to confirm this. Our records of Commoners are limited because they were really the private pupils of the headmaster and so they aren't often noted in the official college records or accounts.

The only records we have of Commoners are annual lists of pupils compiled each October. These show the boys ranked in order of their position in each of the various classes. John Ashley made rather middling progress during his time here – in 1813 and 1814, he was in the senior part of 4th book [class]; in 1815 and 1816, he'd progressed to the junior part of 5th book, and by 1817, he had moved up to the middle part of 5th book.

The top class would have been 6th book.[2]

If it is not possible to do more than guess Ashley's own feelings about, and direct experience of, his time at Winchester, it is possible to obtain a picture of life in the College as it would have been lived by Ashley and his contemporaries. Pupils were divided between 'Foundationers' and the larger number of 'Commoners', the latter were those originally admitted to supplement the incomes of the teaching staff, initially at the Head's discretion, and subsequently forming what was in effect a larger House system. The Rev. H.C. Adams, in his book *A History of Winchester College and Commoners* (1878) despite writing with obvious affection for the College, included some of the darker moments in the College's history, among them a riot.

---

1. Information supplied by Andrew Huckett.
2. I am grateful to Suzanne Foster, Winchester College Archivist, for this information.

Ashley's Headmaster was Henry Dyson Gabell, himself a former pupil. Adams wrote of Gabell that his learning was 'acute, and accurate' and 'as a teacher, if he had any equal, at least he had no superior'. Of his personal character, in society he was 'agreeable and entertaining', and in spite of what follows, generally retained the affection of his pupils. Adams continued by describing him as gullible (for listening to and believing tale-bearers), absent-minded (forgetting tasks that he had set), in punishment unfair (arbitrarily assuming the innocent guilty), and given to favouritism; accusations Adams illustrated with a number of unflattering vignettes.

Adams' view was that Gabell's willingness to listen to tale-bearers in particular was:

> the practice of his that the frequent disturbances which took place under his *régime*, are to be traced, and more particularly the rebellion of 1818 . . . the result of a long series of petty irritations; and the incidents which brought it about, were the slight straws which break at last the camel's back [original emphasis].[1]

Ashley's departure in the summer of 1817 preceded the rebellion of May 1818, but he and his contemporaries were clearly among those in receipt of that 'long series of petty irritations'. Adams' general portrayal of a harsh regime of corporal punishment wielded indiscriminately by the prefects, a fagging system dependent on the vicious treatment of younger pupils, many examples of bullying, and worse, may make the reader wonder at the description of the irritations as 'petty'. Adams' belief that even in his distressing list there were positive things to be found, and that anyway such 'irritations' were common to the great public schools of the day, gives credibility to the appalling examples of ill-treatment he cites, their only fault in his view the unreasonable extremes to which they were sometimes taken. Yet it seems that many old Wykehamists looked back on their time at their college with affection.

After School

Ashley would have left Winchester with a good classical education but more effective for opening doors was to be able to say that he was a Wykehamist, though this is never mentioned directly in his reported speeches or published writing. In contemporary newspaper reports of speeches made when trying to generate support for the Bristol Channel Mission, he sometimes mentioned his first intention, upon leaving school, had been to follow a career at the Bar, something repeated in his pamphlet, *The Church of the Period*: 'I had entered at the Temple but I gave up the Bar for this purpose [of ordination]'.

---

1. Adams, *op cit*, 181. The rebellion was sufficiently serious for the Riot Act to be read and the militia brought in. His chapter XII describes at length the harshness, 'of the roughest', of College life. For the power of the prefects and the fagging system, see 390f.

Middle Temple records show John Ashley, eldest son of John Ashley, of Clifton, Gloucestershire, Esq., to have been admitted to the Honourable Society of the Middle Temple on 18 January, 1819, when aged eighteen. Progress beyond admission is not recorded, but the further silence of Temple records, and his own testimony, make it certain that he did not proceed to the Bar. *Alumni Dublinensis*, recording his entry at Trinity College Dublin on 3 July, 1820, shows his time at most at the Middle Temple to have been eighteen months. Contemporary legal training consisted in some sort of apprenticeship, or 'at worst, serving time and attending dinners'; a system of legal training condemned in 1846 by a report of a Parliamentary Select Committee, and condemned again by a Royal Commission in 1854; examinations were not introduced until 1860.[1]

Ashley's arrival in Dublin in July 1820, prevented his being in Bristol at the time of the visit there of the Baptist pioneer of seamen's mission, G.C. Smith, and made it unlikely that he would have read Smith's 1820 appeal on behalf of sailors in the Bristol newspapers.[2] Ashley's pamphlet of 1879 reveals him to have been, still or again, in Ireland in 1822, 'when I had just come of age'. Here he had been left property by a peer, identified only as 'Lord -------'. Nowhere is it said if the deceased gentleman was a relative but, unless the peer had been an absentee landowner, the legacy is another hint at a network of Irish relatives. It may be said, at risk of sounding like the opening paragraph of a novel by Jane Austen, that the arrival in Dublin (population c.300,000) of a young man of independent means, single, protestant, and newly in receipt of an estate inherited from the unidentified Lord, could hardly go unnoticed, indeed would present him with a significant circle of people keen to make his acquaintance.

The inherited property seems to have been on the edge of Dublin and included a 'noble mansion' with a chapel, and a 'small extent of ground reserved to it', leased to 'nuns', Ashley calling on

> the Lady Abbess there as my tenant, and ever welcome the cheerful old lady made me. . . . One Saturday afternoon she asked me if I would like to attend a service in their chapel. To this I assented; and the next day, a service being over, and the nuns having retired from their gallery, I accompanied the priest through a private door into the mansion . . . in another moment we were in the Lady Abbess's room, to which the youngest nun had been brought down to play the piano for me, a treat I was often permitted to enjoy.

It may be gleaned from this that if the property was not large, at least one building was substantial; also, that if 'a treat I was often permitted to enjoy' was more than a figure of speech, this visit to Ireland was an extended one; perhaps,

---

1. Andrew Boon & Julian Webb, 'Legal Education and Training in England and Wales: Back to the Future', *Journal of Legal Education*, 58 (1) March 2008, 79ff.
2. Smith is dealt with at length in chapter seven.

too, that music was one of his pleasures. If the details of his undergraduate years are correct, the 1822 visit was either not his first, or it was a continuation of one begun in 1820, and probably concluded with the award of his undergraduate degree. A second visit to Ireland took place 'some twelve years later', specifically 1832.[1] This is confirmed by the entry in the *Alumni Dublinensis* which records the award of his doctorate in that year.

His first marriage appears as an entry in the marriage register of the parish church in Millbrook, where his bride, Catherine, was resident:

> The Rev. John Ashley of the Parish of All Saints in the Town and County of Southampton, Bachelor, and Catherine Ward of this parish, Spinster, were married in this church by Licence on the third of August 1824 by William J.G. Phillips A.M., Rector. . . .

Millbrook was adjacent to All Saints, Southampton where Ashley claimed residence. According to the local newspaper Catherine was the 'third daughter of the late Charles Ward, Esq., of Merrion-square, Dublin, and Holly-mount, Queen's country, Ireland', strengthening Ashley's Irish connection. It is tempting to wonder if the marriage was a result or cause of his extended stay in Ireland. The Ward family seems to have been well connected for, in later years, Catherine would claim as her cousin Judge Radcliffe of Dublin.[2] There is no obvious reason why the marriage should have been by licence. Her residence in Southampton, even if after a fairly recent arrival from Dublin, cannot have been too short to allow Banns for, according to her Will, an 'Indenture of Settlement' had been made between her widowed mother, Elinor Ward of Southampton, and Catherine 'of the first part', Ashley 'of the second part' and two of Catherine's brothers (Charles and Vere) 'of the third part', in June 1824.[3] Nor was marriage by licence to ensure privacy, for the wedding was not particularly private; there were four witnesses, three ladies surnamed Ward and a difficult-to-decipher signature, possibly of the Groom's man, and perhaps friends and relatives.[4] Rather, marriage by licence in this period is better understood as an indicator of the leisured position of the Ashleys in society. John and Catherine's first child was born some eleven months later.

Catherine Ward was 'of age' at the time of the marriage, so probably born around 1802. Little is recorded of her beyond successive births of children:

---

1. *The Church of the Period;* . . . *also Sequel to 'Church of the Period' with the Author's Reasons for Leaving the Church of England.* A copy survives in the British Library.
2. *Bath Chronicle*, 6 November 1862, by which time the judge was 'the late'.
3. Elinor Ward died 15 October 1855. The settlement of 1824 included several thousand pounds of Government stock; what remained on Catherine Ashley's death was settled upon the Ashley children. Probate for Catherine's Will records her assets as under £6,000. It would be interesting to know if brother Vere's name indicates a further link with the West Indies.
4. It may read Thos Jennings, a name otherwise unknown.

Catherine, Ellen, John, Jane, Elizabeth, Mary, and Olive.[1] It is known that she died at Bath, on 13 October, 1867. The fruitful nature of their marriage suggests that they were happy in each other's company, at least for the first couple of decades, a possibility supported by her husband's willingness to venture on a second marriage, to Elizabeth Treadwell, within a year of being widowed. This second marriage was not prompted by the presence of small children in need of a mother, for Elizabeth Treadwell was younger (at 29) than the youngest of Ashley's children. It may be supposed that Elizabeth, before committing herself in September, 1868, to a spouse almost forty years her senior, had considered carefully the step she was taking before accepting the role of the second Mrs John Ashley. Ashley offered, under oath, a rather different view of his first marriage when giving evidence in the case of *Ashley v. Haward* in 1874, as will appear in a later chapter. Meanwhile, the mobility of the Ashley family is well demonstrated in the various addresses included in the information provided by Andrew Huckett (see Appendix Four).

Indefatigable Curate

Ashley's switch from the Bar to ordination is nowhere explained, beyond his desire to oppose 'the Evangelical views of the day', but ordination, in theory, should make his progress relatively easy to trace. Records of ordinations and Church appointments can usually be found by consulting contemporary clerical directories, of which in the nineteenth century there were three. One, *The Clerical Guide or Ecclesiastical Directory*, published in 1829 and again in 1836. Ashley appeared in neither of these editions, probably because he was not beneficed. The second, *The Clergy List*, first published in 1841, records only, 'Ashley, ------ , DD, Clifton, nr Bristol'. The DD with which he is here credited would appear attached to Ashley's name from time to time throughout his life and beyond, presumably on the assumption that a DD would be the obvious doctorate to be sported by a clergyman.[2]

The third directory, *Crockford's Clerical Directory*, first appeared in the 1850s. Early entries lack detail; they depended on information provided by their subjects. In 1855, Ashley appeared only as, 'Ashley, John, Heywood Hall, Bristol LLD. deac 1824, pr 1828'. A sample of succeeding editions offers conflicting details:

> 1860 Ashley, John, Grosvenor Place, Bath. Trin Coll Camb LLD 1821; deac 1824, pr 1828.
> 1870 †[3] Ashley, John, Milford Cottage, Greville-road, Kilburn, London NW. Deac & pr 1824.

---

1. Olive is not mentioned in the Will. She may have died.
2. *Exeter Flying Post*, 8 December 1859. He was described as a DD on his death certificate, a description repeated by Strong on the frontispiece of his *Flying Angel*.
3. † Mark signifying a return to *Crockford* not made or imperfectly completed.

1880 Ashley, John, St Germain's Villa, Honor Oak, S.E. Ball. Coll. Oxford afterwards TCD; BA 1822, LLB & LLD, 1832. deac by Bp of Sarum [Salisbury], p 1828 by Bp of B[ath] & W[ells]. Formerly curate of Somersham, Suffolk 1871-75.

The conflicting ordination dates in *Crockford* are difficult to explain, as are the variations in his academic record. Names of those being ordained to the Church of England ministry, as also those of Oxbridge graduates, at this time were usually published in local newspapers, but newspaper searches for references to Ashley's graduation or ordinations have proved nugatory.

A candidate for ordination was required to submit to the bishop evidence of a satisfactory level of education, either as a graduate or a 'literate'. To this would be added the *Si quis*, a certificate that notice of the intended ordination had been read in a candidate's parish church without objection being made, and a *Testamur*, a document countersigned by a number of incumbents, signifying the fitness of the candidate to receive Holy Orders. To satisfy the bishop that the candidate for ordination would not be a burden upon the diocese, a prospective deacon would be required to show that he had a title (i.e., an appointment to a parish which would employ him as an Assistant Curate, or to an Oxbridge Fellowship).

In 1871, Ashley published a pamphlet, *The Church of the Period or the Church of England in my own time*, using the anonymity afforded by his self-description as 'A Wykehamist. A "priest" of 1824'. The British Library catalogue identifies the author as 'J. Ashley LLD'; an identification which agrees with the content. It is not clear why he should ascribe his ordination, whether as priest or deacon, to 1824, a date he repeated in the text of the pamphlet: 'I entered the ministry in 1824, having been ordained by a bishop of the Southern Province . . . as a High Churchman (so called), to oppose the Evangelical views of the day. . . .'[1] Who was this 'bishop of the Southern Province'? *Crockford* offers the Bishops of Salisbury and of Bath and Wells as Ashley's ordaining bishops, the former ordaining him to the diaconate, the latter to the priesthood, both bishops in the Southern Province, and covering Ashley's known geographical locations at the time.

It is certain that Ashley was ordained by the Bishop of Salisbury, but not in 1824 – and not to the priesthood, for the bundle of ordination papers required

---

1. Ashley's description of his 1820s self as 'High Church' in his 1871 pamphlet would be in the sense of Dr Grantly in Trollope's Barchester novels, whose High Churchmanship indicated a high regard for the *Book of Common Prayer* and its requirements, in contradistinction to Mr Slope, whose disregard for it was 'Low' and who was classed as an Evangelical. At this time 'High' did not indicate Ritualism. That the description changed its meaning over time is well instanced by John Benett, describing in the early 1840s a deceased daughter as: 'an enthusiast in matters of religion (*High* Church they now call it) though it used to be called Evangelistic or *Low* Church'. Robert Moody, *Mr Benett of Wiltshire*, Salisbury 2005, 284.

by the Bishop survives, giving November 1823 as the month of his ordination to the diaconate – one may guess, on the first Sunday in Advent. The *Si Quis* for John Ashley, Bachelor of Arts of Trinity College Dublin, was called at the beginning of November 1823 in Clifton parish church, Bristol, suggesting residence at his father's home. As no objection followed this announcement of his intended ordination, the certificate was duly signed by the incumbent and churchwardens. With the *Si Quis* are the Testimonial signed by two incumbents, and a letter from the Rector of Sutton Veny, William Davison, agreeing to employ him as his curate and pay him £100 a year, is also included. The papers show that Ashley was ordained deacon a few days short of his twenty-third birthday, the canonical minimum age for the diaconate.

Sutton Veny, still a small and charming village, situated according to its old milestone three miles from Warminster, is now served by the church of St John the Baptist, dating from 1868, a simple Victorian Gothic affair with a spire. In 1823, the village was smaller, and served by the church of St Leonard in Church Street, a building dating from the twelfth century, now a ruin except for the chancel, and officially redundant. This was the church used by Rector Davison and the parish at the time of Ashley's ordination. Davison came to Sutton Veny in 1812, and remained incumbent until 1854, so his need for a curate was not a result of his age. The absence of Ashley's name from the Sutton Veny registers suggests that he was seldom, if ever, used to perform the occasional offices (baptisms, weddings, funerals), infrequent events but nevertheless occurring during his time in this a small community. The presence of Davison's signature confirms that his curate's appointment was not to cover an absentee incumbent.

Ashley next appears as assistant curate of Downton, Wiltshire, in the same diocese. The gap between his diaconal ordination in 1823 and his first signature as an officiant in the Downton baptismal register on 9 January 1825, with his marriage from a different address in the intervening year (1824), may prompt the thought that the Rector of Sutton Veny had decided either that he did not want a married curate or that the parish could provide a married man with no suitable accommodation. If he was never at Sutton Veny at all, it would make it a paper title. Such things were not unknown.

In Ashley's day, the parish of Downton, some miles out of Salisbury, covered a large area. Until the Parliamentary Reform Bill of 1832, it sent two Members to Parliament annually. Its weekly market continued until a later date. These gave Downton an unusual importance, perhaps reflected in the size of the parish church, a splendid flint building, with tower, transepts and an extended chancel and sanctuary. Unattributed parish notes on the history of Downton church explain that only the transepts and nave of the church were in public use in Ashley's day; until 1860, the chancel and sanctuary were shut off to form a separate chapel for use by the Bishops of Winchester, erstwhile lords of the Manor of Downton, while staying at their nearby house, 'Old Court'. Ashley last signed the baptismal register at Downton on 5 March, 1826, suggesting some fourteen months in the parish.

2. Downton Church, 1833

The search for Ashley's ordination as a priest leads to what seems to have been his next appointment. He was licensed on 9 February, 1827, while still a deacon, by Bishop Law of Bath and Wells to the assistant stipendiary curacy of Croscombe, a village four miles outside Wells in Somerset. As assistant curate he was to receive a reduced stipend of £70 per annum for 'special reasons', perhaps in recognition of his private income, and the accompanying use of the Rectory House (where his second daughter was born) and garden, with the stipulation that he be resident in 'the said House'. The *Si quis* giving notice of his ordination to the priesthood was called in Croscombe church on 30 March, 1828. He was ordained priest on 6 April, 1828, in the chapel of the Holy and Undivided Trinity within the Bishop's Palace at Wells. His Testimonial, duly signed by the requisite three incumbents in good standing, survives together with his *Si Quis*. There is no obvious explanation for the long gap between the two ordinations. Ashley's residence in the Rectory confirms an absentee incumbent in Croscombe. The Rector, Richard Warner (1763-1857) is described in the DNB as an antiquary and great walker, and author of a number of books. He had been collated, between 1825 and 1827, to the parishes of Timberscombe (worth £222 a year), Chelwood by Beth (£200) and Croscombe (£170), so he was well able to afford an assistant curate to ensure his duties were filled in Croscombe.

It is possible to get a glimpse of the new curate at work. In January 1828, a local newspaper reported:

3. Croscombe Church

Christmas Charities – On Christmas Day, being the first anniversary of the establishment of a Sunday School at Croscombe . . . the worthy Rector, the Rev. R. Warner, caused a smile of joy on many an aged countenance, as well as on the younger poor who attend regularly their place of worship on the sabbath, by distributing to each, according to their families, a joint of excellent beef; whilst his indefatigable curate, the Rev. John Ashley, as on the preceding year, invited not only the principal inhabitants to an elegant breakfast, but all those who had attended for the past year regularly their place of worship with the school children. After which with the children they walked in procession to the church, and heard a most impressive sermon preached by the Rev. J. Ashley. . . . [1]

Ashley is seen here, on the second Christmas of his Croscombe assistant curacy, so his first Christmas in the parish and his responsibility for the Sunday School preceded the issue of his license. Croscombe's church of St Mary the Virgin, a gracefully spired, fifteenth-century building in local stone, with its largely intact Jacobean box pews, screen and matching wine-glass pulpit, the whole so little changed, would still strike Ashley as familiar. It served a small village, since grown somewhat, on the busy road between Shepton Mallet and Wells, in Somerset. The church furniture as arranged reflects the infrequent

---

1. *Bath Chronicle*, 3 January, 1828.

celebrations of Holy Communion of its period, the arrangement of the pews affording maximum attention to the pulpit. The village of Croscombe, mostly built in the same attractive stone as the church, was once the scene of local mills using the good supplies of water power to work the wool from local sheep.

Mr Warner, appointed Rector in March 1826 on the resignation of his predecessor, stayed as incumbent only until July 1828. That Ashley's signature first appeared in the Croscombe register of Baptisms on 10 September, 1826, and in that for Marriages on 5 September, 1826, some months before he was licensed, which suggests he arrived in the parish some six months after the incumbent's appointment. The registers reveal Ashley to have been performing these offices regularly, if occasionally giving way to an 'officiating minister', with Mr Warner's name notable for its absence. The newspaper report of the Christmas beef confirms that this 'worthy Rector' was not entirely absent from his parish though the shortness of his time as Rector of Croscombe and his absence from the registers suggest that Warner's visits were rare. It is not clear why The Rev. John East's license appointing him as Warner's successor, unusually, bore the same date as Warner's resignation. The Warner incumbency lasted but two years, Ashley's time as his curate a shorter time. As the new Rector, East, would reasonably require the Rectory to be vacated by the curate. Ashley's overlap with East was less than a month, his signature last appearing in the Croscombe Baptism register on 17 August, 1828.[1] John East seems to have been a popular and conscientious Rector, for grateful parishioners placed a tablet on the north side of the sanctuary testifying to his virtues and the gratitude of those who had erected it; an incumbent sufficiently active not to require a curate's assistance.

It is difficult to discover any other ecclesiastical appointments that Ashley might have had before 1835. Careful examination of Ashley's *Church of the Period* may allow the discovery of a few details which have relevance to this period, though his statement, 'I was ordained in February 1824', and his self-description as 'a "priest" of 1824', among the more obvious difficulties, point to the need for caution when considering anything in his pamphlet. Written some 50 years later, some of the confusion surrounding the version it gives of his early ministry could be explained but the principal purpose, judging by the content, to be, effectively, a rant against Tractarianism and the ritualism that followed, and was not to be an account of the author's early years in the ministry; for Ashley was, at the time of writing the pamphlet, a resident in Kilburn, London, where the unpleasantness in the parish prompted by the appointment of an aggressively Low Church clergyman as incumbent of St Mary's, a parish which had been accustomed to a very different tradition, was sufficient to cause the Bishop of London to create of Kilburn two new parishes in an attempt to calm the situation.[2]

1. Names of Rectors supplied by Andrew Huckett. Other details from the registers held in Somerset and Wiltshire Record Offices.
2. P.F. Anson, *Call of the Cloister*, 1964, 439-40, describes what followed, and gives credence to Ashley's reference in his pamphlet to Sisters of Mercy. The volatility of the situation is well illustrated by the unsuccessful attempt, some years later, of the

One element of autobiography, which seems to be worth salvaging from *Church of the Period*, is his admission of High Churchmanship (not to be confused with Anglo Catholicism) at the time of his ordination. If that is correct, a conversion experience could explain his change of views and his subsequent approach to his ministry. The pamphlet refers to his preaching following an invitation from somebody '[who had] selected me, from a sermon he heard me preach, for a church he had at his disposal', the invited sermon intended to oppose Evangelical views. 'But when it pleased God to open my eyes to the truth . . . I stated at once my convictions to a congregation of upwards of two thousand, who had for seven years been accustomed to hear me opposing the doctrines I that day, with all my heart, proclaimed.' This about-turn, he implies, led to the proffered appointment to that 'church at his disposal' being withdrawn. There is no readily identifiable church in which Ashley might have preached for 7 years nor one large enough to seat a congregation of upwards of 2,000.[1] The sense of this passage in the pamphlet is muddied by the implication that this happened 7 years after his ordination, leading, if calculated from his being made deacon, approximately to the year 1831, or from his priestly ordination to 1835. If the latter, an evangelical conversion might have relevance to his expressed desire to bring the Gospel to the neglected islanders on Flat and Steep Holm in 1835. It would explain his references when speaking publicly on behalf of the Bristol Channel Mission to his having turned his back on the offer of a living (parish), i.e., declined it, but conflict with his claim that the offer of the parish was withdrawn. There are no clues to the identity of the withdrawn parish.

A glimpse of Ashley some years into his marriage and, apparently, between curacies reveals him driving his carriage around the Bristol area with his bulldogs attached to the back, on at least one occasion leaving them outside whilst he was attending church. The memory of this driving his carriage with bulldogs attached surfaced in the 1840s, having taken place almost certainly in the early 1830s.[2] His interest in carriage driving will be shown to take an interesting turn in the 1860s with the registering of his claim for a patent harness.

---

founder of the Protestant Truth Society (1890) to stand as a churchwarden of St Augustine's, Kilburn, the parish carved out of St Mary's in that attempt to bring peace. The liturgy at St Augustine's was one of the things which led to the Public Worship Act of 1874, which attempted to regulate what was permitted in such places, and was followed by – with much discredit – the imprisonment of four Anglican priests.

1. One very large and nearby church at this time would be St Mary Redcliffe in Bristol. Although its *Stranger's Book* lists preachers from, for example, the Church Missionary Society and the Church Pastoral Aid Society, both evangelical in churchmanship, at no point is Ashley mentioned. The same is true of Bath Abbey's records.

2. *Bristol Channel Mission Society. Correspondence between the Committee and the Rev. John Ashley LLD, Chaplain: with an appeal from the chaplain to members of the Society.* Privately printed, 1845. A copy survives in the Bristol Reference Library. A search in *Mathews' Bristol Directory* for the years 1827-1869 reveals only a John Ashley esq, 35 Lower Crescent, Clifton in 1827. No edition lists him among 'Clergy residing in Bristol and its vicinity'.

Mary Walrond placed Ashley working, in the sense of employment, in Ireland at this time, but without detail or evidence, something followed by other authors, with a mid-1830s return for a brief holiday at Weston (within sight of Flat and Steep Holm) preparatory to taking up that offer of a living. Ashley was certainly in Ireland in 1832 in pursuit of higher degrees, but a search for evidence of his whereabouts between his leaving Croscombe in August 1828 and his holiday in Weston in 1835 makes a sustained period in Ireland, such as would be required by Walrond's suggestion of employment there, unlikely. Ashley was, in 1833, in the Clifton area of Bristol, if it can be assumed that he was at home for the conception (July 1832), birth (April 1833), and baptism (June 1833) of son John, while details of the birth of his next child, Jane, born at Banwell in Somerset, and baptised at Weston in November 1835, confirm his presence in Weston early in 1835.

With Qualifications

Tracing Ashley's academic record has been difficult. Searches of alumni records of Oxford and Cambridge colleges in attempts to make sense of the degrees recorded in successive *Crockford* proved unsuccessful. Contemporary newspapers regularly published the names and degrees of men graduating from Oxford and Cambridge, at least for those receiving a First, Second or Third Class degree, but in none is Ashley listed. There is no obvious explanation why Ashley was prepared to allow himself to continue in the misleading entries published in *Crockford* without correction.

A search across the Irish Sea was more successful. Two alumni lists of the University of Dublin, more commonly referred to as Trinity College, Dublin (TCD), testify to his obtaining his degrees in Dublin, confirming the source of the BA mentioned in his ordination papers. The majority of candidates for TCD degrees were intended for ordination in the Church of Ireland, sister church of the Church of England. Given Ashley's claim that he had left the Bar for the Church, a degree from TCD would have provided a sensible route to ordination for someone with Ashley's Irish connections. The *Crockford* of 1882 incorrectly dates his higher degrees from TCD to 1822. Supposing Ashley spent time inspecting the estate of his inheritance from Lord -----, in 1822, there would have been a window for him to graduate from TCD but not to obtain the higher degrees. Nothing currently known about Ashley would militate against his having spent three years in Dublin, studying for the BA, supposing three years to have been a requirement of the university; only the implication in his pamphlet was that his stay in Dublin was for only some months. The question is, in which year was his BA awarded?

The published lists of TCD alumni rely upon TCD records, as against *Crockford* dependence upon a subject's self-description. *A Catalogue of Graduates*

who have proceeded to Degrees in the University of Dublin[1] gives summer 1823 as
the date of his graduation, something confirmed, with more detail, in *Alumni
Dublinensis:*[2]

> Ashley, John S.C. (Dr Maginn), July 3, 1820 aged 20; s. of John, *Generosus*
> [gentleman]; b. Jamaica. BA Æst [3]
> 1823, LLB & LLD Æst 1832.

From this, it may be gathered that he registered for the BA in July 1820,
was awarded the degree in the summer of 1823, and the higher degrees in
the summer of 1832. The abbreviation 'S.C.' seems to be an abbreviation for
Sociorum Commensalis, placing Ashley among the Fellow Commoners. These
sons of the wealthy paid double fees and enjoyed in return certain privileges, in
particular one of being allowed to complete their degrees in three rather than
four years.[4]

The DNB includes a lengthy entry for the Dr Maginn listed as Ashley's
tutor at TCD. It concentrates on William Maginn's early academic success as
an undergraduate but says nothing of his being on the staff of TCD. Maginn
had entered TCD in 1806 at the age of eleven, 'ranking near the top of the
examinations in Latin and Greek, and taking the premium in Hebrew'. He was
later said to have a fluency in 'some dozen additional languages'. He obtained
his BA in 1811, aged sixteen. His father, who had opened an academy in Dublin,
persuaded his son to be its Classics master. In 1819, William obtained his
Doctorate of Law (LLD) at what was considered an unusually early age, and in
the same year, following his father's early death, took his place at the head of his
father's academy. He spent the summer of 1821 in Edinburgh, where he moved
in serious literary circles. When his brother, John, graduated from TCD, he
replaced William as head of the academy, making it possible for William, newly
married in 1824, to depart for London and a career of literary success. His
debt-ridden final years have nothing to do with the story of the undergraduate
Ashley. It looks as if Maginn, doctored a year before Ashley's arrival at TCD,
was supplementing his income as a tutor there. Whatever kind of academic
contact Ashley might have had with him in Dublin is not recorded.[5]

Irish newspaper correspondence columns show 1832 to have been an
interesting year in which to obtain higher degrees, though the corresponding
dates with Ashley's might be no more than coincidence. TCD was Ireland's
equivalent to Oxford and Cambridge universities, all three able to elect
Members of Parliament. *Freeman's Journal*, a Dublin paper, in 1832, published
a number of columns of opinion and a heated correspondence generated by the

---

1. Dublin, 1869.
2. G.D. Burtchaell & T.U. Sadleir (eds), Dublin 1935.
3. *Æst* = *Comitia Æstiva*, indicating summer commencement.
4. I am grateful to Mark MacDermot for elucidating the abbreviation: S.A.
5. I am grateful to Christopher von Patzelt for help with Maginn.

reforming Representation of the People Act (1832) which, among many other things, doubled the number of parliamentary seats available to the University of Dublin in the Westminster Parliament. The right to vote was accorded those with a Master's degree ('after having qualified himself to vote as a Master of Art of TCD . . .') or higher. Candidates intent on election were sufficiently keen to persuade as many graduates to obtain a higher degree, and to register with TCD by the required date, as would agree to vote for them, to the point where one published letter included the claim that some of those standing were offering to pay the cost of potential voters' upgrades in return for a promise to vote for the purchaser. A letter in *Freeman's Journal* (12 December, 1832) claimed that a Master's degree could be bought for as little as ten pounds in these circumstances ('little' is a relative term as that amount in the 1830s would equate with somewhere under a thousand pounds today). Another correspondent wrote, 'a degree might be obtained by a gentleman residing in the remotest part of the country, by simply paying the college fees and the amount of coach hire up and down, at the period of the examinations.' Of these, in the same issue, it was claimed 'which examinations were so much a matter of form, so much a mere farce, that [the correspondent] had never known an instance of any person failing to pass and obtain their honour. . . .'[1] There is little here that would strike anyone in possession of a MA degree from Oxford or Cambridge as particularly unusual.

Fees listed in the Dublin University Calendar for 1833 (the first available volume) were, for the LL.B (*Legum Baccal.*) £11. 15s. 0d and for the LL.D (*Legum Doctor*) £22. 0. 0d . . , sums roughly equivalent to £1,000 and £2,000 today. The academic requirements are not given but Ashley's brief spell at the Middle Temple may have featured in the reckoning.[2] Kverndal described Ashley as a man 'intelligent enough to obtain a doctoral degree', which might be better expressed as a man intelligent enough to obtain it from TCD.[3]

Ashley was by inheritance a freeholder and therefore already in possession of an Irish vote. A higher degree would give him a second vote, this time to be cast for a candidate for a TCD seat, and allow him, if he wished to oblige someone standing, to use it. It cannot be said that Ashley bought, or was bought, his degree; only that Ashley was in Ireland in 1832, had a private income, and that such things were said to be possible. Equally, that the possibility was known, even in the part of England where Ashley had served his curacies.[4] To find him in Ireland, obtaining his degrees of LLB and LLD, against this background may or may not be significant; it is not an explanation for the discrepancies in his academic record in those successive editions of *Crockford*. What is certain, is that from the mid-1830s he was widely and commonly referred to as 'Dr John Ashley, LLD'.

1. *Freeman's Journal*, 13 July, 8 December 1832. The topic appeared in many issues.
2. I am grateful to Christopher von Patzelt for help with financial details.
3. Kverndal, *Seamen's Missions*, 383.
4. Letter of Tom Moore to John Benett, quoted in Moody, *Mr Benett of Wiltshire*, 226.

Chapter Two

John Ashley Discovers a Need

The time between obtaining his BA degree and his higher degrees seems to have been spent by Ashley mostly in England, interspersed with those brief assistant curacies and his marriage, living the life of a man with independent means. That he seems to have been aware of something missing in that life may be suggested by his interest in obtaining a benefice, something also lacking detail, but that was certainly interrupted by the work for which he is remembered.

Ashley, on numerous occasions and speaking to many audiences, repeated the story of how he had become involved with the seafarer. A typical account, here of a Public Meeting in Bristol in 1840 had appeared in the *Bristol Mercury*, which reported him as saying that he had been interested in 'the [Bristol] Channel Islands in the neighbourhood of Weston, where he resided . . . '[1] (see Appendix Four). The report alluded to Ashley saying much the same thing at meetings elsewhere, for example, while on holiday, 'Five years since, whilst staying at a watering place in the Bristol Channel, his notice was attracted during a morning walk with his children to the Islands of Flat Holm and Steep Holm; the sun was rising. . . .' Sunlight reflecting on glazed windows on one of the islands suggested people living there. He decided to investigate.

The islanders, fifteen or sixteen on one island and seventeen on the other, he said, had last been visited by an unidentified minister of religion some twelve years earlier. The 'two Holms formed the south and west extremities' of the County of Bristol.[2] Steep Holm, once attached to the Bristol harbour-side parish of St Stephen, seems to have received little, if any, attention from the clergy notionally responsible for it. Flat Holm, claimed to be the most southerly part of Wales, fell within the parish of St Mary, Cardiff. In 1793, a woman, who kept the lighthouse and farmed an area of land on Flat Holm, had found herself being pursued by the vicar of St Mary's for non-payment of tithes but seems otherwise to have been unvisited by clergy, from Cardiff or elsewhere. Trinity House had taken over the management of the small lighthouse in 1823.

The children accompanying him on his holiday walk would have been Catherine, aged ten in 1835, and her sister Ellen, aged seven; his two-year-old son John would be an unlikely candidate for this sort of exercise. This series

---

1. 6 June 1840.
2. Stan & Joan Rendell, *Steep Holm: the story of a small island*, 1993.

17

of events later became in Mary Walrond's book: Ashley, lately returned from Ireland to search for employment in England, on holiday, walking in summer with his little son, being asked by the boy how these people would go to church; the version repeated in my book. Walrond added, more plausibly, for Ashley often said the same; that he visited the islands for three months and then began to enquire about the seamen he could see in the wind-bound fleets.

Ashley had spent the remainder of his holiday ministering to the islanders, the holiday perhaps in anticipation of taking up the unidentified parish, which he would shortly claim to have turned down or later suggest had been forfeited. In the *Bath Chronicle*, he indicated a more general approach to the islands in the Bristol Channel 'of which there are four; Lunday, Caldy, and the two Holms. . . . After visiting these places several times, his attention was drawn to a large fleet of vessels which frequently lay wind-bound in the Penarth Roads. . . . '[1] 'Five years since', from 1840, the date of the *Bristol Mercury* talk, indicates 1835 as a starting date for his island visits. Ashley would add two other islands to his ministry: Lundy, off the north Devon coast, and Caldey, off Tenby, on the coast of South Wales.[2] These larger islands, with more inhabitants, were also serviced by Trinity House.

'A pleasure-yacht for Dr Ashley to amuse himself': EIRENE

In a typical speech, made in Bath in May 1843, Ashley described:

> the degraded spiritual condition of the Channel Islands before the Mission, the first reception of his ministration, and the happy results, giving an interesting narration of his continued visits for the purposes of preaching to the inhabitants, Dr Ashley entered into an account of his mission among shipping in the Channel, and particularly in the Penarth roads. Speaking of the beginning of his missionary attempts among sailors, he described his first visit among the vessels used for navigating the Severn, called "trows". The state in which he found the river was so deplorable as to the absence of religious feeling, that they refused to hear him or speak to him on the subject [original punctuation].

Persisting in his visits to the trows, he began to win hearers among the crews. Yet, the trows did not distract his attention from those wind-bound fleets of deep-sea vessels, sometimes several hundred gathered at a time. These, he continued to visit, regardless of the weather or the time of day. Here his welcome was warmer, for these ships (unlike the trows beating up the Severn) had crews who, according to the first captain, when asked by Ashley what they did, said that his crew sat around all day, bored and cursing for

---

1. 22 August 1839.
2. Spellings change with time. Today Lunday is spelt Lundy, and 'Caldy' has become 'Caldey'.

lack of occupation, waiting for a change in the wind, and willing to welcome any diversion that might be provided by a visitor. Ashley asked this captain whether anyone had been appointed by the Church to visit these vessels. A negative reply caused him to ask further whether he might be welcome. An affirmative answer resulted in his regular visits to these wind-bound vessels. Ashley's audiences thereafter were regaled with tales of lives changed by provision of Bibles and tracts; tales which suited his gift for preaching and public speaking admirably.

Ashley's visiting of islands and then of those wind-bound vessels by hired boat, proved so necessary that, by 1837, it had reached the point when it could not be continued by private enterprise alone. The London Episcopal Floating Church Society had had an ambitious plan to set up institutions 'in all situations where they may be of service to the object', but if Ashley ever sought its help, neither it nor any other Anglican society was able to offer him assistance; indeed, despite the increasing number of floating chapels in docks around the country, and the provision in some cases of voyage chaplains to migrants, a mission to wind-bound fleets was something never previously envisaged or attempted. Ashley turned to the Archbishop of Canterbury for advice.[1] It seems that Archbishop Howley, a Wykehamist of an earlier generation, suggested that Ashley should form a local society, in due course, named the Bristol Channel Mission, 'under the auspices of the Lord Bishop of Gloucester and Bristol',[2] for which, on various occasions Ashley claimed a foundation date of 1839.[3] In 1845, it was renamed the Bristol Channel Seamen's Mission, a change claimed to clarify its purpose; in fact to distinguish it from the Bristol Channel Mission which in the same year had lost its committee through wholesale resignation, from the ashes of which it had emerged under new management. Perhaps a sign of his increasing involvement following Howley's advice, a house 'now in the occupation of the Rev. John Ashley, at a yearly rent of £45', 4 Woodfield Row, Portishead, was advertised for sale by auction.[4] The published description of the property gives a glimpse of the style in which Ashley's private income allowed his family to live: entrance hall, butler's and china pantry, breakfast room, dining-room, large drawing-room, eight excellent bed-rooms with two closets, front and back kitchen, servants' hall, water closet, and suitable offices.

Ashley relied at first upon the hire of a boat to visit the islands and wind-bound ships. As his involvement increased it became apparent that his visiting needed a purpose-built vessel. The *Bath Chronicle* (22 August, 1839) reported:

---

1. Nothing survives of this correspondence in Lambeth Palace Library's Howley Papers.
2. *London Standard*, 16 February 1841. When addressing the public Ashley was careful to say that he worked with the 'sanction of the Bishops of Exeter, Llandaff, St David's &c.', all of whose dioceses abutted the Bristol Channel. See e.g., *Sherborne Mercury*, 14 Dec 1840.
3. See e.g., *Taunton Courier*, 22 February 1843.
4. *Bristol Mercury*, 8 July 1837.

The Bristol Channel Mission Cutter,
EIRENE,
from a Sketch taken in Pennarth Roads before Morning Service, November 29th 1843,
and Dedicated to the Revd John Ashley, L.L.D. Chaplain to the Mission
BY JAMES EDWARD FITZ-GERALD, Esq.

4. *The Bristol Channel Mission Cutter*, EIRENE,
from a Sketch taken in Pennarth Roads before Morning Service, November 29th 1843,
and Dedicated to the Revd John Ashley, L.L.D. Chaplain to the Mission
BY JAMES EDWARD FITZ-GERALD, Esq.

Owing to the great length of the Channel, its high and rapid tides, and the prevailing west winds, vessels are often detained for many days or weeks at anchor in Kingroad, near the mouth of the Avon, and at Penarth Road, near Cardiff. . . . The advantages of floating chapels to the sailor are well-known, and perhaps even a better opportunity of essentially benefiting him is afforded by the peculiar circumstances of the Bristol Channel. . . . The great encouragement afforded to [Ashley's] first labours led him to continue, and he has now engaged for upwards of a year in constantly visiting these Roads. . . . To extend these operations . . . a Society has been formed . . . a strong and serviceable vessel . . . will amount to about £1,000. The sailors' wages, repairs &c will be about £200 per annum. The clergyman's stipend about the same sum.

The article added that the committee[1] hoped these sums would be forthcoming, but its claim, probably intended as a compliment to Ashley's generosity, that he was willing to work at his own expense if necessary, was

---

1. Names of members of this committee appear intermittently but I have failed to find a complete list.

a detail unlikely to prompt generosity from potential donors. One thousand pounds then would equate with some hundred thousand today, a daunting sum even in a port as wealthy as then Bristol was. It was further hoped that, if successful, it would lead to the 'formation of other Societies on the same model.'

The need for Ashley to be provided with an appropriate vessel became increasingly pressing. It is not clear whether this was built at his own expense or whether he was assisted by the newly formed Bristol Channel Mission, but the vessel was ordered in 1839 and licensed in the same year, being named '*Eirene*, or *Peace*; peace, as expressed at the 14th verse of the 24 chapter of St Luke's gospel – "Glory to God in the highest, and on earth *peace*, goodwill toward men"', as Ashley would tell his audiences.[1] Ownership of the vessel was vested in three Trustees, their names not given. To add immediacy to his correspondence, Ashley would head letters to supporters written whilst on board as from 'B.C.M. Cutter, Eirene'.

On 18 April, 1840, *Felix Farley's Bristol Journal* carried an article:

> CHANNEL MISSION – A considerable delay has been occasioned in the completion of the 'Irene' [*sic*], the vessel destined for the channel mission, in consequence of the greater part of the joiners' work having to be condemned. It was accordingly removed from the vessel, and fresh persons appointed to restore the work. . . . [T]his is now completed, and in a very superior manner, by Mr Wadge, house and ship joiner, on the Quay, to whom it was entrusted to be re-done. . . .[2] Mr Wadge, on his part, has spared no labour, as will be seen when the vessel arrives in Bristol. . . . The vessel will leave the painters' hands next week, and in the course of the following will be brought up to Bristol. It may be well to observe . . . that the joiners' work, which was condemned, had nothing to do with the vessel itself, as built by Mr Morgan – the joiners' work being confined to the *interior* fitting up, and the erection of companion, sky-lights, &c. on deck [original emphasis].[3]

The *Bristol Mercury* (30 May 1840) was equally fulsome:

> The little vessel, the *Eirene*, interesting from the purpose for which she is designed, and beautifully adapted, in every respect, to answer that purpose, continues to attract increasing numbers of visitors. . . . [I]t is gratifying to those who originated the institution, and were connected with the construction and laying out of the vessel, . . . and the adaptation of the

---

1. *Bath Chronicle*, 5 May 1842 is but one example of many identical newspaper reports. Italics original.
2. *Bristol Directory* 1839: Geo. Wadge, ship and house joiner and undertaker. Address: Narrow Quay.
3. *Bristol Directory* 1839: probably Acramans, Morgan & Co, Iron ship builders. Address: Quay.

vessel for the purposes of the society, whether viewed in her superior and seamen-like equipments belonging to the sailing department, which is under the sole charge of the captain of the vessel, William Poole, or the elegant library, or little chapel, in which the chaplain's sphere of duty lies.[1]

The *Mercury* described the *Eirene* as being 45 tons; the vessel's completion 'not withstanding the care bestowed on her construction, had been completed at a cost considerably under that usually incurred by the erection of vessels of her size'. A total cost of 'under £1041' is given but the comparative cost of a commercially-built vessel 'of her size' is not. The *Eirene* was modelled on the cutters used by Trinity House in the Bristol Channel. 'In order to place the ballast in the smallest space possible . . . [it was] necessary to have it entirely of iron', which had cost £115. 3s. 3d; something that would have been much higher 'had not Mr Lewis and Mr Harman Visgar sold them the iron at a very low rate'.[2] That the *Eirene* was requiring much of Ashley's own money to run is implicit in the detail of the 'Bye Laws'.

By the end of May, *Felix Farley's Bristol Journal* was announcing:

BRISTOL CHANNEL MISSION

A PUBLIC MEETING will be held on THURSDAY next, the 4th of June, at the Great Room, PRINCES STREET, when the attendance of all who take an interest in the welfare of seamen is requested.

The Plan of the Channel Mission, and of a school on board the Eirene, for Seamen's Children, will then be submitted to the Public. The Society's flags will be placed on the platform, and the Signals for Service explained.

The Chair will be taken at 12 o'clock precisely

The Eirene will be open to the Public this day, Saturday, and not again till after the Meeting [upper case, original].

The notice on 13 June that the *Eirene* would 'leave Cumberland Basin on Wednesday evening, at half past 7', suggests a good deal of local interest in this novel vessel. It was to prove more than a means of meeting his wind-bound sailors; repeatedly, crowds of potential supporters would come to see what was at the time, the first such vessel: a floating chapel and library. Ashley needed to use that novelty in the pursuit of funds for his work, estimating that running the vessel and its crew would cost around £2,000 a year. Other and earlier societies had acquired redundant naval vessels to fit out as floating

---

1. Ashley claimed the *Eirene* to be 'built for the purpose' rather than adapted. *Bath Chronicle*, 4 May 1843.

2. Alston Kennerley, *British Seamen's Missions and Sailors' Homes 1815-1970*, PhD thesis, CNAA 1989, 65 n105 gave the cost of *Eirene* as £450 to build, £775 for fitting out, £104 for ballast, £13 for provision of small boat; total: £1342.

chapels for dockside use for the benefit of seamen, local employees and their families in a number of ports; something very different from fitting out a vessel to minister to sailors afloat. The *Bristol Mercury* reported Ashley as saying 'at much inconvenience' he would travel on board as chaplain until funds justified the appointment of a regular minister.[1]

One way of increasing the appeal of the *Eirene's* utility would be for the vessel to be used as a school for seamen's children, an idea expanded in the *Mercury* which reported that it was intended to:

> receive and educate on board six youths, giving preference to the sons of seamen in the port, and particularly to those whose fathers had died in the mercantile service. There were already applications for more than the number required.[2]

A General Public Meeting in Bristol's Assembly Rooms on 27 May, 1842, heard that, unless the number and amount of annual subscriptions was increased, the Committee would be unable to 'commence the plan of giving religious instruction and proper training for seafaring life to the orphan children of seamen'.[3] No more is heard of these youths. The idea lapsed into somnolence, to be woken again in 1853 by the Directors of the, by then, re-organised Society at their first London meeting, who proposed that the training opportunity be offered to a different class of youth; one more able to pay its way. Again, the idea failed.

More about the *Eirene* appears in the *Report of the Bristol Channel Mission Society with a list of Donors and Subscribers 1842*. In the *Report*, Letter 1 (17 April 1841) announced that in the two years since the Society's first circulars were printed, the *Eirene* had been built and completed in 1840, its chapel fittings following shortly after, so that in late 1841, it was able to visit different ports in the Bristol Channel as part of a drive to encourage the formation of Branch Associations. The chapel had been furnished, and 'life buoys are preparing, with six of which she will be supplied'. It could seat eighty or ninety people, but visits to the vessel were so popular that '[t]he forecastle was also filled, and every room in the after part of the Vessel, even to [Ashley's] bedroom and the Captain's, was in demand', meaning that numbers attending could well exceed one hundred.[4] A 'valuable Chinese Gong' had been presented for use in case of fog, or in lieu of a bell, to summon sailors to service, as had a masthead signal lamp to serve as a call to 'Evening Service'. A generous lady donor in Bath paid for an awning to cover the deck for the services held there in fine weather.[5]

---

1. 6 June 1840
2. 6 June 1840.
3. *Bristol Mercury*, 30 April 1842.
4. *Salisbury & Winchester Journal*, 20 May 1852 quoted Ashley as saying that the *Eirene* was capable of accommodating 120 or 140 people below with another 250 on deck.
5. *Bath Chronicle*, 22 February 1844.

5. Ashley's flag system

A code of signals was devised (a printed coloured copy is attached to the *Report*), of which Ashley said, 'Our code of signals answers beyond my expectations. The Captains are taking great pains to frame them nicely. These signals are now on board vessels in every corner of the globe'. The signals indicated whether a service would be taking place and at what time. Apart from the *Eirene*'s own flag, the signal flags were essentially standard signal flags. The claim that they were now on board vessels around the globe would certainly be true if meant only in the sense that such flags were commonly carried, but Ashley's meaning seems to go beyond this. He may, like G.C. Smith and the British and Foreign Seamen's Society and Bethel Union, have encouraged captains to hold services of their own on board their ships, but this is something which seems not to be mentioned. Smith's usage followed a practice dating from around 1812, when the master of a Tyne collier hoisted a blue flag bearing the word BETHEL to indicate not only that a service would be taking place on board his ship but also to extend an invitation to others to take part. It had become Smith's custom to issue a BETHEL flag to any captain undertaking to hold services on his ship.[1] The use and recognition of the BETHEL flag seems to have spread quickly. Whether Ashley was unaware of it or chose his own system in contradistinction to something produced by protestant nonconformity is not clear. His system was adopted by the Thames Church Mission (see Appendix One). The later St Andrew's Waterside Church Mission (see Appendix Two) seems to have formulated a different system.[2] For Ashley, the use of his flags on platforms when speaking about his work attracted great interest from his audiences as well as adding colour and immediacy in an age which preceded the magic lantern. Ashley indicated when their use began, in a letter (8 February 1842) to Thomas Kington, writing, 'We commenced among the seamen in March last', i.e., March of 1841. Using the *Eirene*, Ashley began to visit the wind-bound crews. Now 'officially connected with the Merchant Seamen's Auxiliary Bible Society', offshoot of the British and Foreign Bible Society, he was able to offer these men Bibles and Prayer Books at a reduced price.[3]

The *North Devon Journal* (2 June 1842) gives an idea of the popularity of a visit from the *Eirene*, here at the Quay in Bideford for several days, where Ashley held an evening service beneath the vessel's awning for 'a numerous and highly respectable congregation'; so numerous, that people were queuing, and eventually even crowding the decks of nearby vessels. The ship's gong was used to call the people to service. Ashley preached about the need for 'spiritual [not baptismal] regeneration', using a text from John 3:8. In the stern, an easy chair had been placed for the local mayor. On each side of him was a desk, one for Ashley, and the other occupied 'by his clerk'. Apparently many people stayed for a celebration of 'the Sacrament' – presumably the Lord's Supper – in the chapel below. This is the only reference to the Sacrament which I have found during Ashley's ministry. An evening celebration of 'the Sacrament' at that period would signal to those of a similar mind the evangelical churchmanship of the celebrant.

---

1. Miller, *One Firm Anchor*, 129, 140.
2. Miller, *One Firm Anchor*, 170, 183. There may be an issue of churchmanship here, because the SAWCM flag was also adapted for use on North Sea Church Mission vessels. *Ibid*, 173.
3. For the Merchant Seamen's Auxiliary Bible Society, see Miller, *One Firm Anchor*, 120, 124, 140.

Two of Ashley's logs for the *Eirene* survived for many years in the archive of The Missions to Seamen, one covering his work from 12 November 1841 to 11 February 1843, and the second continuing until 22 July 1843.[1] Both give a glimpse of his extraordinary work in the Bristol Channel visiting wind-bound vessels in all weathers and at all hours.[2] The logs show a kindly man concerned for his crew. Sometimes Mrs Ashley accompanied him. The *Eirene* carried Bibles, tracts, and a medicine chest. An extract from the first log (1:13) gives an idea of his industry. On the Thursday, he visited twelve vessels, giving away nine Bibles or Testaments, and three Prayer Books.[3] On the Friday he visited a further eleven ships. On the Sunday:

> Newport River – Torrents of rain – Weather wild and uncertain – Wind shifting about. At eight o'C: hoisted signals for Service at Eleven being the best state of the tide. The morning so very bad did not expect anyone. However men came across from several vessels, and one Woman, the wife of one of the Captains – several came who purchased Bibles yesterday. One of the seamen led in that beautiful hymn, 'When I survey the wondrous cross', and the singing was very sweet and delightful. Preached from Isaiah 56: 6,7. Still raining heavily, and blowing fresh from the S.W. In consequence of the very unfavourable state of the Weather I did not like to hoist signals for the Evening Service. . . . Did not go out in the boat to visit any vessels, being anxious that our crew should have rest, as they had a severe day in the boat with me yesterday, and all hands had been up through whole of the night in consequence of the gale, as well as the whole of the night but one before, when we were in Penarth Roads.

Nothing seemed to daunt Ashley. The same log (1: 23):

> Nov 26th. Got under way from Newport River at 3 o'Clock a.m. Wind down from the Eastward. The whole fleet sailing at the same time there was scarcely room to keep clear of each other – ran down to Cardiff Roads between the Sands – reached them before day – Lead going repeatedly. . . .

The financial state of the Bristol Channel Mission was never good; not surprising given the enormous sums required. Ashley had to spend valuable time away from visiting his ships to attend meetings intended to raise funds, a side of his work illustrated by an extract for part of February 1843.

---

1. The present whereabouts of these logs is not known. I saw them in the early 1970s, when I was able to take notes from them. More recently, I was told that they had been taken for safe keeping to the home of the then General Secretary, after whose death the trail seems to have gone cold.
2. Existing material shows him to understand tides, winds, crews etc. I have failed to find anything to explain how Ashley became proficient on the water.
3. *The Book of Common Prayer.*

From this day [7th] to the 11th was engaged in Bristol and Bath on committee business, and endeavouring to raise funds for the Society. Thus again my time taken away from the duties of the Mission through our not having a Secretary for Bristol. Besides other annual Subscribers which I obtained these few days I got two Subscribers (annual) of *Five guineas* each, and one of these has promised to assist in raising a sum for *endowing* the Society. I did not return home before Saturday the 11th at 1/2 past 5 in the Evening when I found many letters to be answered. At 9 o'Clock the same evening I went down the river in one of our boats to join the Eirene at Kingsroad. Wind East, blowing fresh, and very cold. Arrived on board at 1/4 past 10 at night, when we met for Prayers, and arranged to get under weigh soon after four in the morning for Flat Holm Island [original emphasis].

In pursuit of funds, Ashley took the *Eirene* to visit a number of ports for public viewing, for example, in 1842 to Newport on 17 August, Weston-Super-Mare on 4 September, and Tenby on 27 September. Sometimes Ashley travelled by other means, not specified. In 1843, in one four-day period:

Our sails being sent to be repaired I visited Taunton, Exeter, Torquay, Brixham, Dartmouth, Plymouth, Devonport, Bridgwater, and Bath for the purpose of attending meetings and preaching sermons for the Society.

The second log ended shortly after this entry. There is little mention of sums raised.

Ashley was also pursuing new money further afield, which was less easy without the attraction of the *Eirene*; on 22 June, he was preaching an appeal at Brighton and then three days later at Cheltenham for the same purpose, his journeys perhaps enabled by an extending rail network. The logs record mostly his work afloat, the figures for ships visited and Bibles and Prayer Books given or sold, which steadily mounted. Ashley noted that for the period 1837 to February 1843, he had visited 6,990 ships, all ships afloat, their visitation involving climbing from one moving vessel to another, often in the dark or the rain. He had sold 1,005 Bibles and 189 Prayer Books.[1] His ship-visiting continued until 1850, it was said, by which time, it was said, that the number of ships visited had reached 14,000, with some 5,000 Bibles and Prayer Books sold, though the evidence shows that his ship-visiting had ceased in the mid-1840s, which makes that total of 14,000 questionable.

As Ashley's committee members began to grapple with the task before them, it became necessary to draw up 'Bye Laws [*sic*] for the Management of the Eirene', approved by the general committee according to a Minute of 26 June 1843, and given here in slightly abbreviated form. These Bye Laws reveal

---

1. A sold Bible would likely be valued by the purchaser. The fate of Bibles and prayer books given without charge was less certain.

something of life on board and offer a few details about the ship's geography, for example that the crew was accommodated in the forecastle, usual at the time – but useful to know.

1. Sailing Master not to employ on board close relatives.
2. Sailing Master only to dismiss crew after being given the Chaplain's approval.
3. The crew to remain on board at the Chaplain's will.
4. The forecastle to be kept clean and bedding aired three times a week.
5. The vessel to be kept clean and deck ventilators to be opened, weather permitting.
6. Any damage to be reported to the Chaplain by the Sailing Master.
7. In the absence of the Chaplain, the crew to assemble in the Library morning and evening daily for 'Family Worship'.
8. The Sailing Master to log any damage and the causal circumstances.
9. Omissions of rules 4, 5, and 7 due to bad weather to be recorded.
10. The Sailing Master to use the lead regularly where necessary.
11. The Sailing Master to ensure that a light is displayed at all times.
12. Binnacle and lamps to be kept clean.
13. Sailing Master to keep a notebook of necessities.
14. Sailing Master must order from tradesmen through the Chaplain.
15. Sailing Master to receive no goods on board without a delivery note.
16. Sailing Master to record any rope etc. taken and for what purpose.
17. Proper care to be taken before and during Divine Service for the safety of the ship.
18. No unnecessary work to be done on the Lord's Day.
19. Failure by crew to report accidents or damage to the Sailing Master shall be followed by discharge and payment for damage done.
20. Crew to report any mischief done to the vessel.
21. To take all possible care of the vessel.
22. No matches in the forecastle, or parcels brought on board.
23. No contraband on board.
24. Infringements to be reported by the Sailing Master to the Chaplain.
25. Injuries or sickness to be reported by the Sailing Master to the Chaplain.
26. Crew always to appear on board clean and orderly.
27. No swearing.
28. No drunkenness.
29. Chaplain on perceiving any neglect of duty on board to report it to the Committee.
30. Library once a month, all hands being assembled.

Crewing problems appeared fairly frequently in the Committee Minutes over the next year, mostly involving the Sailing Master, but sometimes regarding equipment.

Chapter Three

John Ashley and his Committee

The Bristol Record Office holds a volume of *Bristol Channel Mission Minutes*, covering the period from April 1843 to December 1844, together with a letter from F.G. Prideaux, the latter illustrating the regard in which at least one section of the public held Ashley at this time.[1] In May, Prideaux wrote to his son who had written him news of his time on a voyage:

> I was particularly pleased with your account of the Bishop doing duty on board the liner. . . .
>
> If I should fall in with Dr Ashley, the Seamen's Friend, I shall not fail to tell him of it. I am sure he will be delighted. We have had lately the annual meeting of the Bristol Channel Mission Society, of which the Doctor is the Chaplain and a most zealous advocate. I really think it is a Society doing great good, and it is gaining ground in the [illegible, possibly 'favour'] of the public.[2]

The Minutes show that Ashley was supported by a small Bristol-based Committee, which was beginning to take its role seriously. At a meeting on 21 May, 1843, two Joint Secretaries were appointed, both Elder Brethren of Trinity House, one (Thomas Porter José) unable to attend morning meetings, the other (W.C. Bernard) unable to attend any meetings. To solve this problem, the appointment was proposed of an Assistant Secretary and Collector 'provided a satisfactory arrangement can be made . . . as to the remuneration for his services'. There was nothing unusual in a charity employing a salaried Collector of Subscriptions. The remainder of the new Committee was elected at a meeting chaired by the Mayor of Bristol on 28 May. These were P.H. Aiken Esq., Isaac Cooke Esq., Captain R. Drew,[3] James George Esq., The Hon. Captain Joby RN, Captain Jenkinson RN, Lieut-Col. Sir Digby Mackworth Bart., Charles Metivier Esq., Rear Admiral Poulden, Chas. Prince Esq., [?] Worral Esq.

Trinity House was responsible for pilotage and the provision of lighthouses in the Bristol Channel area. The lighthouse keepers on some of the islands that Ashley visited were probably glad to see a friendly face in their lonely

---

1. BRO no. 12168/18.
2. F.G. Prideaux to F.G. Prideaux, 12 May 1843. BRO ref: 20535/118.
3. Elder Brother of Trinity House.

work. Trinity House's interest in the Bristol Channel Mission, probably as a consequence, included an annual donation. As already noted, the naval officers on this and similar committees were often in receipt of half-pay for many years, redundant after the Napoleonic Wars; there was a general feeling that officers of the Royal Navy understood seamen and their needs.[1] Other committee members were drawn from the civic and mercantile communities. In short, this was a committee much like other contemporary committees supporting sailors' homes and societies.

There was a Subcommittee to do the work between meetings of the General Committee; effectively a Standing Committee. The details that appear before this committee give a picture of the day-to-day problems faced by a small society like the Bristol Channel Mission. The first meeting (23 May 1843) consisted of four members, one of whom was Ashley. Despite Ashley's kindly concern for the crew, evinced by his entries in the logs of the *Eirene*, the staffing problems he brought to this committee show that he could be a taskmaster.

The committee considered a letter tabled by Ashley regarding a 'distressing situation'. The Captain of the *Eirene*, a man named Thomas (the full name not given), seemed to be looking elsewhere for alternative employment would be the sense of the entry, and in consequence was neglecting his work. Ashley had spoken to him about his neglect and had been rebuffed rudely. Thomas had left in such short order that Ashley had needed to ask the Haven Master for assistance. A further criticism of Thomas was that he had failed to conduct 'family prayer' on board in Ashley's absence. Despite this, he had then asked Ashley to provide him with a 'character to obtain a situation', which Ashley seems to have refused. Meeting again on 29 May, the committee approved Ashley's action regarding Thomas and his appointment of a replacement, Thomas Williams, as Ship Keeper, to be retained as temporary Sailing Master. The Committee further approved Ashley's refusal to accept the return of the *Eirene*'s 'big boat' from Messrs Hillhouse and Company because of its 'ruined state'. Finally, a new Collector, a Mr Powell, was appointed, with Ashley instructed to 'make arrangements with Mr Powell for the immediate collection of the arrears and current subscriptions'.

The Subcommittee continued to grapple with these problems. It considered (6 June 1843) a correspondence between Ashley and Hillhouse regarding the big boat. At this stage there is no particular reason to read anything into the committee's close examination of Ashley's correspondence. The committee went on to consider the regulations for the management of the *Eirene*. When Ashley arrived at this meeting, he explained that what he had observed of the behaviour of Thomas Williams had prevented him from conveying to Williams the resolution of the committee meeting that appointed him as the temporary sailing master. The nature of Williams' shortcoming is not recorded.

---

1. Martin Wilcox, '"These Peaceable Times are the Devil": Royal Navy Officers in the post-war slump', 1815-1825, *IJMH*, 26(3), August 2014, 471ff.

A week later, Ashley reported to this committee that a potential sailing master, 'a young man likely to suit', John Thomas, had been recommended to him by the Haven Master. Perhaps wary after the loss in quick succession of two sailing masters, the committee agreed that John Thomas might be appointed for a trial period. It completed its consideration of the Bristol Channel Mission's Bye Laws. It agreed to pay Ashley the remainder of his £200 stipend as funds allowed 'for the two years ending 31st March 1843'. Ashley had begun receiving a stipend when his private means, derived from family sugar plantations in Jamaica, were reduced as a result of the change in government legislation, which permitted the import of sugar from Cuba. The number of years that Ashley claimed to have worked without pay implies that any payment to him, or intended payment, had only begun after his committee was formed.

The General Committee met at the end of June to approve the Society's Bye Laws. Among these, it agreed to pay the Assistant Secretary £15 for his services; to insure the *Eirene* for half her value; to fix Ashley's salary as chaplain at '----- £ per annum' (*sic*); that the Chaplain should keep an up-to-date journal for presentation to the Committee. A Lay Subcommittee was charged with the appointment of the Sailing Master, to fix wages, which should be paid monthly, and to examine complaints received *via* the Chaplain. It was to meet monthly, agreeing that repairs and stores for the *Eirene* needed prior sanction by the committee except in case of emergency. It would also be responsible for the work of the Honorary Secretaries, and the Assistant Secretary and Collector. The Rules that had been drawn up were approved for the *Eirene*. Finally, it agreed that two thousand copies of *A History of the Bristol Channel Mission* should be printed at the Committee's expense. It was noted that Ashley's Report for the preceding year was overdue.

In August of 1843, the Subcommittee had problems with its Collector and under-secretary, Mr Powell, who 'had lately compounded with his creditors', that is, he had settled his debts by part payment. The committee, 'regretting the circumstances which had occurred, do not think it needs to cancel Mr Powell's appointment but request that he will find an additional security for £50'. This he duly provided for January 1844. A steady income for the Mission was necessary: a policy of insurance for £500 had been opened for the *Eirene* for one year from 1 January of the preceding year and its imminent renewal may be presumed. Added to this, Ashley had submitted a letter to recommend that the Captain's salary should be raised by two shillings a week 'provided he continues to give satisfaction' which indicates that John Thomas, if it was him, had indeed been giving satisfaction. Ashley further suggested gratuities for the remainder of the crew, to which the committee agreed, paying to Wear, one of the original members, a guinea, to Russell fifteen shillings, and to Conningford 10 shillings; incidentally revealing the number of hands working the *Eirene*.

In March of 1844, the Subcommittee, after reviewing the Society's financial position, and apparently arriving at a less than sanguine conclusion, agreed 'the Doctor be requested to complete his arrangements for visiting at once, the Auxiliaries in Somersetshire and Devonshire, and to avail himself of the pulpit open to him at Brighton and Hastings'. The financial position did not prevent the committee from ordering the payment of £50 to Ashley as his salary for the preceding quarter, nor, in preparation for the imminent Annual General Meeting, the General Committee's agreeing in April to increase the Chaplain's salary from 31 March to £250 per annum, perhaps enabled by a donation of £50 from a lady in Bath made for that purpose.[1]

At the Annual Meeting, the Chairman said Ashley 'had won the hearts of sailors, by convincing them that he was their devoted friend as well as their Christian pastor'.[2] P.F. Aiken, presenting the Committee's report, explained that Morning and Evening Prayer were read daily on the *Eirene*, attended by the crew and 'often by strangers'. He described the area covered by Ashley's work and enumerated his statistics: an average of three visits a week to the stations, beside those paid to the lower islands, total 160; visits to vessels 708 (or 14 per week, which seems at variance with totals in the logs) – and since the formation of the Institution, up to 1 April 1843 a total of 7,754 visits made, and 1,963 Bibles and Prayer Books distributed.

In May, dark clouds began to appear. The General Committee Minutes of the 30th refer to a correspondence between Ashley and an occasional visitor to Caldy (the spelling varies) as published in the *Bristol Journal*.[3] The Committee 'deeply regretted' this correspondence and instructed the Subcommittee to meet with Ashley accordingly. Minutes tend to deal with embarrassing material by periphrasis. So it was in this case: the minutes of the Subcommittee's meeting in September recorded only that all had been arranged satisfactorily except for 'the newspaper letter, and with regard to this point, a paper had been left for the consideration of the Doctor . . .'. Two days later, a little more information was revealed when Ashley was asked for his response, in writing, to the committee's request for 'his letter to Mr Bryant and published in the newspaper' to be withdrawn, for consideration at the next meeting, the minutes still avoiding detail of the problem.

At a meeting of the General Committee on 11 October, dissatisfaction with Ashley's response, or lack of, was expressed and the honorary Secretary resigned, the two things apparently connected. A report was given of a meeting with Ashley in September; at this, Ashley had said that he would not have resigned, a resignation not previously mentioned, had he been aware of the full details (which the minutes do not record). Although the committee believed that

1. Alston Kennerley, *British Seamen's Missions and Sailors' Homes 1815-1970*, 65 found that the Bristol Channel Mission accounts showed Ashley accepting travelling expenses for his deputation work and some income (£300 for the period to 13 April 1841).
2. *Bristol Mercury*, 27 April 1844.
3. For Caldey's place in the revival of the Catholic sea apostolate see Miller, *One Firm Anchor*, 294ff.

Ashley was withholding subscriptions, the minutes note that the committee had agreed to let 'bygones be bygones' if Ashley would show confidence in it by handing the withheld subscriptions to the Treasurer. 'We therefore quitted the meeting in the belief that the newspaper correspondence with Mr Bryant was the only point reserved, and that there would be mutual oblivion of all the rest.'

At this point, the minutes' lack of detail is ameliorated by *Felix Farley's Bristol Journal*. The *Journal* issue of 27 April 1844 had devoted two columns to the Annual General Meeting in Bristol, the main part of which was Ashley's report for the year. On the Kingsroad he had visited 35 ships, preached 60 sermons, and sold 238 Bibles and Prayer Books; Penarth: 31 ship-visits, 38 sermons, 278 Bibles and Prayer Books; to the lightships: 36 visits and 35 sermons; The Holm Islands: 58 visits, 63 sermons; occasional stations: 163 Bibles and Prayer Books sold; the Lower Islands and other occasional stations: 42 sermons. Visits to vessels in all 706, to Stations 160 – averaging 3 per week. Services and sermons: 238 – averaging 9 per fortnight. Bibles and Prayer Books sold, in all 679, averaging nearly one per visit. Total receipts for the year £981. 11s. 1d., with £100 in an endowment fund and £27 cash in hand. He explained that the Bristol Channel Mission had been in operation for 3 years, having begun in April 1841. Most of the ships that Ashley visited were carrying products from the Welsh mines, but he had also visited some emigrant ships. His library of books had been well-used and volumes had travelled the globe.

Ashley, expanding on his subject, the meeting lasting two hours, mentioned his warm reception on one of Her Majesty's steam ships, following which, an officer had drawn the attention of Trinity House elder brethren to his work.

> Since then [probably October 1842] he had received a communication from one of the elder brethren . . . requesting to be supplied with the signals and published Reports of the Society, in order that he might lay them before the Bishop of London, preparatory to the establishment of another *Eirene* on the Thames.[1] A nobleman had given his pleasure yacht to use as an *Eirene*, for the Isle of Wight and Portsmouth.[2] Another nobleman in a different part of the kingdom had requested the signals . . . in order that the signals of a similar Institution . . . might be the same.

He then turned to his reception on the various islands in the Bristol Channel. He referred to a vessel driven ashore on an island, which he did not name. 'The islanders came down, climbed up the side of the vessel . . . cut her rigging away, and plundered the vessel' instead of attending to the exhausted crew. The newspaper report continued immediately with Ashley saying that he had encouraged Caldy Island householders to buy, and to meet together to use, Bibles in their homes, which they were now doing.

---

1. Appendix One.
2. To the many wind-bound vessels in the Solent.

An angry response from a pseudonymous 'Visitor to Caldy' appeared in the paper of 25 May in defense of the islanders, its author concluding from the juxtaposition, in the paper, of the plundering islanders and those of Caldy, that the Caldy islanders were the plunderers, and suggesting that Ashley's calumny was unworthy of a clergyman and a gentleman. Ashley asked the paper to include a refutation of the 'Visitor to Caldy's' letter, which the paper published:

> The consideration which I bestowed on the letter in last week's 'Journal' was all that I would give to the anonymous letter of a slanderer – to the letter of a man who would basely calumniate another but who was too mean and cowardly to attach his name. . . .

and so on, at length, pointing out that the newspaper report of his speech was a summary of a two-hour meeting and

> you have imposed upon me the task of delivering the island from the imputation . . . that such low minded conceptions ever found birth on its soil.

With this, he signed himself, John Ashley.

A speedy reply addressed to Ashley from Cabot Kynaston, owner and resident of Caldy, was published:

> I perused with much pain your intemperate attack upon the 'Visitor' who so kindly defended the characters of the inhabitants of my little island from the unjustifiable imputations cast on them by the reports of your speech published in two of the Bristol newspapers. . . . You must be aware that my sentiments . . . coincided with those of the 'Visitor', and would have been published then, had not your timely call at my house prevented it by your saying that you would contradict nearly the whole of the report. You have done so, for which I am obliged. But, Sir, feeling that your conduct . . . is unbecoming of a clergyman . . . I should therefore be compelled to request you to discontinue visiting the Island of Caldy.

Then appeared a letter from Samuel Bryant (the pseudonymous 'Visitor'):

> Having read with much surprise and indignation . . . a most abusive and ungentlemanly letter from Dr Ashley . . . He has since contradicted all the obnoxious portions of his speech . . . and shown extraordinary industry in attempting to remove the suspicion of disorderly conduct. . . .

Bryant continued, referring to an exchange of letters and visits. He had originally called on Ashley before writing his initial letter, to remonstrate with him; then, not able to find him, he had written the letter, as the 'Visitor', to be printed by the *Journal*. But there was more to this than an approach of 'gentleman to gentleman'; Ashley had discovered that only after another paper, probably the *Mercury*, had declined to print a letter signed only with a pen name without knowing the identity of the author, Bryant then approached the *Journal*, which had agreed to publish the letter; a sequence of events that had allowed Ashley to continue his rage.

The correspondence reveals a side of Ashley in controversy that would reappear in the pamphlets of his later years. It is possible to understand his anger at being blamed for something not his fault, namely a reporter's positioning his reference to the wreckers next to a reference to Caldy Island, however, Ashley's visit to Caldy to try to put matters right with the owner confirms that he was aware that the juxtaposition in the printed report of his speech had made it seem, despite his care not to name the island concerned in wrecking, that he was accusing Caldy islanders of callous indifference in the face of shipwreck. His intemperate language makes it a small wonder that his Committee was unhappy with his response.

Although the Committee continued to believe that Ashley was withholding subscriptions as a result of the Committee's response to the newspaper correspondence, the proposal made was 'to let bygones be bygones', if Ashley would show his confidence in his Committee by handing over the missing subscriptions to the Treasurer. The minute read: 'We therefore quitted the meeting in the belief that the newspaper correspondence with Mr Bryant was the only point reserved, and that there would be mutual oblivion of all the rest'. But Ashley failed to satisfy the General Committee, meeting again on 11 October, with his response. It was then that the Honorary Secretary had resigned. His resignation was followed at the next meeting (31 October, 1844) by a letter of resignation from Charles Pinney.[1] Nevertheless, the Committee, which continued to deal with Society business, turned to the *Eirene*, approving a plan for it to be placed temporarily in Cardiff for repair, and then to return to Bristol as soon as possible. A resolution was adopted unanimously that all disagreements to date be obliterated and 'the Committee concur in the expectation that their Chaplain . . . will continue his useful services . . . on boardt he "Eirene"'.

'Mutual oblivion' proved wildly optimistic. A letter from Ashley on the matter, written on 6 November to The Rev. H. Montague, and read to the General Committee meeting of the 14th, 'positively and finally rejected that pacific offer'. The meeting minuted that as 'The Secretaries and one other member of the Committee had given their resignations' another General Meeting would be called, this time for 18 November, as it was agreed that only a General Meeting could accept the resignations. As on the 14th, so on

---

1. It is not clear when Charles Pinney (1793-1867) joined the committee. According to the DNB, he had West Indian interests as a merchant and slave owner; was a Whig and an Evangelical, and a Clifton resident. A Bristol Common Counsellor (1822-35), Sheriff (1823-4), Mayor (1831), Alderman (1835-53), as Master of the Society of Merchant Venturers (1844-5) at the time of this disagreement, his resignation was of particular significance.

the 18th, Ashley absented himself from the meetings. It was resolved at this meeting that there would be a 'Special General Meeting of the members of the Society . . . "For the purpose of receiving the resignations of certain members of the Committee and Officers, and of appointing others in their room"', to be held on 5 December or as soon as possible. In the meanwhile, a meeting of a 'Special Sub-committee' ordered the Assistant Secretary to recover and discharge as soon as possible all outstanding accounts and to prepare a short statement of the Society's finances, which suggests either that the Committee had financial worries additional to the resignations or was preparing for the winding up of its affairs. Negative publicity may in part have been the cause of the downward turn in the Society's income. Perhaps, too, concern about Ashley withholding subscriptions remained.

The General Committee, meeting on 3 December, heard from the Secretary that no reply had been received from Ashley regarding the removal of the *Eirene* from Cardiff, beyond 'an intimation on the 29 November that [the Secretary] should receive an answer shortly'. Implicit here is the thought that another asset had been withheld, for a letter from the Assistant General Secretary had already told of Ashley forcibly removing a book from the office on 29 November. A summary of the situation recorded that most of the Committee had, by now, resigned and that Ashley had stated his intention of publishing his account of proceedings. Those present acknowledged their failure to arrange their difference with their Chaplain in an amicable manner, he having ceased to correspond with the Committee, and resolved that the Committee purposely 'abstain from any statement which might provoke oral controversy. . . .' The total of resignations consisted of the Treasurer, the Honorary Secretaries, the Archdeacon of Wells, and fourteen other members.

Two days later, a Special Meeting repeated all that had been said on 3 December, this time with Ashley present, accompanied by a number of supporters, mostly female, and some of them members of the Ashley family.

> It was announced that by the Fifth Rule of the Society the Clergymen on the Committee were empowered to fill up vacancies . . . it only remained for the members present to appoint eleven laymen in the room of these Gentlemen. . . . The Rev. Dr Ashley said he was prepared with a list of Gentlemen to fill up the vacancies.

But, as lack of due notice had been given, he declined to name them 'now'. The Minutes of this meeting note that the Treasurer, Thomas Kington, was willing to continue only until 31 December, 1844, and would be the person with whom the books were to be lodged. An attempt by Ashley to arrange a meeting of subscribers in January 1845 was not approved. Here, the Minute book ends.

What followed was a battle fought on paper, for on 5 April, 1845, the *Bristol Mercury* carried an advertisement:

BRISTOL CHANNEL MISSION SOCIETY

A further appeal from the Rev, John Ashley LLD, Chaplain to the members of the Society; with an answer to the Certificates and Statements contained in the Pamphlet of the Members of the Committee who have resigned, will be published on Wednesday next, the 9th of April. Copies will be sent to Subscribers gratuitously. Non Subscribers [*sic*] may obtain them from Mr Rose, Printer, 20 Broadmead, Bristol. Price Sixpence.

A copy of Ashley's Pamphlet survives in Bristol Reference Library. The pamphlet of the Committee Members who had resigned has not been traced.

John Ashley States his Case

Whether Ashley was wise to publish all that had passed between him and his Committee, the reader may judge from his published account of events. In his introduction to this account of his disagreements with his Committee, Ashley referred first to an annual donation to the Bristol Channel Mission of twenty guineas by the Bristol Board of Merchants which had ceased in 1844.[1] It had been reported to Ashley that the stoppage followed a Board of Merchants meeting, at which members had been told of 'the inutility of the Society [Bristol Channel Mission]' and because '[Ashley] used to drive about with dogs after my carriage'. He admitted that some dozen years previously, it had been his custom to drive his carriage with his bulldogs attached,[2] only one of which remained, in old age, and his servant had been instructed never to let it out of the grounds of his house.

It was Ashley's opinion that the donation was stopped because he had protested against 'Sabbath-breaking' by the shipowners who were members of the Board of Merchants, that is, the shipowners had allowed loading and repairs to take place on their vessels on a Sunday, preventing crews from attending his services by having them work instead. In his published letter to the Bristol Channel Mission Committee, Ashley had offered to resign if he was an obstacle to obtaining donations from 'some of the old members of the Society', an offer which might be summarised as, 'back me or sack me'.

The Bristol Channel Mission Committee responded with a vote of confidence in its chaplain – but this failed to satisfy him. His response:

A public body, in their public hall in the city, had publicly made objection to me as Chaplain of the Society, and our Committee had conveyed this

1. The Society of Merchant Venturers Finance Committee *Minutes* (Bristol Records Office SMV/2/2/1/1). The first book begins in 1842. It records details of disbursements, including to religious groups. I have found no reference to Ashley or the Bristol Channel Mission over the period 1842-45.
2. The breed of dog might interest those who share the view that owners can sometimes resemble their dogs.

objection to me, showing me they could not get the funds they sought for in consequence. However I might disregard the breath of slander in the street, this objection . . . required to be met and sifted for the sake of the Mission itself. . . .

Ashley's pamphlet noted that time passed and yet nothing had been done. At his Committee's June 1844 meeting, as the Board of Merchants' subscription had still not been received, Ashley again tendered his resignation. The Secretary thought Ashley's response 'overstrained'. Ashley responded by saying that subscribers were now asking that money given to him be returned, with others delaying their payment until the matter with the Board of Merchants was settled. The Committee expected him to pass on the donations he had been asked to hold, accusing him of lack of trust in it.

In an attempt to break the impasse, it was agreed to hold a conference, which duly took place. The General Committee Meeting was held on 25 September. Ashley, the Committee was told, was willing to withdraw his resignation but that he was still not satisfied with the Committee's response. At a further meeting of the General Committee, on 11 October, The Lieutenant Rev. Horatio Montagu was deputed to write to Ashley 'to remove all misunderstanding' by asking him to state in writing his point of disagreement. Montagu referred also to the 'Visitor' letter in the *Bristol Journal*. Ashley replied on 18 October, the waters still very muddied, 'I honestly tell you, that I regard the whole principle on which the Committee acted . . . as opposed to every principle of justice'.

Ashley's pamphlet continued with what was claimed to be the full correspondence. In this, he complains of publications and accounts being withheld from him 'a minister of the Gospel . . . not in [the Committee's] opinion, to be trusted in the selection of books for his flock' – apparently in reference to some comment made about books on the *Eirene*. Worse still, the Committee was delaying the provision of necessary equipment for the *Eirene* (oils, rope, sails), which required crew members to go ashore unnecessarily: 'It appears to me desirable that our men should be given as little occasion as possible for going ashore. This has been so studied in the Thames Mission, that, to prevent it, they find men in provisions.'[1] Meanwhile, Ashley claimed that the delay in solving this disagreement had prevented him – for seven months – from making appeals for donations and subscriptions.

The pamphlet continued with Ashley's version of events. On 30 October, he wrote to his Committee:

In proportion as I pressed my resignation, *other ground* than my letter to the 'Visitor' was sought for, on which to establish charges . . . And yet these are the very gentlemen who assert my resignation, which long preceded my letter to the 'Visitor', was sent in because of their animadversions on that letter [original emphasis].

1. This suggests that the crew of the *Eirene* had had to find their own food.

Notwithstanding, he claimed, the next day the Committee had resolved that the *Eirene* should be temporarily kept for safety at Cardiff, there to be repaired, and then brought over to Bristol's Cumberland Basin 'as soon as weather will permit'. It had then turned its attention to Ashley's latest letter:

> In consideration of the complicated nature of the correspondence between the Chaplain and the Committee of the Bristol Channel Mission since the 14th of March to the present date, and the unintentional and almost unavoidable mistakes on both sides . . . Resolved, that the whole records of the above correspondence be completely erased, expunged, obliterated and removed from the Society's Minutes; and further, that the Committee heartily concur in the expectation that their Chaplain . . . will continue his useful services as heretofore . . .

Ashley replied to the Committee on 6 November, pointing out that, despite the intention that records be destroyed, those members of the Committee who had resigned were noising the problems abroad. Accordingly, he would reject the Committee's offer and publish all the correspondence because the Bristol Channel Mission 'was commenced under a course very different from this'. Then followed a long account, perhaps reflecting whatever legal training he had once received, of inaccurate and dishonest Minutes and meetings, and accusing the Committee of intending, once the *Eirene* was back in Bristol, for the vessel to be paid off and sold. He claimed he had had to threaten to call the police before the Secretary (Mr José) would let him have necessary papers. And for good measure, he returned to accusing the ship-owner members of the Committee of being disaffected by his charge of Sabbath-breaking.

An appendix of letters followed. Ashley presented a sequence of letters, not all in chronological order, given here in Ashley's order of printing. Letter II (19 June 1844) referred to Ashley's position as Chaplain.

> I very reluctantly entered upon the office, hoping the formation of the Society would have afforded me an opportunity of retiring from the Channel, and again engaging in the care of some parish ashore . . . From the first, I have had to experience from persons in Bristol (but in Bristol alone) the most bitter opposition. . . . A Member of the Board [of Merchants] . . . replied that "the *Eirene* did nothing, that she was only kept as a pleasure-yacht for Dr Ashley to amuse himself" . . . I beg to resign the office of Chaplain, . . . to retire again to duty on shore, after having been engaged in the work nine years.[1]

In Letter III (6 August 1844) Ashley reported a split mainsail that necessitated a replacement. This was something that required Committee approval. Ashley explained that he could not continue on board or with the

---

1. I have failed to find Ashley in the Society of Merchant Venturers [i.e., the 'Board'] in the SMV archive at Bristol Record Office.

Bristol Channel Mission if his request was not attended to. He seems to have been offering this example in illustration of his claim that Committee was withholding things necessary to his ministry.

Letter IV (9 August 1844) touched on the issue of his being given the fees for subscriptions, which carried a caveat from those subscribing that he should not forward them to the Treasurer 'till [*sic*] the Merchants' business was so settled that I could continue to serve as Chaplain.'

Letter V[1] was written to Ashley by John Hensman,[2] his new Chairman, explaining 'such groundless calumnies cannot seriously operate either to your own or this Society's disadvantage; far less do they afford a substantial reason for the abandonment of a post of duty'. Hensman turned to Ashley's 'Visitor' letter:

> The ardour of feeling . . . we can understand and excuse; but we cannot defend or justify expressions of which many of your friends read in the newspapers with pain and regret. . . . We conferred with Mr Bryant, and . . . obtained from him this admission – "that he would not have written the letter which gave offense to Dr Ashley had he been aware of the real state of the case".

Despite this, it will be recalled that Ashley had refused to agree to the withdrawal of letters by both sides.

Hensman added that Ashley's letter contained 'severe reflections on the conduct of some member of this committee, whose name you do *not* mention. You thus make each of us in some degree obnoxious to your indefinite rebuke . . . [original emphasis]', adding, in the matter of withheld subscriptions, that Ashley was effectively accusing the Committee and its Treasurer of being 'not worthy to be trusted'.

> We entreat you, dear Sir, by all the regard you have ever expressed for us; by that which we have unfeignedly cherished towards yourself; above all, by the sacred cause whose interests are now at stake, that you will seriously and calmly review the facts, and the sentiments we have been compelled to submit to your consideration.

Letter VI (7 September 1844) was written by Ashley to W.C. Bernard, the Honorary Secretary. His Committee must have thought a corner had been turned, for Ashley wrote, 'I see clearly where the Committee were misled, and am sure their intentions were the best'. He added, 'With much pleasure I accept the proposal to seek the adjustment of these, and other matters . . . in a Christian spirit. . . .'

---

1. The date of this letter is not clear.
2. Hensman (1780-1864) had served a curacy in Cambridge under Charles Simeon. According to the DNB, Curate in charge of Clifton 1809-22, returning in 1847 as Vicar of Clifton on the nomination of the Simeon Trustees, notable builder of Bristol Churches, a senior figure in the diocese, and an influential Evangelical.

Bernard replied to Ashley in an undated letter (Letter VIII), referring to the 'Visitor' letter and Bryant's response. He asked Ashley to withdraw his letter and agree to a short notice being inserted in the *Bristol Journal*. In addition, he copied Committee resolutions dated 8 June: 'That this Committee deeply regret the correspondence . . . which has appeared in the *Bristol Journal*' and 'That the Society's Chaplain be requested to abstain for the present from visiting Lundy and Caldy Islands. . . .' Letter IX (15 June 1844) seems to be Ashley's reply to this. In it, Ashley emphasised his main objection in the matter of the 'Visitor' letter was to the anonymity of its writer.

Bernard's reply (Letter X, 20 June 1844) reflected the frustration felt by the Committee:

> All that you have written fails to convince us that it is the duty of the Chaplain of the Channel Mission Society to enter upon a crusade against anonymous scribblers. . . . If you are not prepared to carry out our proposition, perhaps you will let us know what you are prepared to do. . . .

Ashley replied (Letter XI, 2 July 1844) to Bernard: 'not one line of my letter, nor one expression throughout it, will I relax against any anonymous traducer in the land . . .', with more in a similar vein.

It is difficult to see what any member of the public, sufficiently interested to buy the pamphlet, would see in Ashley's intended defense against what he perceived as an unreasonable Committee, beyond the Committee having done everything in its power to bring to a peaceful conclusion an unhappy episode, during which, the Chaplain had at no point been open to reason. Ashley's objections, apparently sparked by the Merchants' withheld subscription, had swung variously between his view of anonymous letter writers, Sunday working, his Committee's delay in sanctioning necessary supplies, and, generally, a failure to support him in the way that he thought he should have been, leaving the reader to wonder what his real problem was. A charitable diagnosis might be that Ashley was showing the effects of the years of unrelenting work in extreme conditions by an exhausted man. The knowledge of his Court evidence in the 1870s may prompt the reader to wonder, if there was any truth in his claim made there of his wife's insistence on making him 'live like a widower' from this time, whether this might have played a part in his mood swings. Then, there is the irony, which is hard to escape, of somebody fulminating against 'anonymous scribblers' then later writing pamphlets under the pseudonym of 'A WYKEHAMIST'.

Dr Crossley Evans, with some charity, after reading the *Minutes* and the pamphlet, described Ashley as a 'man of great pride, and very difficult to deal with. . . . Dr Ashley was a man of hot temper, and unstable temperament.' If his description of Ashley is accurate, it might explain the short durations of Ashley's curacies and the lengthy gaps between them; perhaps, too, his change of diocese between ordinations; even his frequent changes of address.

With such a reputation going before him, if a man was to seek another church appointment, success might require the passage of years and relocation to a distant diocese before he would meet with success.

As at this point, Dr Crossley Evans, all the records available to him being exhausted, concluded that after all those resignations and unpleasantness, the Bristol Channel Mission had ceased to be.

Chapter Four

The Bristol Channel Mission: Lame Duck or Phoenix?

It is extremely difficult to piece together what happened after the 1844 General Meeting, at which Ashley's intransigence had caused all the Bristol Channel Mission Committee to resign. Mary Walrond says nothing of this major disagreement. A few items survive in local newspapers. The British Library holds two pamphlets giving reports of the 'British Mission to Seamen on the Coast of England and Wales, in the Bristol Channel', dated 1851 and 1853.[1] Following what appears to have been a four-year gap, brushed over with a reference to Ashley's health, this new Mission seems to have emerged, at a date never made clear, clad in the mantle of the original Bristol Channel Mission. There was more to it than a change of name, for the Mission's bankers were now to be located in London, Bristol and Bath, and the whole backed by a Board of Directors rather than a General Committee.

It seems that an accident had involved the *Eirene* and had affected Ashley's health, explaining the vessel's extended presence in Cardiff in 1844 but offering little in the way of detail of what happened to the *Eirene* or to Ashley between 1844 and 1849. The Directors wrote, 'It is with deep regret the Directors have to mention the severe illness of the esteemed Chaplain of the Mission . . . since the publication of the last Report, which necessarily obliged him to suspend, for a time, his valuable labours. . . .'

Two accidents appear in Ashley's Letter VII (in the same 1851 Report), the numbering a continuation of the Letters produced in Bristol Channel Mission days, addressed to the Subscribers of the Bristol Channel Mission. Letter VII, headed Heywood Hall, Ashley's address, dated 31 December 1850, provides details of the accidents which had prevented him from working. 'No sooner had I recovered from an accident, by which I was laid by from my duties in the Channel for a considerable time, than a fresh event occurred'. It is the 'fresh' event that is given a date and more detail.

In July 1849, the *Eirene* was returning up-channel from the Helwick light-vessel when at 3:00 a.m. 'I was startled out of my sleep by hearing our vessel hailed' – followed by a collision. Ashley rushed on deck in his flannel

---

1. Walrond, 46, says that the Bristol Channel Mission was revived in 1855 as the Bristol Mission to Seamen.

night-wear at 3 o'clock in the morning, to discover a gale driving rain 'almost horizontally across the deck'. Finding the *Eirene* locked in the rigging of a schooner, he supervised the business of separation, which took some fifteen minutes. Damage was prevented by 'our large cork fenders'. 'My good sailing-master' told Ashley, "It will be the death of you if you don't go below'. Yet it was, Ashley noted, the Sailing Master who, but a month later, had 'passed from sublunary scenes and vain shadows, to enter upon the realities of existence.'

The accident took a toll on Ashley who, having been chilled to the bone, soon claimed he could move only with the aid of crutches. 'In this state and nearly bent double I kept to the sea till the latter part of November'. A further gale left him in bed for a further thirty days unable to turn or lie except on his back. Nevertheless, he was able to report that he was now back at sea. The story thus far is repeated in abbreviated form in Mary Walrond's book, *Launching out into the Deep*.

The Directors of the 'British Mission to Seamen on the Coast of England and Wales, in the Bristol Channel', added to a Treasurer's Account for the period to December 1850, which revealed Ashley's society to have been running at such a loss for the preceding four and a half years that Ashley, although still working, had been doing so without a stipend and with a reduced crew on the *Eirene*. It is hard to reconcile this statement with the reference in the following Treasurer's Account to the sale of the old vessel and Ashley's continuing indisposition. Lately, it was said, Ashley had been reluctant to leave his ministry to the men to make appeals on their behalf.

> But the present position of the Mission requires the Directors candidly to state, that for the private losses of Dr Ashley (in consequence of the measure introducing slave grown sugar in 1846), even to the complete ruin of a valuable family estate in Jamaica – he is now rendered unable from a sense of duty to his large family, to continue the sacrifice that he has hitherto so generously made for the Mission.

The accounts reveal non-payment of his annual Chaplain's Stipend of £200 since 24 June 1846.

In the years between the collapse of the Bristol Channel Mission committee and 1850, it appears from the *Gloucester Journal* (7 December 1850) that Ashley's ministry had not been without its supporters. The paper recorded 'another munificent donation of 50 [pounds] from Mrs Jenkins, of Caledonia Place, Clifton. This is the *fifth* donation presented by that lady to the mission since 1845 [original emphasis]'. Five generous donations over five years imply the existence of a continuing bank account, but whether handled by Ashley himself, or by a rump of the old Bristol Channel Mission, is nowhere explained. The financial statement in the Directors' Report of 1851 only records a small balance received from the 'old Society'. It is surprising to find the existence of even a small balance as the Treasurer had reported in Letter VII, in December 1850, that annual expenses were expected to be seven or eight hundred pounds, against an annual income since 1846 of a mere two hundred pounds.

In fact, receipts and payments from 31 March 1846 to 9 December 1850 had a total of just over £1687. This included: 'Balance on sale of the old vessel after paying the debts of the Bristol Channel Mission Society £110. 10s. 4d.' and: 'Expense of building Vessel and Boats, Furniture, and fitting up Chapel to 9 December 1850, £654. . . .' From this, it seems reasonable to conclude that a small group, Ashley's friends, judging by the list of Directors, which respected his work had been willing to pick up the pieces; indeed, perhaps had been handling the Bristol Channel Mission's affairs since the debacle of 1844. As a benison, their Chaplain offered the Archbishop of Dublin's description of the Bristol Channel as Ashley's 'floating Diocese' and the latter's own thought that his floating chapel was the '*cathedral* of my diocese'. The financial statement's references to the 'sale of the old vessel', and the 'expense of building Vessel and Boats . . .' make one wonder whether the original *Eirene* had been replaced. There is no obvious answer.

Those Directors of the new Society, who had replaced the committee of the old Bristol Channel Mission committee, were Richard Greville Esq., The Rev. Ralph Lambton Hopper, The Rev. Richard Croly (the Partis College Chaplain who had been Treasurer of Ashley's Bristol Channel Mission Bath Auxiliary), W.T. Hawke Esq., and The Rev. John Betts. They reported that, 'It is with deep regret the Directors have to mention the severe illness of the esteemed Chaplain of the Mission . . . since the publication of the last report', for which report no date is given. The emphasis on Ashley's health may reflect its unreliability, but it conveniently deflected attention from the circumstances surrounding the passing of the Bristol Channel Mission, while avoiding the necessity of referring to the resignations that were provoked by the behaviour of their 'esteemed chaplain'. At this point, the *Eirene* seems to have been in use. The Directors drew attention to the vessel's significance:

> Nor should it be forgotten that this Mission is, as far as we know, the first effort *of the kind* ever made for seamen, and the *Eirene*, the first vessel *of the sort* ever equipped for such a purpose. While we have had our floating Chapel moored *in port*, for that *particular port*, we have never before had a *sailing* vessel fitted up with a Chapel within, to meet the seamen in the Roadsteads after they had left their several ports, and to move then from Roadstead to Roadstead – affording, at the same time, an opportunity of visiting the Islands and Light Vessels in the Bristol Channel [original emphasis].

Ashley did not withdraw entirely from opportunities to appeal on behalf of his work. At a meeting in Poole on 23 December, 1851, 'Dr Ashley delivered a most excellent as well as a prolonged address . . .', raising a collection of nine pounds.[1] At Bath, on 15 April, 1852, according to the sympathetic *Bath Chronicle*, at a meeting of friends in the Bath Assembly Rooms, Ashley gave

---

1. *Salisbury & Winchester Journal*, 27 December 1851.

the standard talk of how he had turned down a much-desired offer of a small
country parish sixteen years earlier, and had begun visiting ships instead. After
five years, he had, on the advice of the Archbishop of Canterbury, established
the Bristol Channel Mission to support his work. As his hearers had probably
come to expect, he dwelt on the work of the *Eirene*:

> a large powerful cutter . . . one that could beat to windward in all
> weathers . . . built for the service . . . so good a vessel that never, during
> the whole period of sixteen years, had she been weather-bound for the
> space of five minutes. . . .

And, implicit, nor had the speaker been. Some of his Bath audience
might have known that for some of those sixteen years, she had certainly
been laid up. If 'Sixteen years' is to be taken literally it would have meant the
Eirene was sailing before she had been built.[1] 'The character of the vessel was
suggested by that of the cutters of Trinity House to convey oils and other
stores to the lighthouses', the invocation of the name of the Trinity House
and its worthy work instantly casting a cloak of respectability over Ashley's
work. Even so, as subscriptions and collections covered barely a seventh of
the cost of running the vessel and Society; Ashley told his audience that the
Eirene was now laid up. This talk prompted a retiring collection of sixteen
pounds and the names of several people expressing a willingness to subscribe
annually.

Sunday preachments in Taunton, according to the same journal (22
November 1851) realised nineteen pounds from services, which were 'both
well attended, and addressed at considerable length by Dr Ashley.' More
preachments appeared in other local papers. The *Hampshire Advertiser* noted in
November of 1851 a 'numerous attendance', leaving almost twenty pounds on
its departure. In the following January, a public meeting in Romsey produced
forty-four pounds. In March 1852, Ashley received just over nine pounds in
Southampton. The laying up of the *Eirene* was expected to end by December
1853, for the *Bristol Mercury* (3 December 1853) reported: 'The *Eirene* is now
so far refitted that it is hoped she will in a few days be ready for sea.' This still
leaves unanswered the question, what was the 'old boat' mentioned as having
been disposed of in the 1851 accounts?

The second Report of the Mission to British Seamen, dated April 1853,
inevitably started with the story that Ashley,

> while crossing a headland projecting into the sea on the coast of
> Somerset, obtained a view of a house on an island a few miles removed
> from the shore, the windows being seen glittering in the beams of the
> sun. Judging that the island must be inhabited, although apparently just
> a barren rock, he engaged a boat to take him to the island.

---

1. Cp Bill Down, *On Course Together*, 1989, 25: 'For fifteen years he visited the ships in
    all weathers'.

At the expiration of three months, during which time he had been preaching to the inhabitants of these islands, Dr Ashley proceeded to pay them a farewell visit – as a church had been offered to him which he was about to accept. Having visited the Steep Holm island, he was walking up the beach of the Flat when, the day being bright, his attention was particularly drawn to a large fleet off the coast of Wales.

Ashley mentioned the building of the *Eirene*. Then, passing lightly over what must have been the gap between his falling out with his Bristol Channel Mission committee and the establishment of its successor, he explained, 'Except, therefore, on an occasion once now and then (at one time for more than three years), he did not withdraw himself from the work to advocate the cause on shore'.

The Report, repeating the loss of the Ashley family's Jamaican estate, continued by explaining the genesis of the resurrected society:

At length, however, he was obliged to yield. He brought the vessel to her moorings. . . . At this juncture Dr Ashley was asked if he had any objection to lay the subject before the public at large. . . . This he undertook to do, and large and influential meetings have been held in various parts of the country. . . .

What was proposed to him was

not for the seamen of the Bristol Channel, but for British seamen, FROM EVERY PART OF THE UNITED KINGDOM. . . . That the subject, therefore, should be taken up in a proper manner, it is necessary that a meeting should be called in London . . . [original emphasis].

The Directors chose to think on a national scale, following a more ambitious route but one not dissimilar to that used in the establishment of the original Bristol Channel Mission. A 'proper manner' envisaged the recruitment of two chaplains, the first hint of succession planning, who would require stipends of a thousand or twelve hundred pounds each, sums, which, even if running costs and housing are included, are sufficiently extraordinary (when an incumbent might receive two hundred pounds a year, plus a house) to suggest a mistake in the report. To achieve this, it would be necessary to hold meetings in London, which, by now, had become more readily accessible with the extension of the railway that had opened the way to Bristol residents in June, 1841. There was a return to the idea of a school-master on board, but now not for orphans; rather, unsaid but clearly meant, for those whose fees would underwrite the cost of the proposed vessel.

It is intended for the future that two Clergymen shall be employed . . . then might a vessel of a larger size be used and by the addition of a school-master on board, a limited number of gentlemen's sons who are going into the Royal Navy might be taken on board, for two or three years previous to their being of age to enter the service, and there be brought up, instructed, and prepared for that service under advantages never before enjoyed by youths in a similar position. . . . This is no new idea, for it was suggested by Dr Ashley at the commencement of the Mission.

This larger vessel would thus depend to an extent on what would now be considered child labour. There is no mention here of Ashley's original intention of providing religious instruction as part of the curriculum for these young recruits but it would be odd if this was not intended.

The Payments Column in the Report (1853) includes, for the first time, payment for steam towing, the significance of this tocsin for a ministry to wind-bound sailors was, at the time, unremarked and probably not appreciated.

A public meeting duly took place in London. The *Morning Post* (11 June 1853) was generous in the space it afforded the event, as were some West Country papers. It was held in the Freemason's Hall, Great Queen Street. The Earl of Shaftesbury took the chair. Dr Ashley explained at some length how his mission had come about, how he could no longer afford to carry the expenses involved and, never one to allow modesty to prevent his seizing an opportunity for financial support, invoked in his talk the name of Sir John Franklin. Franklin was famous at the time as an Arctic explorer. His last expedition, to discover the long-sought North West passage (between the Atlantic and the Pacific Oceans), had resulted in the disappearance of ship and crew, the weight of public opinion in 1848 causing the Admiralty to begin a search for the missing expedition. Soon British and American ships were participating, encouraged by the offer of a finder's reward. By 1854, a number of relics and reports were beginning to appear, ensuring that Franklin's name was on many lips.

> [Ashley] denied that the moral and religious condition of sailors was a matter for the consideration of shipowners only; and related that previous to his departure on his last voyage, Sir John Franklin intimated his wish, as one of his last injunctions to his family, that they should continue his contributions to the "Bristol Channel Seamen's Mission,' and do all in their power to further its success and prosperity. They would, he asserted, do more towards sending the gospel to the heathen by granting 1000*l* a year to the "mission", than had yet been done to the accomplishment of that object.[1]

As in the Report, Ashley argued now for 2 clergy to be employed, on the salaries suggested, to allow that 'the mission might effectively be carried on', a proposal supported at the meeting by the Bishop of Llandaff, who mentioned his peculiar interest as 'the coasts of his diocese were washed by the Bristol Channel'. Captain Maude RN of the Thames Church Mission, seconding the proposal, explained that the Thames Church Mission had begun as a result of

---

1. *Gloucester Journal*, 18 June 1853.

the 'success attending the Bristol Channel Mission'.[1] 'The noble chairman, in putting the resolution, after referring to the aid to the cause of religion given by the mission, passed a high eulogium on the character and zealous exertions of the Rev. Dr Ashley'. How the salaries were to be achieved was not said; the receipts between 9 December 1850 and 31 March 1852, amounted only to £898 13s. 9d., leaving a balance of a modest 87 pounds.

Mary Walrond's version of what had brought things to this point, somewhat at variance with details available elsewhere, can be given briefly. She ignored Ashley's contretemps with his committee, pointing instead to the Bristol Channel Mission's financial position, claiming this had made the last five years of Ashley's ministry the most difficult; though Ashley himself received no pay, his crew and the vessel's maintenance required funding. His financial worries, long hours, late nights and the energy required for his ship-visiting brought him to the point where ill health forced his retirement. She wondered that he had been able to keep going for so long, a marvel of energy and diligence. Her view seems to have coloured the picture of Ashley which thereafter prevailed in The Missions to Seamen.

Mary Walrond further claimed that when Ashley did retire the work fell into abeyance for 5 years, to be revived as the Bristol Missions to Seamen. It was hoped that a spin-off from this revival would be a ministry to vessels off the Isle of Wight. The Rev. Thomas Cave Childs, who, as Vicar of St Mary, Devonport, had been involved in visiting emigrant ships at Plymouth for some 6 years, resigned his benefice to take up an appointment as chaplain to the English Channel ports, with his base at Ryde, on the Isle of Wight.[2] Additionally, Walrond noted that The Rev. C.E.R. Robinson, interested in Childs' work in the English Channel, was moved to start visiting emigrant ships on the Thames from his parish of Milton next Gravesend, eventually founding the St Andrew's Waterside Church Mission in 1864.[3] It was Childs, following Ashley and inspired by his work, who had so impressed W.H.G. Kingston with his ministry to emigrants at Plymouth, that Kingston was prompted to try to bring about an amalgamation of those various Anglican works for seamen that he had been able to discover to form what became The Missions to Seamen; an amalgamation, which, at this stage, included neither the Bristol Channel Mission nor the Thames Church Mission.[4] For a brief period, in 1855, Childs' assistant was The Rev. Clement Dawsonne Strong. While Childs was working off the Isle of Wight, Strong was attempting to revive Ashley's work in the Bristol Channel. Strong would come with the successor organisation of the Bristol Channel Mission into The Missions to Seamen and stay to work among seamen for 23 years. Childs resigned on being appointed to the benefice of

1. See Appendix One.
2. Kverndal, *Seamen's Missions* 387.
3. See Appendix Two. Miller, *One Firm Anchor*, 168ff.
4. The sense of its being an amalgamation was lost when the society changed its title to the (singular) Mission to Seafarers.

Nympton St George in Devon in April 1857, where he remained as incumbent until 1868. His departure, according to M.R. Kingsford, was due to the Bristol Channel Mission's not having the funds to pay him. A different explanation appeared in The Missions to Seamen Minutes.[1]

Mary Walrond's summary is sufficiently wide of the mark to be misleading rather than completely inaccurate. The newly reconstructed Mission to Seamen (successor to the Bristol Channel Mission, not to be confused with The Missions to Seamen) did begin to get things moving again. The *Exeter Flying Post* (7 September 1854) reported a further meeting in aid of this Mission to Seamen, held in London at the Athenaeum, with Captain Bingham RN in the chair, and an assortment of clergy in attendance. Ashley, as always, outlined the origins of his ministry, before referring to the London meeting of June 1853 'when the Society was reorganised'. The Archbishop of Canterbury had agreed to become its Patron, and Lord Shaftesbury the President. A Managing Committee was formed in Bristol 'and resolved that the mission vessel should be at once refitted, which had since been done at an expense of £200'. Childs and Strong filled the two chaplaincy positions that Ashley claimed had long been in his mind, though nothing was said to indicate how they were to be funded; Ashley remained as the new society's chaplain.

---

1. Kingsford, *The Work and Influence. . .*, 132. For the different explanation see Chapter Five below.

Chapter Five

John Ashley and The Missions to Seamen

In an address made at Southampton in 1850, W.H.G. Kingston described meeting The Rev. T. Cave Childs, then Vicar of St Mary's, Devonport (1846-52), and being shown Childs' work among emigrants at Plymouth.[1] He noted how Childs visited the emigrant ships, held services on board, organised those emigrating into classes, encouraged those who could read to teach those who could not, and so provided occupation during the tedium of a long sea voyage. Kingston, a publisher and prolific author, particularly of children's stories, had first taken up the cause of emigration in the 1840s while he was Secretary of the Colonization Society, a treatise, *A system of General Emigration and for the disposal of Convicts in the Colonies* (1848). Another of his works was *How to Emigrate* (1850). As he was touring ports in his yacht to investigate provision for emigrants, Kingston had been impressed by what he saw of Church work among emigrants, particularly in Plymouth and Bristol, where chaplains were including both seamen and emigrants in their visits to ships. His regularly published *Kingston's Miscellany* provided a platform on which to present his thoughts on their work to a wide audience.[2]

The Missions to Seamen's foundation resulted from Kingston's interest. Childs, now based in Ryde and serving the English Channel, was attempting to rebuild the work of John Ashley. According to M.R. Kingsford, Kingston's biographer, the link between the two men had allowed Childs to try to attract Kingston's interest in those Bristol Channel Mission debts, which had caused its work in the Bristol Channel effectively to cease.[3] His initiative in drawing Kingston's interest was timely, for by 1856, the work of Kingston's Colonization Society having been taken over by the Church of England's Society for the Propagation of the Gospel, Kingston was left free

---

1. M.R. Kingsford, *The Mersey Mission to Seamen*, 1957, 16.
2. The only biography of Kingston seems to be M.R. Kingsford, *The Work and Influence . . .* based on his Oxford BLitt thesis. Material in this chapter, particularly the detail of Missions to Seamen Minutes (now in Hull History Centre) used previously in my book, *From Shore to Shore*, is supplemented with material on W.H.G. Kingston, and information obtained from newspapers as indicated. See M.R. Kingsford, *Life of W.H.G. Kingston*, 1972, 2.
3. Kingsford, *Mersey Mission . . .* , 17: 'Childs suggested to W.H.G. Kingston that he should organize a National Society'.

to concentrate on achieving an amalgamation of Church of England groups working among seamen. Kingsford made this claim by citing Kingston's own words.

> Soon after this, from the urgent appeal of Mr Childs, I was induced to endeavour to form a Society in London. This, with the aid of earnest friends was soon accomplished; though they, in consequence of its debts, refused to date their origin from the Bristol Society. The union of the two societies was, however, for some months supported by us; but after a time Mr Grant (the local Bristol Secretary) seceded, and recommenced the old society.[1]

Kingston called a preliminary meeting of interested parties on 20 February, 1856.[2] With the luxury of time and the means to cruise in his yacht around a number of ports, and having noted what he saw, he began trying to bring the various agencies together through a committee recruited from the great and the good, with a predominance of naval men. His connection (as a grand-nephew) with Admiral Sir Harry Burrard Neale, erstwhile Commander-in-Chief in the Mediterranean, can only have helped. The recruitment of senior naval officers for such committees has already been noted.

That the foundation of The Missions to Seamen was largely down to Kingston's interest is clear from the Minutes of committee meetings preliminary to a Public Meeting.[3] Kingston seemed to have chosen a fortunate moment, for out of the few small and gradually absorbed groups that he had discovered grew quickly a busy society. While The Missions to Seamen seems never to have had large sums of money, neither was it plagued by the financial difficulties of the earlier societies nor, as with the later Saint Andrew's Waterside Mission (1864), did it have to create work; appeals for its help came quickly enough, evidenced at regular intervals in reports presented by the General Secretary at successive Church Congresses.[4] Kingston had discovered and responded to a genuine need.

Kingston did not seek to dominate meetings. Yet his skill as an organiser can be seen in the way regular meetings very quickly established a working framework for what was intended to be a society with ambitious aims. At that first meeting, 20 February 1856, in the chair was Captain Scott, accompanied by Kingston, Captain Waugh, J. Richardson Esq., M. Benson Esq., and J.H. Tate, laymen all. They formed a provisional committee, which would include the Duke of Manchester, and Captains Caffin, Fishbourne, and Sullivan, to start a society in London to support missions to seamen.

At a second meeting, 28 February 1856, it was agreed to form a central association to work on the lines of the Bristol Channel Mission, which it was

---

1. Kingston, *A Cruise on the Mersey*, 43.
2. Kingsford, *The Work and Influence . . .* , 122ff.
3. Minutes can be found in Hull History Centre.
4. Miller, *One Firm Anchor*, 144ff.

hoped would become a member while continuing its work previously established and executed.[1] Despite Kingston's sensitivity in choosing the word 'association' to describe the venture, in March an approach to the Thames Church Mission was rebuffed. The Bristol group seems also to have expressed reluctance.

On 5 April, the committee drew up working guidelines. The first section, *Laws and Regulations*, proposed that the title of the society should be, 'The Society for the Promotion of Missions to Seamen afloat, at home and abroad'; the 'afloat' in its title lying behind Church Congress speeches suggesting work among seamen ashore would fall to others, i.e., the parochial clergy who were supposed to be responsible for the ports in their parishes. The society would have Patron(s), Vice Patron(s), a President, Vice President(s), and a committee of twenty-four. Other paragraphs dealt with subscriptions, General Meetings, and regulations to govern the committee. Kingston and The Rev. T.A. Walrond were named as Honorary Secretaries and the Hon. A. Kinnaird and Admiral W.B. Hamilton as Treasurers.

A week later, *Bye Laws* were drawn up and accepted. There were ten of these, which placed operations of the society under the central committee in London, but allowed for provincial committees, corresponding members, as well as Foreign and Colonial Port Committees. The central committee was to organise other committees, select and appoint staff, communicate with the Government, receive chaplains' reports, and handle subscriptions and other monies. The provincial committees were intended to create interest and raise money; the port committees to oversee vessels and boats employed in the work of the society and assist port chaplains; the Colonial and Foreign Port Committees to have a similar function. Chaplains and other agents were to keep journals of their work for submission to the central committee. The central committee would pay stipends quarterly.

Negotiations with the Bristol Channel Mission

Details of those stumbling negotiations with the rump of the Bristol Channel Mission now begin to appear. On the 25 April, 1856, The Missions to Seamen committee asked for clarification of the objections of the Bristol Mission to merge, in the hope that the two societies could be brought closer. The Minutes of 2 May reveal that the Bristol Mission was highly suspicious of the London committee, fearing an attempt to encroach upon its Bristol activity, something 'indignantly repudiated' by The Missions to Seamen. London, for its part, declined to accept the Bristol Channel Mission's debts, for which there was, at this stage, no certain figure, reasonably arguing that it was unable to give 'undefined aid and assistance'. Further investigation (13 May 1856) into the income and expenditure of the Bristol Channel Mission stations at Bristol

---

1. From this point references to the Bristol Channel Mission effectively refer to its successor body, the Mission to British Seamen.

and Ryde prompted, five days later, a compromise proposal, effectively for the Bristol work to become a provincial committee. This too proved unacceptable to Bristol. On 17 May, a London proposal for the dissolution of the Bristol association was accompanied by another that suggested the opening of two subscription lists, one for the general purposes of the new Society and the second to pay off the debt of the Bristol Mission. The next meeting (28 May) of the central committee, considered what appeared to be a Bristol Channel Mission debt of £1,000 and concluded that to give more than ten per cent of its present income towards removing the debt was impossible, a statement that gives an idea of the expected income of the London society in its first year.

In an attempt to overcome the impasse, for the Bristol Channel Mission The Rev. D. Coper and its Hon. Secretary, Henry Grant, travelled to London to meet the central committee and supervise the transfer of all papers. To amorticise the Bristol debt, now revealed to be a more manageable £450, London agreed to use a percentage of its income – to be paid by installments. A month later, Mr Grant wrote to say that the Bristol Committee ('the Mission to Seamen off the Coasts of Great Britain') had been dissolved. The national society, accepting the dissolution, appointed The Rev. Theodore A. Walrond as Secretary of the combined society, agreed to pay him £200 a year, and ordered him to obtain office premises. In early July, an office was taken in Fenchurch Street, in the City of London. Plans were made to launch a major appeal for funds. Dr Ashley was contacted regarding his handing over the *Eirene*. The Rev. C.B. Gribble was approached about the possibility of absorbing the Wells Street Sailors' Home and St Paul's Church into the association. The Wells Street Home declined to be absorbed.

An independent picture of the situation at this stage survives in the *Bristol Mercury* (5 July 1856). At a meeting, at which Ashley was not present, held in Bristol's Victoria Rooms to receive 'a farewell report from the committee and dissolving the local society', the newspaper reported:

> the Society . . . under Dr Ashley's chaplaincy, had got deeper and deeper into debt. This circumstance led to a representation in the month of June, 1855, to Dr Ashley, who then agreed to resign, and to date back his resignation to the month of April, up to which time his full stipend of £400 per annum was paid to him. The *Eirene* mission cutter was then sent out to the South coast, where she had not long appeared, when, without any effort of the part of the committee, a powerful Metropolitan committee began to be formed, the nucleus, it was hoped, of a noble society.[1]

Optimism was expressed. 'After ten years of depression, the mission at length enjoys a prosperous year, and one which closes with the happiest prospects for

---

1. The offer to Ashley of £400 at a time when a curate could expect £200, though usually with accommodation, may have been intended to sweeten his withdrawal from the affairs of the society.

5. W.H.G. Kingston from M.R. Kingsford, *The Mersey Mission to Seamen*, 1957

6. 'The Mission Ship *Eirene* Bristol Channel 1843'

the future'. This optimism was based on 'the extensive and increased efficiency of the mission', better finances, and this 'immediate expectation of establishing a national society'. The extolled efficiency came from three stations, one based at Ryde for the English Channel, its chaplain The Rev. T.C. Childs, the Bristol Channel Mission under the chaplaincy of The Rev. C.D. Strong, and a third for the 'Great Harbour of Malta' with an honorary (i.e., unpaid) chaplain, The Rev. R.B. Howe. As to the improved financial situation, 'The [Metropolitan] society thus constituted is prepared to take our debt, estimated at £450 (to be gradually paid off). . . .'

> Feeling then that the time is come – that already the adequate discharge of our duty as a mission to the seafaring population of Great Britain is entirely beyond our strength as a small local committee, we propose that this society is now dissolved in favour of the society for promoting missions to seamen at home and abroad'.

The report was adopted on the motion of The Rev. W. Mansell.

> The Rev. R.A. Taylor proposed a resolution declaring the local mission dissolved, and merged in the central association. The motion, which was seconded by The Rev. C. Strong, was unanimously adopted, and the proceedings terminated.

Having made enquiries (9 July 1856) about the rate at which a vessel, like the *Eirene*, could be hired for the months during which she could cruise in the English Channel, there being some delay in Ashley's delivering up the *Eirene*, the London committee resolved (17 July 1856) that Childs should be authorised to continue his work in the Channel. He was to use Ryde as his base, with an assistant named Hall, the use of three boats, and should publicise the work while raising funds locally; a Port Committee would be formed to support the work. The *Eirene* was not considered suitable for use at Ryde, as it was too expensive to maintain. It was decided to employ a ship keeper until the *Eirene*'s ownership was decided; a decision which confirms that there were a number of grey areas requiring resolution between the London and Bristol societies, for which the *Eirene* seems to have become a token. This is confirmed by the London committee's decision (1 August 1856) to write to Ashley to enquire on what grounds he was claiming the *Eirene* as his property, when it had been understood to be part of the package transferred to London by the Bristol society. It is not clear whether Ashley received a letter from the committee; no record of a reply seems to have survived. The appointment of a ship keeper suggests that the London society had access to the vessel; the Minutes are otherwise vague about both vessel and ownership.

In August, continuing disagreement over the *Eirene* caused the Bristol Channel Mission, apparently now a provincial committee of the larger society, to show signs of independence; Bristol was being asked to give up that upon which it had been built, the *Eirene*. Meanwhile, London decided (8 August 1856) that there were places more in need of missionary efforts than Ryde, for which insufficient funds were available. It was concluded that the Resolution of 17 July, which authorised Childs to continue his work should be rescinded; a resolution that caused Childs, the real link with the remnants of Ashley's work, the man who had brought W.H.G. Kingston into the equation and indirectly to the formation of The Missions to Seamen, to complain of breach of engagement. His decision to opt for the quieter life of a small Devon parish will be readily understood by numbers of mission staff who, over the years, have had a similar experience. The proposed changes at Ryde caused those signs of Bristol's independence to harden in August, prompting from Bristol a lengthy correspondence complaining of 'the Committee having deviated from their proposed mode of action and avowed object, by relinquishing the Ryde Mission', and, as will appear below, in consequence viewing itself again as a separate society (Minutes, 10 September 1856).[1]

Elsewhere, the London committee continued to make progress. The Archbishop of Canterbury agreed to serve as a Vice Patron as did the Bishop

---

1. This was not to be the end of The Missions to Seamen's involvement in Ryde. In 1929, a cutting from an island newspaper surviving among the Society's papers reported the naming and commissioning of *Eirene IV*, the numbering indicating its succession from the original *Eirene,* at Ryde pier head on 12 June. The local Bishop, missing the ferry, had had to find a fast boat to take him across the Solent to arrive in time to conduct the ceremony. Somebody told the reporter that the original *Eirene* had been used by John Ashley, 'really the pioneer of Missions to Seamen', from 12 March, 1841.

of London; the Archbishop of York deferred his decision for no obvious reason. Sir James Duke MP and Captain Gambier became Vice Presidents. In his *Cruise on the Mersey* (1856-1857) Kingston gave a slightly different list of names, but all from a similar mould. On 29 October, 1856, the London committee reported the receipt of its first appeal for assistance, from Odessa, served from the Embassy Chaplaincy in Constantinople.[1]

The London committee entered 1857 with plans for a large Public Meeting at which Lord Shaftesbury had agreed to take the chair.[2] It amended the Constitution to make absolutely clear that the society belonged to the Church of England. The Public Meeting, booked for 10 March, to be held at Willis' Rooms (a venue also favoured by the Thames Church Mission for meetings), recognised the neglect of its seamen by the Established Church, commended the work of the new society, and replaced what had been a provisional committee with a regular one. Ashley's name did not appear.[3]

This new committee met on 11 March, 1857, and appointed The Rev. J. Nagle Gillman as Travelling Secretary. From this date, it may be said, the society 'got under weigh'. Grants were made to several ports and others were investigated. Gillman travelled widely to publicise the work. He seems to have been involved in some way when the (by now) totally separate Bristol Channel Mission re-opened negotiations with London at the end of May. Despite the unhappiness of the Bristol Channel Mission with London's attitude to Ryde, to Childs and to the *Eirene* (though lack of funding was The Missions to Seamen's favoured explanation for the rift) an amalgamation of the two societies again began to appear a possibility, though the financial situation of the Bristol Channel Mission at one point appeared so bad that The Missions to Seamen Committee again had to emphasise that it could not claim the Bristol society's foundation date as its own, lest it be rendered liable for Bristol's debts.

There is no doubt that the existence of two societies using 'Missions to Seamen' in their titles caused public confusion, something compounded by the Bishop of London's official connection with both. Despite slow progress in bringing the two societies together, this seems largely to have been achieved by St Peter's Day, 29 June 1857, and marked by Ashley's election as a Vice President of The Missions to Seamen in September, 1857. Details are sparse. Whether Ashley had had a role in discussions is not known. His absence from surviving records suggests that he had become increasingly detached from the Bristol committee; however, his election was important as a symbol. Mary

1. Miller, *One Firm Anchor*, 181.
2. *Minutes*, 18.2.57, 25.2.57.
3. Captain Caffin RN, CB; J.C. Colquhoun Esq; The Rev. W.B. Daubeny; Montagu Gore Esq.; Captain W.H. Hall RN, CB; W.H.G. Kingston; The Rev. W. Light; Captain Nolloth RN; Captain Scott; Admiral Sir William Carroll KCB; H.D.P. Cunningham Esq.; Captain Fishbourne RN; The Rev. C.B. Gribble; The Rev. E. Kingston; Captain Liardet RN; Captain Mangles; J. Richardson Esq.; Captain Waugh.

7. Somersham Church, 1844

Walrond implied that Ashley had retired to a parish but this is unsupported by any evidence; parish work only claimed his attention in 1871 – fourteen years later, while he covered an interregnum in Gosfield, Essex, for a three month period, before moving to a curacy-in-charge in Somersham, Suffolk, in 1872. In the meantime, he remained in Bath. As he appears neither in the list of Bath parochial clergy nor in the local newspapers as officiating anywhere, it seems safe to assume that he was without parochial duties.

The London committee's first report, for 1856-7, indicated that it had established a first permanent station on the Cork River and Queenstown Harbour. It had also a missioner working on that part of the Thames not served by the Thames Church Mission. Honorary Chaplains represented the society on the Mersey, the Bristol Channel, the Isle of Wight, Milford and Swansea, Cork, the Sussex Coast, Great Yarmouth, Plymouth, the Tyne, Malta, Leghorn, and the Elbe, while Scripture Readers served the Tyne, Yarmouth, Brighton, Plymouth, Portsmouth, Swansea and Madras. A number of these derived from the Bristol Mission's work, leaving Bristol little to report.

In 1858, complete unification was accomplished between London and Bristol following another move to bring the two societies together under the suggested title *Missions to Seamen* as being 'more free and open'. Four points were discussed: the question of the name of the combined societies, the combining of committees, the pooling of resources, and the honouring of outstanding engagements entered into by the Bristol Channel Mission. The London committee had drawn up a circular by the end of April 1858, and had sent copies to the Archbishop of Canterbury, Lord Shaftesbury and the Duke of Marlborough for their consideration. The circular proposed that both committees should resign and a new committee should then be formed; there would be two representatives from each society to select a committee that they found mutually agreeable; the Vice Patrons of both societies who were Prelates, Peers or Admirals to be retained; the General Committee to meet quarterly in London supported by two standing sub-committees, one in London, the other in Bristol (in effect a local committee). The first three of these points were agreed. Anything outstanding was left for consideration by the new committee. On this basis, The Missions to Seamen and the rump of the Bristol Channel Mission achieved permanent union on 19 May, 1858, the Minute Book of The Missions to Seamen Central Committee carrying this entry for 1 June 1858: 'Resolved: That an advertisement be twice inserted in the Times, Record & Shipping Gazette announcing the union of the Bristol Society with the London Society – & that this union is also announced in the circulars of the Society [original emphasis]'. The Minutes of the Annual General Meeting in the summer noted, 'This meeting received with pleasure the announcement of a union of the London and Bristol Societies'.

Subsequently it was noted, 'Resolved: That the Members of the late Managing Committee at Bristol, now members of the [Central] Committee be appointed to act as Sub-Committee of this Society [original emphasis]'. On 14 September, Bristol agreed to accept the proposals of the Central Committee, among them 'That the foreign Stations of the Society hitherto under the management of the Bristol Subcommittee be transferred to the care of the London Sub Committee', which would leave Bristol responsible for the Bristol Channel, the Kentish Coast, the Isle of Wight, Plymouth, Milford and Swansea.

A permanent solution regarding the *Eirene* remained to be found. The Minutes for September, 1858, recorded:

> Rev. L.A. Walker having given an account of the state in wh[ich] the *Eirene* is at present & the necessity of some steps being taken respecting her, it was Resolved that Dr Ashley be requested to give his consent that the Central Committee may do with her whatever they judge best [original emphasis].[1]

The outcome of the Committee's request is not recorded. Silence, and Ashley's disappearance from the Minutes, may indicate that Ashley had decided to wash his hands of the problem. Marital difficulties could also have taken his mind off the *Eirene*; the suggestion is only a possibility.

What resulted, as it was described by Captain Gambier RN at a meeting in Southampton in 1859, was a society which 'was not only an extension of the old Bristol Channel Mission to the whole coasts of Great Britain, but to seamen all over the world'. In other words, the London society had begun already to see itself as a successor to the Bristol work, despite resolutions to the contrary

---

1. Hull History Centre DMS/1/2, *Minutes of the Missions to Seamen Central Committee from 1858.*

so recently made. In reality, the Bristol Channel Mission had joined the larger society.[1] That said, teething problems continued: on 8 January, 1859, General Secretary Walrond in his letter book copied a letter 'addressed to each member of the Bristol Committee'. To each, he had written:

> Sir, owing to the retirement of Mr Cooper & Mr Grant from the Bristol local Committee Mr Walker writes me that it is *de facto* non existent – It w[oul]d greatly simplify our course of action if you w[oul]d kindly inform me . . . whether you will in future be able to take an active part in the Sub Committee or w[oul]d prefer retiring from it. . . . [2]

The departure of Mr Grant and Mr Cooper can only have eased the working relationship between London and Bristol.

In 1858, The Missions to Seamen in London began producing a small monthly account of its work, *Word on the Waters*, mostly drawn from chaplains' reports.[3] The account this gave of the Society's origins is rather wide of the story as it appears in the Minutes. The January issue noted that the Bristol society had requested Dr Ashley 'to make [his work] known by sermons and public meetings; and wherever the Mission was introduced to public notice, funds were poured in with liberality and cheerfulness', before introducing readers to Ashley's financial problems: 'Thus a work, which had been carried out for upwards of sixteen years . . . was brought to a close'. It touched on Ashley's successor, 'The Rev. T. Cave Childs . . . until the spring of last year . . . he and the Committee parted with mutual kindly feelings and good wishes . . .'. It mentioned 'that excellent institution "the Thames Church Mission Society" [which] commenced in 1844. Adapting our [*sic*] system of sending the Gospel to seamen afloat . . .', a statement that may have surprised supporters of the Thames society. Throughout 1858, it referred to itself as 'Missions to Seamen', a title still to be agreed. Several issues offered Ashley's version of his encounters with seamen, sanitised by the omission of the various difficulties which the Bristol Society's Committee had had to face. Not until July 1858 did Ashley begin to appear, albeit as the final name, on its list of Vice Presidents. As names seem to have been listed by order of appointment, his position is not without significance.

The same issue gave an account of the coming together of the two societies. Here, it is possible to source some of the misinformation in the various books, Mary Walrond's the first, about The Missions to Seamen (published in the twentieth century).

> Our readers are aware, that for some time there have been in existence two Societies for the promotion of Mission to Seamen, namely, that named simply 'Missions to Seamen', having its base of operations in

---

1. *Hampshire Advertiser*, 23 April 1859.
2. Hull History Centre DMS/1/2, *Minutes*. . . .
3. A bound volume, 1858-1863, survives in the British Library.

Bristol, the birthplace of the original Society . . . and the 'Society for Promoting Missions to Seamen Afloat, at Home and Abroad', having its committee sitting in London. . . . Both of these Societies . . . originated in the 'Bristol Channel Mission Society', which dates from the year 1835. . . . In 1844 a brief interruption of the work took place; it was revived in 1845, by the formation of a Society called 'The Bristol Channel Seamen's Mission'. . . . This extension [*viz.* Childs on the Isle of Wight] . . . to the south coast led to the formation of a Society in London. . . . The relation, therefore, in which these two Societies stood to each other, could not but prove a source of pain and anxiety to the Christian men acting on both Committees.

To these anxious and pained Committee members, it was able to report that the two Societies were beginning to work together, followed by the news, in August's issue, that the London Society's Annual Meeting on 29 June, 1858, had been told 'that a union had been effected'. By the issue of January 1860, matters were sufficiently advanced for it to be announced that 'the arrangements and direction of all the stations is in London. . . .'

Ashley was not entirely removed from the work for seafarers. The *Exeter Flying Post* (8 December 1859) reported a meeting in aid of The Missions to Seamen, which had been held at Exeter's Athenaeum on 5 December, Captain Bingham presiding, as he had done in 1854. 'The Rev. John Ashley DD [*sic*], chaplain to the Bristol Channel Mission of the society, attended as a deputation.' Ashley 'gave the meeting an interesting narrative of his experience during the twenty-one years which he had been connected with seamen afloat', a total of years suggesting that he saw no discontinuity in his work for the seafarer. In June 1860, Ashley, at last present at the Annual Meeting in London 'moved the second Resolution – "That this Society will with God's help . . . earnestly avail itself of the great openings for usefulness . . .'", and continued with the oft-told account of his starting the work in Bristol, in 1835, after seeing the wind-bound fleets in the Bristol Channel.

Chapter Six

John Ashley's Later Years

Ashley's name is associated with the Thames Church Mission, The Missions to Seamen, and the St Andrew's Waterside Mission but features little in their records. Where his name does appear, it is usually in a reference to his Bristol Channel work as an inspiration. Mary Walrond's book touches on his later years but her information is not always accurate. This means that tracing him from the 1850s is quite difficult. Newspaper reports offer examples of his public speaking, usually on behalf of the revived Bristol Mission, later and less frequently, for The Missions to Seamen. Newspapers are not ideal sources but they do offer useful nuggets of information, which allow some key dates and his whereabouts, if not always his occupation, to be traced. Just occasionally, the difficulties of these years appear in eye-catching columns.

The *Salisbury and Winchester Journal* carried a number of reports of him speaking at various places in the South West, on the lines of 'Dr Ashley delivered a most excellent as well as prolonged address', mostly in the early 1850s.[1] The *Gloucester Journal* (5 February 1853) reported a speech in Gloucester. In each case, his talk was on behalf of the revived Bristol Channel Mission. Later in 1853, the *Morning Post* (11 June) reported Ashley speaking at a Public Meeting in London, in the Freemasons Hall ('Tavern' in the *Gloucester Journal* of 18 June), with the Earl of Shaftesbury ('who, we regretted to observe, seemed in indifferent health') in the chair. Ashley proposed that the revived Bristol society should employ two clergy to extend its work, his proposal supported by the Bishop of Llandaff, and seconded by The Hon. Captain Maude RN.

In September 1854, at a meeting at Exeter's Athenaeum, Ashley informed his audience that 'a meeting was held in London in June last year, when the [Bristol] Society was reorganised. The Archbishop of Canterbury became Patron and Lord Shaftesbury president . . . a managing committee was formed in Bristol . . .', the implication being that Ashley was party to these plans.[2] In

---

1. *Salisbury and Winchester Journal:* 22 November 1851 'well attended and addressed at considerable length . . .'; 27 December 1851; 23 May 1852. *Bath Chronicle* 22 April 1852. Much the same material appears in the *Hampshire Advertiser*, 22 December 1851, January 1852, March 1852, etc.

2. *Exeter Flying Post*, 7 September 1854. Anthony Ashley-Cooper, Lord Ashley until he became 7th Earl of Shaftesbury, great 19th century reformer, was president of

1856, the year of The Missions to Seamen's foundation, Ashley was missing from the *Bristol Mercury's* report of a similar meeting in Bristol's Victoria Rooms (2 July 1856):

> for the purpose of receiving a farewell report from the committee dissolving the local society. . . . The *Eirene* mission cutter was then [1855] sent out to the South coast, where she had not long appeared, when, without any effort on the part of the committee, a powerful Metropolitan committee began to be formed, the nucleus, it was hoped, of a noble society.

And then, in December 1859, there was that report in the *Exeter Flying Post* that 'The Rev. John Ashley DD [*sic*], Chaplain to the Bristol Channel Mission of the society, attended as a deputation', on that society's behalf in the local Athenaeum.

A number of things might have contributed to Ashley's very reduced involvement in the Bristol Mission's work, among them, the death of his father in 1850, his own poor health after the collision of the *Eirene*, or the general turmoil following the re-emergence of the Bristol Mission. Occasionally, and without evidence, it has been suggested that his wife's health was giving cause for concern. It is hard to imagine that he would not have been involved in the refitting of the *Eirene*, noted in the *Bristol Mercury* of 3 December 1853 as 'now so far refitted. . . .' The *Bristol Mercury* reported his formal resignation as chaplain of the Bristol Channel Mission in April, 1855.

Contemporary street directories for Bristol and Bath give few clues to his place of residence in this period. Letter VII to subscribers of the Bristol Channel Mission (31 December 1850) gave his address as Heywood Hall, Bristol, as did the 1855 *Crockford*, but neither Ashley nor Heywood Hall appear in Bristol's 1850s street directories. At some point, he moved from Bristol to Bath. The Bath directory first mentions him as a resident of 13 Grosvenor Place, Bath, in 1860, an address repeated in the 1860 *Crockford*, which suggests that he was a Bath resident, at least from some point, in 1859.

Grosvenor Place was in a good, if not the best, part of Bath, and in the (then) very large parish of Walcot; a parish served by an incumbent and two assistant curates. No evidence has been found to suggest that Ashley was exercising his ministry in any Bath parish. His house in Grosvenor Place was described in an advertisement as an 'elegant and spacious Mansion' with generously proportioned rooms, among them library, breakfast and dining rooms, 'two splendid drawing-rooms . . . ten bed chambers, bathroom, billiard or music-room, domestic offices; greenhouse and flower garden'. Ashley's application for letters patent in 1861 also gave Grosvenor Place

---

the British & Foreign Bible Society (1851-85) and the Evangelical Alliance, among many agencies. It can have done John Ashley no harm to share the famous surname though there is no evidence of kinship.

as his address.[1] Entries in the *Bath Chronicle* mention Ashley there in 1860 and 1862; later Bath street directories add nothing more. His wife was mentioned as living at the Grosvenor Place address in the *Bath Chronicle* of 6 November, 1862. The 1865 *Crockford* continued to give Grosvenor Place as his address.

That Mrs Ashley died in Bath, at 28 Gay Street, on 13 October, 1867, suggests the continuing presence of Ashley's family, if not at Grosvenor Place, at least in Bath until that year. At his court case, pursued while at Somersham in 1874, Ashley said that they had been separated for some time, though his evidence under cross examination seems to have drifted from what can be demonstrated from independent sources. The Ashleys ceased to share the same roof from early 1865; 13 Grosvenor Place was advertised in the 'To Let' column of the *Bath Chronicle*, without success, almost continuously from May 1865 until 1868, at which time it seems to have been taken by Admiral Sir W.F. Martin, Bart., KCB.[2]

It is apparent from the newspaper reports that followed Ashley's court appearances in Bath that his income was sufficient to maintain a cook (and where there is a cook there is usually at least a house maid) and groom, at least until (if required) it had to serve two households. Dublin's *Freeman's Journal* (7 July 1863) reported a petition which came before the Carlow Quarter Sessions from Ashley and others, joint tenants of lands in the Queen's County, regarding 'The Estate of the Rev. John Ashley D.D. [*sic*] and others . . . praying that the chairman might sanction the granting by them of an improvement lease' to the tenant in possession. It is not certain that this John Ashley was the subject of this book, but it seems probable, and if he was, the likelihood is that some income remained from his Irish inheritance.

Newspaper reports of meetings imply that Ashley's life before 1865 would have appeared little changed to those around him. The *Chronicle* reported his presence with many other clergy at the annual meeting of donors, patrons and friends of Grosvenor College in June 1860. At the January 1862 Annual General Meeting of subscribers and governors of Bath United Hospitals, he was invited to move a vote of thanks to the physicians and surgeons. A week later, he sat with the clergy at the General Meeting of the Bath Auxiliary of the British and Foreign Bible Society, another very public occasion. His presence in each case was probably because he was a subscriber.

---

1. Ashley's patent, no 2771, dated 4 November 1861, 'Improvements in Apparatus for attaching Horses to Carriages'. It will reappear in a newspaper interview during Ashley's time as curate of Somersham. The preamble reads: 'The shafts and poles presently in use for attaching horses to carriages in single or double harness cause great distress to the horses. . . . To obviate the evils and the risks from the use of long shafts and poles heretofore employed, and to relieve horses from the strains . . . according to the present Invention very short shafts are used, coming only to the horse's waist or middle. . . .'
2. *Bath Chronicle*, 26 November 1868.

The *Chronicle* of 13 August 1860 reported a prosecution brought by Ashley against his cook, Elizabeth Randle. At his behest she was 'charged with stealing a quantity of bread and butter, meat, dripping, a piece of cloth, &c.' from 13 Grosvenor Place. Apparently Ashley had discovered her on the morning of Saturday 11 August giving the stolen goods to a boy at the door. She was charged on the following Monday and sentenced to three months' imprisonment with hard labour. Courts of the period, a time when those involved in the administration of justice depended upon an army of domestic staff in their homes, tended to deal harshly with dishonest servants.

A year later, it was Ashley himself who was called before the court. The *Bristol Mercury*, 28 September 1861, in a paragraph, COUNTY POLICE, SATURDAY, reported that The Rev. John Ashley, of Grosvenor Place, was 'summoned for having on the 11th of the month' refused payment of a toll. The *Bath Chronicle*, 26 September 1861, carried more detail. Ashley had been summoned by Thomas Young, keeper of the Lime Pit turnpike for leaving his carriage and horse in the turnpike road 'whereby payment of the toll was evaded'. 'The defendant drove up in a carriage with a young lady in it within fourteen yards of the gate'. They alighted from the carriage, walked through the gate, and went into a nearby house, 'leaving the carriage and horse in charge of a groom'.[1] On their return, some half an hour later, Ashley refused to pay the requested toll, handed the keeper his card, and told him he might summon him. In court, Ashley argued that as the horse was a young one, he had not dared drive through the gate, 'because there was no convenient place in which to turn it'. He added that he would have left the horse where he did, even if there had been no gate nearby. The magistrates' clerk said that there was no liability to the toll unless the carriage passed through the gate, so the Bench dismissed the case; something of a storm in a teacup, but affording a rare glimpse of Ashley's manner, particularly towards those of another social class.

There is a possibility that Ashley was using his pen at this time. Together with Ashley's 1870s pamphlets in the British Library Catalogue published under the pseudonym 'A WYKEHAMIST', several other works, but from the 1860s, claim the same pseudonym. The possibility that these others were written by Ashley needs consideration. *Papers on Preaching* (1861) can be dismissed on internal evidence, as, for example, the author quotes with approval (p.34) Dr Pusey and John Mason Neale, Tractarians both; something inconceivable for a man with Ashley's protestant views. Several books of school day memories are written in a style unlike Ashley's. A more likely proposition, given his Irish trips, a book entitled *Paddyland*, the catalogue ascribes to F. Gale. Although Ashley's Irish connection makes his authorship of *Paddylands*, a discursive travelogue written by a Protestant, a possibility yet the presence of humour and the lack of Ashley's increasing bigotry suggests a different author. In short, a reading of these 1860s books makes it hard to credit that any are his.

Where Ashley lived from 1865 seems not to have been Bath. The Bath street directory offers nothing to suggest continued residence there. It is

---

1. It is implicit in both papers that the groom is Ashley's.

possible that he remained in Grosvenor Place, ready to leave as soon as a tenant could be found. It is more likely that he moved to Kilburn in London, at least according to his testimony in his 1874 prosecution, but exactly when or why is not certain. His whereabouts in 1866 and 1867 have to be guessed. In 1867 the *Chronicle* announced in its deaths' column: 'on Oct. 13, at her residence in Gay-street, Catherine, the wife of The Rev. John Ashley LL.D, daughter of the late Charles Ward, Esq., of Holly Mount, in the Queen's County, and Marrion-square, Dublin, Ireland.'[1] The wording, that the Gay Street address was 'her' rather than 'their' address, supports Ashley's claim in court in 1874 that the couple had separated.

The 1869 *Post Office London Street Directory* listing for The Rev. John Ashley LLD at 23 Greville Road, Kilburn (allowing for the delay between compilation and printing) implies his residence there from 1868, the year of his marriage to Elizabeth Treadwell, while the 1868 *Crockford* listing of his address as Milford Cottage, Greville-road, Kilburn, could push his residence in Kilburn back to 1867, presumably, if there is any truth in his statement in *Ashley v. Haward* that he was paying for his lodgings in Kilburn with a 'woman named Treadwell', at that address. Assuming this was the same Miss Treadwell who married him in September 1868, it is odd that he was named as the principal resident in 23 Greville Road in the *Post Office Directory*. This would not have been the case had she been his landlady. The 1870 *Crockford* repeated his Kilburn address. It is possible to speculate that the couple had known each other in Bristol, where Elizabeth had been born and successive censuses record her return as a visitor, from whence is unsaid, or that, on arrival in Kilburn, Ashley had lodged with her until he found the house in Greville Road; whether to rent or to buy is not known – but if rented, it could explain the shortness of their stay in Greville Road. At the time Ashley was referring in court to Elizabeth as 'a woman named Treadwell', his newer Will was referring to her as 'my dear wife'. Neither reference can be used to establish whether the marriage was one of convenience or affection, or both. What is certain is that it was entered with a measure of celerity.

Nineteenth-century Kilburn, on the main road north from London, was still being developed. Early in the century, there had been some hope that a local spring might allow Kilburn to become a health resort; something never achieved. Although the railway company had opened Kilburn and Maida Vale station (now Kilburn High Road station) in 1852, a horse bus into London continued to run. Businesses were opening but at the time of Ashley's arrival, there were still nearby open spaces and fields. Greville Road remains a pleasant tree-lined avenue in the better part of Kilburn, though much of the original housing, including that of the Ashleys, has given way to flats. St Mary's church,

1. *Bath Chronicle*, 17 October 1867. The registration of Elizabeth's death adds to the newspaper notice that she was aged sixty-four and giving the cause of death as paralysis and an intestinal obstruction.

gracefully spired and built in the newly fashionable early decorated Gothic style in 1856, is a fifteen-minute walk away; the walk to the railway station perhaps ten minutes. A signpost at the end of Greville Road indicates Marylebone as two miles distant.

On 13 September 1868, the date of his marriage to Elizabeth Treadwell, i.e., before Ashley had managed to let his Grosvenor Place address in Bath, the marriage register of Marylebone Parish Church listed 'St Marylebone' as his place of residence. Ashley's marriage to Elizabeth, as to Catherine was 'by Licence', so gives no evidence of the duration of Ashley's residence there. If evidence of anything, it is rather an indication of gentrification. Marylebone was fashionable as a wedding venue; perhaps, too, easier than Kilburn for friends to reach. Whatever the reason, it does not prevent his living in Kilburn.

The couple's marriage certificate described Elizabeth Treadwell's father, Jabez Treadwell, as a gentleman. According to the *Bristol Mercury*, Jabez died on 16 June 1869, aged seventy two. He had been born in 1798, and so was two years older than his new son-in-law. Successive census returns confirm his residence in various parts of Bristol. Jabez Treadwell had married Elizabeth Beard in 1824. Of their six children, Ashley's bride – also Elizabeth – was apparently the youngest.[1] The Marylebone marriage register listed three witnesses, Jno. Treadwell, [Annie?] O'Neill and Thos Flintoff. The officiating minister was an assistant curate of St Marylebone, Henry N. Collier. Jabez Treadwell's age, and his death just nine months after the wedding, suggest he may not have been in London for the ceremony.

At Kilburn, the incumbent, The Rev. Mr Kennion, a man with similar religious views to Ashley, had been appointed, initially as Perpetual Curate, then Vicar, of St Mary's in 1867; he remained in the parish until 1879. It is possible, since Kennion had been Curate of Eastington, Gloucestershire from 1855, that Ashley and Kennion were already known to each other.[2] Things had come to such a pass in Kilburn in the three years since Kennion's arrival that the then assistant curate of St Mary's, The Rev. Richard Carr Kirkpatrick, unhappy at Kennion's attempts to impose his markedly protestant views upon a parish hitherto used to a more Catholic tradition, took himself and many of the parishioners off to found in 1870, what would become St Augustine's, Kilburn. The Bishop of London divided the parish in an attempt to ameliorate the situation. The new church of St Augustine, designed on a very grand scale by John Loughborough Pearson RA (1817-1897), with a spire to dwarf that of St Mary's nearby, indeed said to be the highest in London, had been begun in 1871. Ashley's 1874 pamphlet, in which he fulminated against the state of the Church of England and its Catholic revival, is full of detail which would describe very well the liturgical and extra-liturgical practices that followed at St Augustine's, though Ashley does not name the parish.

---

1. I am indebted to David Huckett for some of this Treadwell information.
2. *Crockford* 1868.

A guess that Ashley went to Kilburn to support a fellow Protestant must remain a guess; other possible reasons present themselves. While London would have removed the newly-weds from the gaze of Bath residents interested in the marriage of a clergyman just shy of his 68th birthday to a bride aged 29, within a year of the death of his first wife, Kilburn may also have introduced a small measure of economy into their accommodation when compared with his larger house in Bath. Where the newly-weds spent 1869 was probably still at the Kilburn address. By the time of the 1871 census, they appear briefly in Gosfield in Essex.

In Gosfield, Ashley was involved with the parish church at which, since the parish was vacant for the several months of his residence, he seems to have been covering an interregnum.[1] The Gosfield baptism register, which he signed as 'Officiating Minister', shows his first baptism as 15 January 1871 and his last, 26 March 1871. The *Essex Newsman* (29 April 1871) reported that on Thursday, 20 April, the churchwarden, Mr Alexander Ferguson, presented the departing Ashley with 'a purse containing 17 sovereigns . . . from the congregation'. Unusually, the newspaper printed the full text of a letter of gratitude received by Ferguson from Ashley written 'In all the hurry of packing up'. The presentation had been made privately and it was, as Ashley wrote:

> more than I deserved, and what I never expected. It was a pleasure to me to minister to them in the church, and from house to house; and amply had I been repaid . . . *by the assurance of many that the 'blessed truth as it is in Jesus' set forth in weakness, was made by the Holy Spirit's teaching "the power of God to the refreshment of some, and to the salvation of others believing"'* [original emphasis].

This letter to his 'fellow sinners' continued at length in the same vein before concluding: 'my dear wife desires with me to express the deep sense we entertain of the affectionate reception we have met with in our daily work . . .', the whole well-larded with suitable scriptural allusions. It is not known how Ashley had been recruited to cover the interregnum in the parish. His letter, giving an indication of the churchmanship that he brought or found in the parish, may hint at one possibility. Through Kennion he would have had access to a network of like-minded people. Alternatively, it is known that Ashley was a reader of protestant periodicals, among them, as he described it, 'that faithful paper *The Rock*'.[2]

Early in 1870, possibly before that, Ashley began work on his pamphlet, *The Church of the Period*, which the British Library catalogue dates to 1871. He published it as by 'a Priest of 1824', which he was not, and using the pseudonym

---

1. *Crockford* 1870 places Gosfield in the Diocese of Rochester. A part of Essex in the Rochester Diocese was later transferred to St Albans. The Vicar, Stephen Wilkinson Dowell, incumbent of Gosfield since 1848, was succeeded in 1871 by Henry Lettsom Elliott.
2. A markedly protestant journal.

THE

CHURCH OF THE PERIOD;

OR,

PRIESTCRAFT AND THE CONFESSIONAL
IN THE CHURCH OF ENGLAND;

ALSO,

SEQUEL

TO THE

"CHURCH OF THE PERIOD,"

WITH THE

AUTHOR'S REASONS FOR LEAVING THE
CHURCH OF ENGLAND.

BRISBANE:
PUBLISHED BY WILLIAM ROWNEY, QUERN STREET.
MDCCCLXXIX.

7. Title page of *The Church of the Period or the Church of England in my own time*, (reprint, 1879)

A WYKEHAMIST. It is this that contains descriptions of Anglo-Catholic events, which most surely describe what would have been seen in Kilburn at this time. It seems to have had some acceptance, at least in evangelical and protestant circles, for it was reprinted with his *Sequel* of 1874. The two combined were again printed in Brisbane, Australia, in 1879 by a protestant publishing venture as one of a series, disingenuously titled *Tracts for the Times*, and offering works by hands other than Ashley's of which *Priest, Woman, and Confessional* (1880) and *Papal Idolatry* (1888), by Charles Chiniquy, and *Mitred Mountebanks* (1879) and *Lay Surpliced Lunacy in Contention with Sound Principles and Common Sense* (1879), by David Buchanan, are four among the titles. His description of the 'present state of things' included

> the childish effeminacy of tawdry finery, and changes of gaudy vestments. . . . Choirs – then professional singers – then intoning . . . crosses, vestments, candles, flowers, incense-burners, and processions of decked-out men and women bearing lights, with scenes that throw Drury Lane and Covent Garden Theatres into the shade. Whilst this movement was going on, came the "Tracts for the Times", giving the whole an impetus in the direction of Romanism.

Those against whom he fulminated, he accused of filling

> their churches with processions of hundreds of men and women, boys and girls, meretriciously decked out – some with coronets, others with veils, with countless lighted tapers – "magnificent banners" – clouds of incense – and "sisters (sisters?) gorgeously attired". I do believe we shall shortly have "footlights" to what they now call their "altar" [original punctuation].

These extracts give an idea of the whole. Ashley argued that good Protestants in the Church of England were being forced into Presbyterian and other churches in London by such practices because weak-willed Bishops were failing to exercise their authority. His 1871 pamphlet, and the *Sequel* (apparently written whilst in Somersham) and the Australian version of 1879, give the author's 'reasons for leaving the Church of England', beginning with a reprint of a letter, written in similar vein and first published in the *Christian Standard*. He repeated his claim to have been ordained in February 1824. He enlarged upon his 1832 visit to Ireland, which he said had left him convinced that 'there are no "good" Catholics in existence'. He saw the National Church 'sinking into Popery . . . because the Bishops "love to have it so"'.

> Seriously taking all this into consideration, I cannot but regard the National Church of this day as APOSTATE; and though in the first year of my ministry I was offered a large sum per annum, with a guarantee that it should never be less, if I would leave the Church of England and come up to London – which I positively refused to do – I must now, after having been a minister of that church for fifty-three years, renounce all

connection with her till she is presented to the country pure from the defilement of Popery, and willing to admit within her pale only those who can say they take the Word of God as their rule, and hold to the simple truth as it is in Jesus, worshipping 'in spirit and in truth'. . . . I have hitherto subscribed myself as 'A WYKEHAMIST'; it must now be JOHN ASHLEY, LL.D [original emphasis].

The 'large sum', suggested for a not very clear purpose, seems to have as much credibility as his 1830s claim to have had an expectation of a benefice before preaching to a congregation of two thousand, an expectation apparently dashed in consequence of his espousal of an Evangelical position. Whether he left the Church of England will be considered in a later chapter. For the time being, however, until the summer of 1875, and despite this claim to be leaving the Church of England, he remained as Curate in Charge of Somersham.

Consideration of these pamphlets to confirm what may have been the religious attraction of Kilburn, and to explain the religious opinions expressed in his letter to the Gosfield churchwarden, has run far ahead of Ashley's residence in Kilburn, which seems to have continued until the end of 1870. He left Gosfield in early April 1871. Where the Ashleys stayed in the months between Gosfield and Somersham has yet to be discovered. It is likely to have been in south-east England, for an advertisement, which may have been what drew to his attention the needs of Somersham, appeared in the *Ipswich Journal* of 16 September, 1871:

> Wanted immediately, for a Rural Parish and a small Church, a Curate in Priest's orders offered a good house, not large, unfurnished, with a fair stipend. – address: The Rector, Somersham, near Ipswich.

Somersham's Rector, The Rev. Newman John Stubbin, according to an inscription on an etching of the church commissioned by Stubbin in 1844, was the husband of 'Mrs Stubbin', the Patroness; that is, his wife had the advowson, and presumably had appointed Stubbin as Rector of Somersham in 1833, where he remained until his retirement in 1875. Whether Mrs Stubbin had bought or inherited the right to appoint is not known. Stubbin was now at least the same age as Ashley, and, if beginning to fail, perhaps in need of assistance; probably, too, a widower by the 1870s, if *Crockford* in 1874 is correct in listing him as his own Patron. Ashley, at this time, was showing signs of needing an income to supplement what was left of his inheritance. The two needs coincided. Nothing survives of Ashley's relationship with the incumbent. Mrs Ashley managed to make friends in the parish, and evidently enjoyed the company of the young female friends she invited to stay in the parish house.

Ashley made his first appearance in Somersham's baptismal register on 17 March, 1872, ascribing himself 'Curate in Charge'. Ashley's seventeenth baptism on 23 November, 1873, was followed by an absence from the register, which ended on 12 July, 1874, then eight more baptisms followed with the last on 6 June, 1875. The reason for the break in parish duty may have been the ill-health claimed in Ashley's 1874 court case (below), but may only have been a reflection of a rural birth pattern. The appointment of The Rev. Goodrich Langley as Rector of the parish in succession to Stubbin meant that Ashley's services were no longer required. Langley preached his farewell sermon in his church of St Mary Elms late in September of 1875, that parish having been informed of his impending departure earlier in the month, and by the year's end Langley had been installed as Rector of Somersham.[1]

The local newspaper affords a couple of glimpses of Ashley while Curate in Charge. An interview with Ashley appeared in the *Ipswich Journal* of 20 July, 1872. His willingness to place an advertisement in the paper for his patented harness probably influenced the generous number of column inches given to the interview about it, following a local demonstration of its use. The advertisement, perhaps another indication of his need to increase his income, was the first, indeed would be the only, advertisement for his invention so far discovered. The *Journal* described him as 'a skilful whip and a lover of horses', reporting him as saying that he had been a 'four-in-hand driver from his earliest years'. His attention in 'his earliest driving days' had been drawn to 'the necessity for making an effort to save the horses' forelegs and to increase the safety of human beings in the vehicle'. Consequently he had

> invented a system of double harness in which the pole is dispensed with, and the horses' work on the forelegs so much lightened that he claims that horses descending a hill in this harness have no more distress than the leaders in a four-in-hand would have.

The reporter noted that a group of gentlemen, among them the Rector of Blakenham, The Rev. Mr Cookson, the Mayor of Ipswich, and others, had been invited to witness a demonstration of his invention by Ashley, using models and a harness attached to a stuffed horse. This stuffed horse ensured good copy for it had been shot under a Danish officer in the war of Schleswig-Holstein, and its skin preserved at Copenhagen.[2] A detailed description of Ashley's invention followed, including what Ashley called 'the LLD double shafts', and the reporter's wry comment, '[i]ndeed, from first to last, there is not a point which Dr Ashley has overlooked'.

The harness advertisement appeared in the same paper, headed:

CARRIAGES IN DOUBLE HARNESS without Poles;
AND PERFECT EASE TO HORSES IN
SINGLE HARNESS Going downhill with the Heaviest Carriage
[original emphasis],

---

1. *Ipswich Journal*, 11/9/75 and 28/9/75.
2. Associating the name of Copenhagen with his stuffed horse was a shrewd move by Ashley. Copenhagen was the name of the horse on which the Duke of Wellington had been seated at Waterloo.

with an accompanying explanation:

> The present system of the Pole and Old Shaft is cruelty. L.L.D's Patent
> may be seen every Wednesday, from Two to Five o'clock, on application
> to Mr David Green, The Griffin, Somersham; or arrangement for
> private inspection may be made to L.L.D Somersham, Ipswich [original
> emphasis].

It is not known if this advertisement attracted any sales.

John Ashley in Court Again

The *Ipswich Journal of* 4 April 1874 carried a six-columned report of an action,
Ashley v. Haward, for trespass and assault, before a 'Special Jury empanelled to
try the case'. Ashley, the plaintiff, was represented by two lawyers, one a QC and
MP, and the defendant by a similar duo. The whole affair, as it unfolded, was
worthy of reprinting as a chapter in Charles Dickens' *Pickwick Papers*. Laughter
in court was reported on frequent occasions, mostly at the expense of the
plaintiff. Many of the autobiographical details elicited during the questioning
of Ashley conflict with information already established in this book, not least a
claim never to have driven a four-in-hand.

Introducing the case, Mr Bulwer QC, explained that his client, Ashley, was
an elderly gentleman, aged 75 years, who 'had never known what it was to have
a day's illness in his life. . . . He was a gentleman on whom fortune had not
smiled. At one time he had more money than at present; but he lost it through
no fault of his own.' His position in Somersham brought him £150 a year,
with a house worth another £50. For this, he was dependent upon the Rector
of Somersham. In the course of evidence, 2 maids and a cook are mentioned,
which suggests a certain standard of living. Ashley argued that it was important
that he was able to maintain his health if he was to maintain his livelihood.

The defendant was a local farmer. When Ashley arrived in Somersham an
'acquaintance sprang up' between the Ashleys and the Hawards, a mother and
son. Mrs Ashley had a young lady staying as her guest, later named as Miss
Spencer. The defendant, Frederick Haward, frequently occupied the Ashleys'
pew in Somersham church, initially it had seemed attracted by Ashley's
preaching, but now apparently by the charms of the Ashleys' guest. In October,
1873, Ashley and his wife left home to visit a 'neighbouring watering place'
(Aldeburgh). The young lady remained in their house. On his return, Ashley
discovered that visits had taken place and the defendant had kissed the young
lady.

> I want the date of the kissing. (*Laughter*) – No pleasant matter in a
> gentleman's house. I think it was in July 1872. Did she ever complain to
> you? No, but she did to my wife. . . .
> Did not the defendant once walk home with her? – I should not have

allowed it if I had known of it. I told Miss Spencer that I did not like to do anything painful to Mrs Haward, and I told her to preserve with the defendant the most distant reserve.

An occasion followed, when Miss Spencer complained that Haward had given his attention to another young lady inside a carriage with her, returning by night with Ashley and his wife riding on the box, on a return trip from Felixstowe. Miss Spencer told Ashley when the carriage had lurched and Haward had put out his hand to protect the other young lady. Ashley told the court that Miss Spencer had said, '"I did not know what to do; I was hot all over" (*Much laughter*)'. After which, Ashley claimed that he had treated Haward coolly.

Next, when Ashley was officiating in Somersham church on a Sunday afternoon, Haward had attended a service at his own church in the neighbouring parish, the incumbent of which had told Ashley that Haward had left the service shortly after it had begun, apparently for an assignation in Somersham, apparently not with Miss Spencer. Ashley's cook told him that she had heard Haward 'talking to the same young lady that had complained of him [not Miss Spencer, who was at Ashley's church service] . . . in the drawing room . . . and she knew that she had not opened the door for him (*laughter*). The window was open.' Apparently there had been two other young ladies staying in Ashley's house who had attracted Haward's interest; seeing from upstairs Haward coming through the garden, one had come down to open the window for him.

Ashley wrote a strong letter to Mr Haward on November 8th, demanding that Haward never enter his grounds again, but he gave no explanation. Ashley was asked why he had sent this letter. He explained that before he and his wife had set off for their three days in Aldeburgh, he had cautioned Miss Spencer not to admit Haward into the house. 'She was offended and said of course she would not do such a thing (*laughter*).' On Ashley's return, 'I noticed a marked difference in her manner'. When asked if Haward had been to the house she denied it,

> but afterwards I found that he had been, and that they were on intimate terms such as was only due from one to whom she was engaged. They walked about together, and she brought him into my house, and they were shut up in a room for some time. (*Laughter*) After that I thought it right to send the young lady home, and I wrote to the defendant.

When Haward came to the Ashleys' house to discover what had led to this intemperate letter, Ashley ordered him to leave and tried to shut the door, but Haward kept the door open with his foot, continuing to ask what had prompted the letter; pushing and shoving ensued. Ashley denied taking him 'by the whiskers and collar' and forcing him towards the gate. Rather, he called for a maid to send for the police (something Haward managed afterwards to forestall by a word with the maid).

Ashley told the court that after the assault he had performed his Sunday morning and evening services with difficulty, thinking on three occasions when he felt faint that he was about to die. The following morning his leg was sore when it touched the sheets; on examination, he claimed to have found a long wound on the side of his knee, 'a blood mark five or six inches long'. He claimed his shoulder pained him considerably, prompting counsel for the defence to ask, 'Do you gesticulate as much in the pulpit as you do in the witness box? (*laughter*)'. Eventually, Ashley took professional advice from two medical men, one of whom told him he must give up his work and rest, the other that he could find nothing wrong. Ceasing to work meant that he had to pay somebody two pounds a week to supply his Sunday duty. Mrs Ashley, in her testimony, said that, 'At that time he was a hale, strong man, the strongest man I ever knew. Up to the Sunday in question he was a very strong man.'

Ashley was questioned about his life before he came to Somersham. He was asked where he had obtained his doctorate, answering, Trinity College, Dublin 'but I entered at Balliol'.[1] 'I first had a living[2] at Sutton Deane in Devonshire.[3] I then went to Clifton to my father's house. I subsequently went to Gloucester in 1868.[4] I did not go into any parish after that, but gave my services freely. I went over to Ireland.' Then asked if he was in the habit of driving a 'coach and four', he said that he would 'swear I never kept a coach and four'. His first marriage was to an Irish lady, he claimed without a 'fortune', by whom he had 10 children (5 boys and 5 girls), who had been living with him in 1859-60, when he lived in Grosvenor Place in Bath, but he claimed not to have seen them since 1862.[5] His wife, having 'transferred her affections to another', left his house in 1865 and died in 1867. For 25 years, she had, he said, made him live as 'a widower', in other words, without a physical relationship. He denied that he had ordered her out of his house, saying that it had been her choice to leave; that she had not liked the house in Grosvenor Place and he had allowed her to choose the house to which she moved, and for which, he said, he had paid. His next move had been to lodge in London 'with a lady there named Treadwell', whom he paid for his accommodation. It was mentioned at this point that he had previously been threatened with action for libel, and later another for passing on unpleasant remarks to a third party, though neither had been proceeded with; the newspaper report had given no information about either. When asked by the judge, Ashley claimed not to remember details of these actions.

1. Balliol College had not previously appeared in his academic history.
2. Technically, this would not have been a 'living'. Ashley would have relied on the money from his father.
3. Sutton Deane, Devonshire, should be Sutton Veny, Wiltshire.
4. Parts of Bristol were originally in Gloucestershire. The year given as 1868 may have been the reporter's mistake as Ashley had already moved, by this time, to London.
5. His seventh, and apparently final, child had been born in 1844. The first Mrs Ashley's Will indicates that she had brought to their marriage several thousand pounds of Government bonds.

The Ashleys' relationship with the Hawards was pursued in detail. Mrs Ashley often took tea with Haward's mother.[1] Ashley described their relationship as like that of mother and daughter. He admitted that he had borrowed money from Haward, while Haward had asked for the loan of one of Ashley's kicking straps, apparently, the day before Ashley's first letter to Haward. Ashley was also pressed on the subject of Miss Spencer's being kissed in his house, as was his wife who, in her reply, clearly thought the incident to be of such insignificance that she claimed most of the details had passed from her memory. Ashley described Miss Spencer as 'a dear friend of my wife, who looks upon my house more than her own home'.

The two doctors who attended Ashley were called to give evidence, the first initially suspecting him to be suffering from a cold; the second claiming to have told Ashley that he could find 'no mechanical injury . . . no organic disease. . . .' A surgeon, noting dropsy, had suspected pericarditis, but had recommended no change in his treatment.

The following day, it was the defendant's turn to be questioned. His counsel argued that the whole business was based on an untruth. Haward mentioned his visits to the Rectory to dine, often three times a week, with the Ashleys. He explained that it was necessary to pass through their grounds to attend the church and he also referred to games of croquet in the Rectory grounds.

On 9 December, Haward had received the first letter, which he thought arose from Ashley's belief that he had referred to Ashley as appearing to be something of an ass. Haward had apologised for this misunderstanding. Apparently not satisfied with his apology, Ashley had sent a second letter, in which he wrote:

> Mr F Haward seems to be utterly insensible as to the enormity of his conduct when he expressed regret for annoying Dr Ashley. His ungentlemanly and outrageous conduct to ladies under Dr Ashley's roof tonight might have called forth something different. If Mr Haward wishes to find women whom he can subject to such treatment, he must betake himself to the streets of Ipswich. . . .

On the 12th, Haward had received another letter, which was also made available to the court. In this, Ashley was more specific, allowing the court to hear more of Haward's behaviour towards the young ladies. Ashley wrote:

> Dr Ashley again and again had representations made to him by rich and poor, and by more than one clergyman, that 'Mr Frederick Haward

---

1. A peculiar feature of the questioning of the plaintiff by the defence counsel is the intimate knowledge it contained of Ashley's past, surely something little known beyond Bath and Bristol. Some memorable words of Gerald Vann OP (*The Divine Pity*, 1949, 50) may hint at an answer: 'characters have been taken away to the tinkling of tea-cups', and so it turned out. When questioned in court, Haward confirmed that he was the source of the information that Ashley's first wife had left him. He denied saying anything about the plaintiff's having driven a coach.

and the ladies of Somersham Rectory' were the talk of the whole neighbourhood. . . . It was exceedingly hard and cruel that Mrs Ashley and her friends should be subjected to this annoyance through Mr Haward's conduct at this house by getting into it at the time of afternoon service . . . [then] an outrageous insult on another occasion offered to a young lady (who had just come on a visit to Mrs Ashley, and with whom he was left alone for a few minutes in the drawing room). . . .

The character of the young ladies that Mrs Ashley had as her friends was not deliberated, though there was a point at which Ashley told the court that earlier, he had cause to caution Haward against getting involved with two of them who, having been rather forward with him, were later overheard saying that they had no intention of marrying him.

On receiving Ashley's letter of 12 November, which Haward claimed had come without warning or indication of what might have prompted it, he had gone to see Ashley. Ashley had stood at his door and immediately ordered him off the premises. Haward said, 'Why, doctor, I came to see what this letter was about.' Ashley had replied, abruptly, 'Get off, sir, you will hear from my solicitors tomorrow morning'. Haward described Ashley as attacking him and his need to defend himself. His coat had been torn, his whiskers unintentionally grabbed. Ashley had pushed him a couple of yards down the path. The letter that he had received from the curate spoke of the 'enormity of his conduct. . . . His ungentlemanly and outrageous conduct to ladies under Dr Ashley's roof. . . .' When asked by counsel what the nature of the outrageous conduct was to the young lady in the drawing room, Haward replied that he thought he had kissed her; when pressed, he confirmed that this was indeed the case. Whether the second young lady was kissed is not recorded. The one in receipt of a kiss seemed to have raised no objection. 'Is that your usual mode of making an acquaintance with a young lady?' Haward replied, '"Well . . ." (*laughter*).'

The parish clerk was called to give evidence, he affirmed that Ashley had given up doing his Sunday duty only some four or five weeks after the accident, having had his arm in a sling for a fortnight, which had not stopped him throwing his arms about when preaching.

Speaking for the defendant, his counsel said that he thought he had 'brought out sufficient to show that Dr Ashley was a man whose evidence must be received with the utmost caution'. He told the court that Miss Spencer's displeasure seemed to have arisen over what she perceived as Haward showing interest in another female on an occasion when Haward, Miss Spencer and another young lady were sharing a carriage. The evidence was his moving to protect the other as the carriage lurched. Neither her displeasure nor Ashley's letter had prevented Haward from visiting Miss Spencer subsequently in her own house. Ashley's letters to Haward were read aloud in court.

Counsel for the plaintiff criticised his opponent's manner of questioning but had little positive to say on behalf of his client. The judge thought the whole case could have been resolved with a lighter touch. The jury retired for fifteen minutes before returning a verdict for the plaintiff, awarding fifty pounds as damages, and expressing its disapprobation of the cross examination of the plaintiff by the defendant's counsel. A more temperate man than Ashley might have resolved the issue with little, if any, expense, and without loss of face.

The cost of bringing this prosecution, surely requiring of Ashley considerably more than the fifty pounds he was awarded, raises a question about his supposed shortage of money, something first mentioned in his Bristol Channel Mission days. Other details of the affair are reminiscent of Ashley's behaviour at that time: his abusive replies to the author of the anonymous letter in the Bristol *Gazette*, his consequent falling-out with his Committee, and his claim to have been bed-ridden and unable to move for all those weeks following the *Eirene* collision.

There were other inconsistencies in his evidence. Asked whether his first wife had ever sued him for a judicial separation, despite his higher degrees in Law, Ashley claimed never to have heard of such a thing. The number and gender of his children that he remembered is puzzling. His view that Haward's kissing of his guest was an abuse of hospitality, something he thought particularly inappropriate to have taken place under a clergyman's roof, though common of its period, makes one wonder how Ashley had gone about his own courting of the second, very much younger, Mrs Ashley. The situation suggests, if not a willingness to depart from the truth, perhaps a measure of confusion.

Leaving the Church of England?

Somersham's reception of its Curate in Charge after his days in court can only be guessed at. It is not difficult to imagine a measure of interest among the villagers, who would have been made aware, for the first time, of the very personal details of their curate's earlier life exposed in the *Ipswich Journal*'s account of his cross examination. Some might have wondered, if copies of his pamphlet claiming that he was leaving the Church of England had also reached the parish, to what sort of pass things had come. Nevertheless, Ashley remained in Somersham until the following summer, certainly until 6 June, 1875, when he made his last entry in Somersham's baptismal register, leaving the parish shortly afterwards on the appointment of the new Rector of Somersham.

To discover where he went on leaving Suffolk, and what he did, is not entirely straightforward. If the question of whether he remained in the Church of England is added, the obvious place to search is *Crockford's Clerical Directory*. Unfortunately, while successive issues of *Crockford* give clues, taken together, they also raise as many questions. It is important to remember that *Crockford* made no claim to infallibility, relying as it did on the occupants of the pages of each edition to provide accurate information and to correct published inaccuracies. The 1876 edition listed Ashley for the first time without his degrees, although it may have been coincidental that the preface to this edition of *Crockford*, after dwelling at some length on the subject of clergy sporting bogus or worthless degrees, added a caution that degrees claimed from Oxford, Cambridge, Dublin or Durham were 'verified by the published lists of Graduates of those Universities'. The 1878 edition continued to list him as Curate of Somersham, three years after his departure. His entry in the 1880 edition (it was published in alternate years) restored his degrees and gave them in unusual detail, despite the threat in the 1876 edition of the requirement for verification now including the entry at Oxford; Ashley's attendance having been mentioned in his court case but not found in Oxford records. The 1876 entry for Ashley read: 'Ashley John, St Germains, Honor Oak SE, Ball. Coll. Ox, afterwards TCD; BA 1823; LLB and LLD 1832. d.1824 by Bishop of Sarum, p.1828 by Bishop of B&W.' The lack of any mention of Ashley in later volumes of *Crockford* covering his remaining years, 1884 and 1886, could, but may not, have indicated that he had asked to be excluded on leaving the Church of England, but the general confusion caused by other details given in previous editions suggests the need for care before reaching any conclusion.

It seems the Ashleys, on leaving Somersham, returned to London to settle with a measure of economy south of the river. *Kelly's London Suburban Directory (Southern Suburbs)* of 1872 (i.e., before the Ashleys' residence) placed the St Germain's Villas on the Lewisham Road. The *Post Office London Suburban Directory* of 1876 listed Ashley, minus his clerical title, which was something hitherto included in every street directory in which he has been traced (i.e., in Bristol and Bath), still sporting his LLD, but with a minor variation in his address, here St Germain's Villa, Peckham Road, Forest Hill, SE, rather than the Honor Oak of the 1880 *Crockford* entry.[1] The census taken on Sunday, 3 April 1881, gave the Ashleys' address as '1, St Germain [*sic*] Villa, Honor Oak Road, Lewisham', and described him as a 'Clergyman of the Church of England' and head of the household.[2] Also in the house were Elizabeth Ashley, Matilda Fulton (a visitor, widow, aged 64, born in Ireland), Rose Preston (an attendant/companion, single, aged 27, born in Hull), Hannah Thompson (servant, widow, aged 41, born in Manchester), and 2 locally-born servants, Fanny Julian (aged 18) and Rhoda Greenhead (aged 19). The number of staff suggests that their circumstances were still reasonably comfortable. The 1886 *Blackheath, Lee, Lewisham and Greenwich Directory* also placed St Germain's Villa in Honor Oak, SE. Despite the confusion of Lewisham, Honor Oak, and Forest Hill, it seems to be the same address listed, unless – an unlikely possibility – in his eighties he was constantly moving within a small area,

1. As street directories list only the principal resident, those for Lewisham do not mention Mrs Ashley. This makes one look back with more interest at Ashley's claim in court that he had earlier lodged with 'a woman named Treadwell' in Kilburn, which, if she was the landlady, should have been confirmed by her listing in Kilburn as the principal resident, whereas she does not appear in Kilburn at all.
2. Ashley's age is given as 50, an easy misreading of the 80 which should have been the census taker's record.

8. Ashley's grave at Holy Trinity East Finchley

accompanied by his house name and number. Neither Lewisham Reference Library, the London Metropolitan Archive, nor the two in tandem, offers a complete run of directories. Two points of interest emerge: that 1 St Germain's Villa seems to have remained his address until the year of his death (1886), and that he came to St Germain's in 1875, that is, on leaving Somersham; 1875, suggested by his being listed in the main text of the *Post Office London Suburban Directory* of 1876, rather than being among the entries listed as sent too late for inclusion in the main text of the Directory.

According to his death certificate, Ashley died at 6 The Grove, Clapham Common, on 30 March, 1886, Clapham being adjacent to Lewisham, in the borough of Lambeth. This is another address that is difficult to trace in street directories.[1] It is not clear when the move to The Grove took place. His removal seems not to have been a measure intended to address the 'senile decay' present on his death certificate, for when his widow was granted Letters of Administration on 10 May, 1886, The Grove was given as her address, indicating that they had moved as a couple. His age was given as 85. The person registering his death was Caroline Clark, of 1 Carpenters Cottages, High Street, Clapham; listed as present at the death but otherwise, her name was unknown. The cause of death was certified by J.A. Tapson MRCS. The death certificate says nothing of Ashley being a clergyman, giving his 'occupation' only as 'Doctor of Divinity'.

The brief newspaper notice of his death, silent on the subject of a funeral, suggests that the service was intended to be a quiet affair. It took place in East Finchley. The burial register of Holy Trinity Church, Finchley, recorded his burial in the small parish cemetery on 3 April, 1886, gave his age as 85 years old and his abode as Clapham. The officiant was H.N. Collier, Vicar of Holy Trinity. As clergy of the Established Church are called upon to conduct funerals for all sorts of people, neither a Church of England officiant nor burial in a cemetery attached to a Church of England church need indicate the denominational allegiance, if any, of the deceased. A baptised resident has a right to burial in the cemetery of his parish church. Finchley was not, nor had it ever been, Ashley's place of residence, which prompts the question: why should a Clapham resident be buried in Finchley?

Ashley's 1868 marriage certificate may provide a clue. His marriage to Elizabeth Treadwell took place in St Marylebone Parish Church on 15 September, 1868. There was some sort of connection between Marylebone (its cemetery long over-full) and Finchley, also between Ashley and Marylebone, at least in part, as his 'Residence at time of Marriage'. The clergyman who officiated at the Ashleys' wedding was Henry N. Collier, described in the Marylebone register as 'Curate'; according to *Crockford* a curate attached to Holy Trinity, St Marylebone, in 1868. This church now redundant, prominently situated on the

---

1. It appears in *Kelly's* of 1872 but I have failed to find it elsewhere. If The Grove was anywhere, it was most likely on the north side of the Common.

Marylebone Road, was one of several built after Waterloo as daughter churches to St Marylebone's parish church (another was St Mary's, Bryanston Square) to serve the needs of the rapidly expanding population. Again according to *Crockford*, from his Marylebone curacy, Collier went to Finchley in 1870 as the incumbent. It looks as though Ashley and Collier had maintained an acquaintance, though whether it was one built on shared churchmanship, friendship, or through Miss Treadwell in some way, is impossible to say.

Following her husband's death, Elizabeth Ashley (née Treadwell) had to obtain Letters of Administration, which she did on 10 May, 1886. Ashley's original executor was George Boughton Hume, a solicitor of 10 Great James Street, Bedford Row, London, otherwise absent from Ashley's story, who had drawn up Ashley's Will in 1874, whilst his client was still at Somersham. The Will left 'to my dear wife' all Ashley's 'real and personal estate', and to Hume 'all such real estates as are vested in me as Mortgagee or Trustee'. Elizabeth made her application as residuary Legatee, and was granted permission to administer the Will in Hume's place 'until he shall become of sound mind'. The application described Ashley as 'Clerk Doctor of Laws'.[1] The gross value of the personal estate was given as £1553. 0s. 0d.

By 1891, according to the census, Elizabeth had moved to Bournemouth. At some point after the burial, Ashley's grave stone was erected, presumably at her behest. It is likely that the inscription it carries was her choice and, one may guess, indicative of her understanding of Ashley's early life; almost certainly, given her age, an understanding derived from her late husband's version of his past.

---

1. 'Clerk' was a title normally used for clergy of the Established Church.

Chapter Seven
John Ashley in Context: Early Modern Seamen's Missions

Ashley today is remembered for his pioneering work among merchant seamen. Though his chosen method was without precedent, the class of men among whom he began his work, merchant seamen, were, in the early part of the nineteenth century, in receipt of an increasing amount of attention from a variety of Christian denominations. Though things seldom occur in a vacuum and Ashley can be placed in the evangelical revival of his church, it is difficult to link his interest in seafarers either with developments on the national scene or, more locally, in Bristol, using the surviving evidence; rather, his initial concern was with islanders who were not reached, as it seemed, by the Gospel, and only then with the crews of the vessels he could see from those islands. In the 1820s, at the point at which the seafarer had become an object of Christian interest in Bristol, it is likely that the young Ashley was a student in Dublin. There is some evidence of church work among seafarers in Dublin in the 1820s but none to suggest that it was known to Ashley. His ministry, however, whether a pioneering one or not, would have benefitted from some of those early efforts.

The nineteenth century saw every English Christian denomination experience a growing missionary movement, the reasons for which are complex, the detail rather beyond the scope of a study of John Ashley and the Bristol Channel Mission. The increasing distance between that century and the troubled years of the Reformation may be one reason, as the identity of the Established Church encouraged a growth in confidence. The cessation of the Napoleonic wars, in 1815, allowing improved global communications, became another factor in a rising concern to spread the Gospel. A time of war would not prompt religious revival, as a first thought, yet Kverndal has described a major religious revival in the Royal Navy between 1793 and 1815, calling it the 'Naval Awakening'.[1] With the coming of peace, the consequent dispersal of thousands of naval men carried that revival into the merchant fleet where it became a factor in the succeeding phase, the Thames Revival.

One major factor in the 'Naval Awakening', and what followed in the merchant fleet, was the rise of the Bible and tract societies. Some of these societies, for example the British and Foreign Bible Society (a nondenominational society,

1. Kverndal, *Seamen's Missions*, 71-132.

founded 1804), began to distribute tracts during the Napoleonic wars among French prisoners as well as to British soldiers and sailors. Other significant producers of Christian literature were the Society for Promoting Christian Knowledge (a Church of England society, founded 1698), the Naval and Military Bible Society (a nondenominational society, founded 1779), the Religious Tract Society (a nondenominational society, founded 1799), the Prayer Book and Homily Society (a Church of England society, founded 1812), and the Merchant Seamen's Auxiliary Bible Society (a nondenominational society, an offshoot of the British and Foreign Bible Society, founded 1818), together forming a cluster around Kverndal's 'Naval Awakening'. Each was providing tracts, initially to the Royal Navy, then to the merchant fleet, and to particular groups such as the men of the revenue cutters, before 1820. Those who distributed the tracts became aware not only that seamen could be brought to religious faith but that an almost exclusively lay-led revival was taking place among them.

The Naval Awakening produced the seminal figure of George Charles Smith (1782-1863), a Baptist minister attached to a chapel in Penzance, who had served in the Royal Navy before his conversion. In 1809, circumstances led to his conducting a Naval Correspondence Mission, which involved an extensive ministry by letter to men of the Navy in the five years that followed, and ending, as the war ended, with the departure of Napoleon for Elba. The dramatic reduction in the size of the Navy on the outbreak of peace led to a corresponding growth of the peacetime merchant fleet, with numbers of Christian naval officers moth-balled on half-pay, and rendering older naval vessels surplus to requirement. In 1818, Smith, with some of these officers, bought a former naval vessel for use as a floating church in the port of London, starting the nondenominational Port of London Society for work among seamen.

Thus, there appears to be a natural progression in the early years of the century from Christian neglect of the seaman to a developing, if not yet wide-spread, missionary movement for his conversion. With the Thames Revival, which followed the 'Naval Awakening', groups of men on colliers began meeting in what Kverndal has described as 'cells'. Enthusiasm in English religion at this time was suspect, with a division in the Church of England between those who were of the High Church, a description which the young Ashley espoused, and those who were of the Low Church or Evangelical; the latter terms often treated as equivalent and more associated with enthusiasm. Kverndal traced the Thames Revival to Wesleyan Methodists in Rotherhithe, particularly to Zebedee Rogers (baptised 1774, d.1833), a shoe maker familiar with collier brigs, who began regular prayer meetings on board some of these colliers in 1814, following, what was described as, an emotional encounter with a captain after a prayer meeting in the Silver Street Wesleyan Chapel, Rotherhithe. In his work, Rogers was supported particularly by Samuel Jennings, a timber merchant.[1]

---

1. Kverndal, *Seamen's Missions*, 151ff. Kverndal, *George Charles Smith of Penzance*, Pasadena 2012, 50ff.

Smith's foundation of the Port of London Society followed his engagement with some of these groups. In the following year, a combination of tensions and opportunity had led him to found the nondenominational British and Foreign Seamen's Friend Society and Bethel Union to extend the work of the Port of London Society beyond London to meet the spiritual and welfare needs of the wider maritime community. His foundations, mainly due to his character, proved to be fissiparous, and seldom remained long within the orbit of their founder. The movement, however, grew, with Smith encouraging local groups to copy the work of the British Seamen's Friend Society and Bethel Union. In each case, the encouragement had come mainly from the central production of a magazine, through which local groups maintained contact by correspondence. Recognition that they belonged to the parent society was indicated by the bestowal and display of the BETHEL flag.[1] This had emerged in 1817 as the preferred signal for worship on the Thames colliers, originally only with the word BETHEL in white sewn on a blue ground but soon with the addition of a white star and dove. This flag, adopted by Smith is, by now, well recognised and was also accorded to captains who were sympathetic to the movement and intending to hold prayer meetings aboard ship and in foreign ports. There was also, at least in London and Liverpool, a parallel effort by the Church of England. Elsewhere, for example in Dublin, were more peripheral societies of uncertain denominational status, of which the barest details have survived, but all part of the general movement. The work of G.C. Smith needs to be set against the background of both the 'Awakening', and the rise of the Bible and tract societies, which will be considered further. Smith's work receives a full measure of attention in Kverndal's monumental book, *Seamen's Missions: Their Origin and Early Growth* (1986). Kverndal subsequently published a small book with emphasis on the character of Smith but little attention to context.[2]

The Bible and Tract Societies

In considering the various societies that paved the way for dedicated work among seamen, it is necessary to return to the eighteenth century and look at the work of a number of Church of England or nondenominational protestant-leaning societies. For the Church of England, the Society for the Promotion of Christian Knowledge (SPCK, 1698) and the Society for the Propagation of the Gospel (SPG, founded in 1701) found that their work of reaching out to emigrants brought them into contact with the crews of the emigrant ships, but the work of both was limited to emigrants by charter. Evangelical dissatisfaction with charter limitations led to the founding of the Society for Missions to Africa and the East in 1799, which was renamed the Church Missionary Society in 1812. The foundation of the Church Missionary Society reflects the increasing confidence, at this time, of the Evangelical movement, which was responsible also for other foundations, directly or indirectly involved with the sea, as, for example, The Bible Society (founded in 1779) which

1. Kverndal, *Seamen's Missions*, 156ff.
2. Kverndal, *George Charles Smith of Penzance*.

initially provided Bibles to the Army (shortly after 1779, the society's name changed to the Naval and Military Bible Society, NMBS), and had begun to distribute religious material to the Royal Navy, eventually to be incorporated into the nondenominational Scripture Gift Mission (1888).[1] The NMBS, with a Council of Anglican bishops and Evangelical worthies drawn from the senior ranks of the Royal Navy, had among its objects the dissemination of the Scriptures to sailors and soldiers of His Majesty's Service, or in the service of the Honourable, the East India Company, and to fishermen and all mariners, whether connected with inland or general navigation; objects to be achieved through a network of auxiliary societies.

The 48th NMBS Report in 1826 (chairman: Admiral Lord Gambier), had given a breakdown of ships and corporations supplied with Bibles or Testaments to illustrate its work, and included bargemen and others at Weedon, the Seamen's Friend Society, Edinburgh; Merchant Seamen, Lynn; Merchant Seamen and Fishermen, Norwich; the Mariners' Church Society, and Mariners, Torquay. The list of auxiliaries indicated how such groups multiplied in this period, including Dublin (1817), Edinburgh, Portsmouth (1819), Cork, Stirling (1820), Deptford, Greenwich, Woolwich (1824), Blakeney (1825), Bath, Bristol (1826), Plymouth, Devonport, Stonehouse (1826), Torbay (1826), plus Cove and Fermoy. The 1827 Report added Southampton, Sheerness, Chatham, Gloucester, Witham, Braintree, Halsted and Sudbury. Of these places, some served ports, some canals, while those inland functioned as supporters' groups.[2]

A similar society, the Religious Tract Society, with a committee consisting of equal numbers of Anglicans and Nonconformists, was founded in 1799; at a time when the Anglican body for tract dissemination, the SPCK, was at a low ebb.[3] Details surviving from the foundation of the society confirm that seamen were soon in receipt of its tracts. By 1817, it was supplying the Navy, as was the NMBS, plus the hulks moored at Sheerness on the River Medway, and in 1818 'colliers on the Thames, the crews of four ships proceeding towards the North Pole, to the convict ships, . . . to the Committee for the Relief of Poor Seamen.' Succeeding copies of the *Missionary Register* add details, among them, that the society's most popular tracts, *Conversation in a Boat between Two Seamen* (Richard Marks, 1818) and *The Swearer's Prayer* (William Rust, 1839), sometimes prompted remarkable conversions after even a casual reading.[4] From 1819, the Religious Tract Society had a regular ship visitor distributing tracts in the Port of London. The success of his work soon led to the formation of smaller tract societies in Aberdeen, Sunderland, and the Isles of Scilly, which were likewise printing and distributing tracts especially for seamen. The later history of the Religious Tract Society goes beyond the interest of this book.

1. Kverndal, *Seamen's Missions*, 71ff.
2. Miller, *From Shore to Shore*, 48.
3. I follow custom in referring to Protestants as Nonconformists, but am aware that Catholics also do not conform to the State religion.
4. *Missionary Register*, 1818, 403ff.

The Port of London agent alone reported visiting between eleven and twelve hundred ships during 1821, at which, usually, his tracts were well received.

In 1814, the SPCK began providing Bibles and copies of the *Book of Common Prayer* (1662) to six quarantine vessels at Milford Haven, and various convict and prison ships, augmented in 1816 by the addition of 2 bound volumes of Bishop Wilson's sermons to its distribution of Bibles, Testaments, and Prayer Books to each of the 62 Revenue Boats established around the British coast for the prevention of smuggling. The sermons were distributed without charge because the men's work on the revenue boats prevented their Sunday church attendance, thus from hearing a sermon, which was required to be given by a suitably authorised person, the absence of such a person being filled by Bishop Wilson's sermons.[1] This gift prompted an appeal from the Inspecting Commanders of H.M. Revenue Cutters (42 being supplied) for a similar grant, they expressing their intention not only to read the 'Church Service' (presumably Morning or Evening Prayer) on Sundays for the crews, but also to include one of Bishop Wilson's sermons.[2]

The BFBS, like the Religious Tract Society having a committee of Anglicans and Nonconformists (15 of each), was founded in 1812, in part because of the SPCK's failure to print a Welsh Bible.[3] This Bible Society should not be confused with The Bible Society of 1799. By 1816, the BFBS was providing Scriptures to bargees on the Grand Junction and some other canals.[4] By 1818, the society's work among seamen had grown sufficiently to create the Merchant Seamen's Auxiliary Bible Society (MSABS), which relieved the parent society of Bible distribution to seafarers, the MSABS intending to 'provide Bibles for at least 120,000 British Seamen, now destitute of them'. In the first 2 months of MSABS operating, a total of 1,721 men on 133 outward-bound ships were visited at Gravesend by the MSABS' agent, Lieutenant Cox, who distributed 580 Bibles and Testaments.[5] John Ashley would source his Bibles from this society. To extend Bible distribution to seamen, 4 depositories were established in Liverpool, while a year later, another BFBS auxiliary, the Hull Marine Bible Society, was founded.

Statistics were beginning to be kept by these societies, their circulation intended to encourage supporters. The first year's report of Lieutenant Cox showed him to have supplied Scriptures to '1,681 vessels, having on board

1. Bishop Wilson, Bishop of Sodor and Man (1698-1755), was known to have been concerned about the spiritual welfare of fishermen in his island diocese.
2. *Missionary Register*, 1816, 348.
3. Bullock, *Voluntary Religious Societies 1520-1799*, 232.
4. *Missionary Register*, 1816, 278.
5. *Missionary Register*, 1816, 175; 1818, 503; 1819 etc. In early-1818, SPCK referred an application from the Society for the Aid of Destitute Seamen in London for a supply of 'suitable books' to the MSABS, which responded with a hundred each of Bibles and Testaments in assorted languages. Gordon C. Cook, *Disease in the Merchant Navy*, 81.

24,765 men, of whom 21,671 are reported able to read', his statistics a rare indication of scripture ownership and literacy levels. On these vessels, he found 1,475 Bibles and 725 Testaments, all in private ownership and not for common use. They were unevenly distributed: as many as 590 ships, having 6,149 men on board, of whom 5,490 were literate, had neither Bible nor Testament.[1] The MSABS was able to issue, for free, 1,075 Bibles and 4,068 Testaments to foreign-bound vessels, selling a further 390 Bibles and 207 Testaments at half price, yielding £89. 4s. 10d. All these vessels were alongside.

Cox reported his approaches as being 'contumeliously rejected' on only four occasions. More often, his offers were met with pious responses, later usefully brought to the attention of supporters by the BFBS in its reports. Many, but not all, the vessels he boarded, were smacks with small crews. Cox did encounter examples of religious practice, which were sufficiently exceptional to be reported. A Dutch ship with a crew of twelve held on board daily prayers and singing, with grace said at meals, and every crew member in possession of a Bible.[2] The Mate of the *Sprightly* from Arbroath (eight crew), with his Captain's permission, gathered men aft every evening to hear the Scriptures read, while Captain Baignie of the *Timanda* of London (eighteen on board), concerned that his men should be able to read and write, promised they 'shall learn to read the Scriptures' on their voyage to Bombay. The MSABS was encouraged sufficiently to produce a sample letter to captains, offering Bibles at a subsidised price, and suggesting for crews of eight or nine, one Bible and three testaments, and for larger crews, a Bible for each watch, and a testament for every three or four men. As an inducement, the letter continued: 'The Committee beg to call your special attention to this subject, as suggesting the best means of improving the moral character of seamen, and promoting among them the habits of regularity and subordination'.[3]

In 1820, the *Missionary Register* reported that 7,803 seamen on 789 ships had been saved from sailing without Bibles by the MSABS. The National Bible Society of America, perhaps encouraged by such statistics, called upon its coastal auxiliaries to become Marine Bible Societies providing Scriptures to seamen. In 1824, The National Bible Society of America drew attention to the Calcutta Bible Association's second annual report, which announced the formation of a Marine Subcommittee to help establish Bible associations actually onboard ships. The success of the MSABS allowed the NMBS to direct its work more specifically to the armed forces. Initially financed by the BFBS, money for the MSABS came from many sources, including a donation of 100 guineas from Trinity House. After seven years' existence, the MSABS

1. Ashley seems nowhere to have commented on the ability of the seamen he visited to read, only on numbers of Bibles and Prayer Books requested but these imply at least some of the crews being able to read.
2. *Missionary Register*, 1819, 167f.
3. BFBS Annual Report, 1818, 251. BFBS archives are held at Cambridge University Library.

claimed to have provided 9,275 Bibles and 10,647 Testaments. Its income for the year was £911. 4s. 7d and expenditure £860. 8s. 6d; a happy state of affairs.

The 1826 MSABS's Annual Meeting, presided over by Admiral Viscount Exmouth, heard that a further 1,555 Bibles and 893 Testaments had been distributed. Annual meetings ran to a pattern, reporting similar statistics. A point of interest is the names that appear, overlapping frequently with other Anglican or Nonconformist meetings concerned with seamen: The Rev. Andrew Brandram,[1] Captain Colin Campbell C.B., RN, John Petty Muspratt Esq.,[2] W. Parker Esq., Captain G. Gambier RN,[3] The Rev. Professor Shedd of New Orleans, Captain Edward Parry RN, and Captain Bazalgette RN. The work of the society continued for many years; as late as 1849, the Liverpool Auxiliary engaged a colporteur to work with local shipping. He reported distributing 2,471 Bibles in his first year, only 7 in English, suggesting that the pattern of this ministry had broadened; of these Bibles; 928 were sold to Roman Catholics and 1,543 to Protestants. No indication is given of the languages of the Bibles sold; of more interest to supporters would be those sales to Roman Catholics.[4] Ashley touched on similar sales but without reference to editions in other languages, which may say something about the origins of the majority of the crews which he visited.

The specifically Anglican society in this field was the Prayer Book and Homily Society (PBHS), founded in 1812, which appeared regularly in the pages of the *Missionary Register*. It began to disseminate tracts, Prayer Books and the *Book of Homilies* at reduced prices among seafarers in 1825, largely through the efforts of individual committee members. The *Book of Homilies*, like those sermons of Bishop Wilson, would be to provide sermons in the absence of a preacher. The PBHS agent was sick for his first 6 months, limiting sales, but when his total for 14 months was announced, it revealed 1,261 ships visited, the distribution of 1,614 Prayer Books, 19 copies of the complete *Book of Homilies*, and almost 1,500 canvas-bound copies of the shorter *Book of Select Homilies*, of which those given free for the use of ships' crews cost the PBHS about £100. It was reported that the visits of committee members and agents had prompted some masters to resume the practice of reading Divine Service (Morning and Evening Prayer from the *Book of Common Prayer*) for crews on Sundays.

The *Book of Select Homilies* was considered sufficiently admirable a medium for Church teaching that in 1827 its distribution was extended to Naval vessels, allowing the society to report that all H.M. Ships in ordinary at Sheerness, Chatham, Portsmouth and Devonport had been supplied with the 'Formularies

---

1. Newly appointed Master of the Queen's Chapel of the Savoy.
2. Possibly a director of the East India Company.
3. Son of Admiral Lord Gambier, a Methodist, whose ship, the *Defence*, in 1793 suspected of being a 'prayer ship' had proved itself also a fighting ship.
4. W. Canton, *The History of the BFBS*, vol II, 164. Such sales would be hoped to draw the purchasers away from the iniquities of Rome.

of the Church'; additionally all prison hulks had been visited; the chaplains were given free volumes of the *Book of Select Homilies* to offer to the prisoners. The same report drew attention to a neglect of fishermen, particularly of river fishermen. Expansion continued, with 40 representatives being appointed in various ports in 1828, amongst them, 7 clergy, the remainder laymen under clerical supervision (as supporters would wish to be assured, and guaranteeing the PBHS its cloak of ecclesiastical respectability), most new to the work and functioning in an honorary capacity. These representatives were able to report Bibles, testaments and '8,788 Homily Tracts, and Festival Services in the same form, principally in Foreign Languages, distributed among sailors who have visited English ports'.[1] It is possible that the PBHS was the earliest of the agencies working among seamen to make a serious attempt to respond to the presence of non-English speakers. The languages chosen are not indicated.

Cox's statistics for Bibles and literacy levels on board merchant ships visited are supplemented in the 1828 PBHS Report with figures relating to religious observance on board 590 ships visited in the Port of London, where 891 Prayer Books were sold, and 1,500 copies of the *Book of Select Homilies* given.[2] On these 590 ships, Divine Service was held regularly when at sea (weather permitting) on 207, occasionally on 5, and never on the remainder. John Ashley made no mention of using these books nor of levels of religious observance. What he did offer those who attended his public speeches were impressive stories of sailors, after being encouraged to read the Bible, reforming their lives, and extending that reformation to their families; beyond numbers of ships visited and Bibles and tracts issued, Ashley left no statistics.

The books and tracts of the PBHS sound unappealing to modern ears. The passage of time has made it easy to forget how cheap printing and increasing levels of literacy had allowed the tract to become a popular medium for Gospel sharing. Sailors, with little to fill their leisure time at sea, welcomed reading material. The tract could go where ministers could not, passing from hand to hand, and continuing ministry until discarded, worn out or washed away. The tract avoided the whim of the ship's master and could impart sound teaching; well-written, it could even be exciting. Equally, tract scattering could be a hindrance to the Gospel; there are hints that these early agents of the PBHS had to discriminate when placing tracts.[3] Dissemination of tracts had got visitors on board ships, and these visitors were among the men who started the early societies.

---

1. *Missionary Register*, 1828, 372ff.
2. The extraordinary figure for the *Homilies*, which required considerable concentration, may be explained if it is understood to refer to the homily tracts of the preceding paragraph. At this time, Church of England clergy at their ordination were required to assent to the *Book of Common Prayer* and the *Book of Homilies*.
3. Cp Basil Lubbock, *Round the Horn before the Mast*, 22f. See also, Miller, *Priest in Deep Water*, 92. Tracts were not always well received. Charles Hopkins in the 1880s was scathing about what he called 'tract mongers'.

G. C. Smith[1]

An agent of the Religious Tract Society remarked, in 1821, upon 'the active zeal of the Port of London Society for preaching the Gospel among seamen in a noble chapel on their own element', adding that when he observed 'The British and Foreign Seamen's Friend Society and Bethel Union' holding prayer meetings on the River Thames he detected the hand of the Lord at work. In this case, the Lord's hand was largely working through George Charles Smith, already briefly noted. Smith was born in London in 1782, raised as an Independent Christian, and, at age fourteen, he was apprenticed to Captain Clark of the brig *Betsey* of Salem, Massachusetts, sailing for Boston, until pressed by HMS *Ariadne*. This experience did not deter Smith from returning to the Royal Navy, voluntarily joining HMS *Agamemnon*, on which he served five years. He witnessed the Nore Mutiny, served under Duncan at the Battle of Camperdown (1797) and Nelson at the Battle of Copenhagen (1801). He led a disparate life until his own illness, followed by the death of his mother, ended in a conversion experience in 1803. Now twenty one, having returned to London, he was drawn to a Baptist Chapel, then began preaching in the Plymouth Dock at Devonport among his former naval mates while undergoing training for the Baptist ministry. In 1807, he was called to be pastor of the Octagon Chapel, Penzance, which was to be his base for the next seventeen years while he preached widely among seamen in West Country ports.

Smith's oratory was not without effect, a ministry continued in the printed word when he was asked to correspond with some sailors, in 1809 founding the Naval Correspondence Mission following an invitation to preach on board a ship at Penzance; effectively his first mission to sailors.[2] Then, in 1812, he was called to London where he preached in the open air.[3] London, seat of empire and a busy port, was notorious for the conditions in which its sailors had to live; press gangs, brothels, crimps and much else made them very vulnerable. The *Weekly Dispatch* carried an item on 30 April, 1837, which could as well have been written in 1812:

> It is really heart-rending to hear of the various ways in which the 'British Tar' is imposed upon as soon as he is paid off. The harlots and a variety of other wretches in the vicinity of Wapping, &c., pounce upon him like so many hyenas. It is a pity so little protection is shown to that noble body of men. . . .

---

1. Kverndal, *Seamen's Missions*, 113ff. His book, *George Charles Smith of Penzance*, adds little.
2. Kverndal, *Seamen's Missions*, 121f.
3. In addition to Kverndal, a useful source of information was the *Soldiers' and Sailors' Magazine*, 1862.

The paper printed details of seamen being flogged, kept up the mast or on the poop almost to the point of death from exposure, bound and trailed overboard until nearly senseless, clapped in irons, given the cat-o'nine tails, swindled by boarding house keepers, involved in drunken debauches and murders, pressed and carried aboard ship, and more. There were opium dens in Limehouse, brothels on the Ratcliffe Highway, as well as gin palaces and public houses at every turn, waiting to welcome the returning sailor, newly paid off and carrying the accumulated wages of perhaps a year or two.

It was against such a background that those prayer meetings began on vessels in the Port of London early in the nineteenth century, the first apparently organised by that master of a Tyne collier for his crews and those on neighbouring vessels in 1812.[1] Soon a BETHEL flag would be hoisted when a service was about to be held. Though Smith's main ministry, a preaching tour on the Continent excepted, remained in Penzance, he continued to make his name as a fiery preacher in London; it is hard to imagine that he was not involved in the steps that led to the increase of these services. The 1819, formation of the undenominational but protestant Port of London Society followed, soon to be associated with the MSABS and similar societies, and the obtaining of a floating chapel, for which plans had been laid in 1817; the work of Smith and R. Marten Esq.

The movement spread; for by 1825, according to the Annual Report, appearing in the *Missionary Register*, 'this Meeting rejoice[s] . . . in those zealous exertions at Liverpool, Leith, Dublin, and other out-ports – at Gibraltar, Calcutta, and other of our Foreign Dependencies – and in America'. London's floating chapel flourished at its mooring off Wapping.[2] It is illustrative of the overlap of supporters of early kindred societies that, here, Mr Sheriff Brown moved a motion, doing so again at the London Episcopal Floating Church Society meeting; the Gambiers, earlier seen at the MSABS Annual Meeting, were also present. Such meetings heard of the perennial concern about money (1826: income £375. 15s. 5d; expenditure £539. 3s. 5d) and how owners and insurers of ships might benefit by supporting this evangelical outreach, which would result in the better behaviour of merchant seamen.

Smith's work increased as need unfolded. His foundations were numerous, but in most cases their substance is difficult to assess. In 1819, he founded the British and Foreign Seamen's and Soldiers' Friend Society and Bethel Union; in 1820, the first *Sailors' Magazine*; in 1825, claimed the first mariner's church in England, the while continuing to conduct a number of preaching missions. The British and Foreign Seamen's and Soldiers' Friend Society and Bethel Union was supported by most of the people who supported the Port of London Society and seems to have grown in a similar way. In 1826, a motion was approved 'to

---

1. M.R. Kingsford, *Life of W.H.G. Kingston*, 125. See also Smith's tract, *Bethel or The Flag Unfurled*, 1819.

2. *Missionary Register*, 1825, 251.

give every possible stimulus to the Foreign Operations of the Institution' by, among others, the Gambiers, Professor Shedd, The Rev. Mr Crosbie of Dublin, and The Rev. John Jack 'missionary from Astrachan'. In 1822, Smith founded the Watermen's Friend Society for giving religious instruction to watermen, bargemen and coal-whippers; in 1824, the Shipwrecked and Distressed Sailors' Family Fund (which coincided with the start of the undenominational London City Mission and the opening, according to one source, of a Mariners' Church in Wellclose Square); in 1826, the first Shipwrecked and Destitute Sailors' Asylum and Sailors' Home.[1] In 1829, he was claimed as responsible for the first temperance mission to sailors and the foundation of the Maritime Penitent Female Refuge. Although a Baptist, Smith attracted support from other denominations, among them the Established Church.

The Port of London Society and the British and Foreign Seamen's and Soldiers' Friend Society and Bethel Union, sharing a common president and working harmoniously, merged in 1827, to form 'The Port-of-London and Bethel Union Society, for Promoting Religion among British and Foreign Seamen', renamed in 1925 the British Sailors' Society, in 1995 the British and International Sailors' Society, and, since 2007, the Sailors' Society. It is implicit in the early annual reports that all went well; they would hardly suggest otherwise. The 1828 meeting heard of another of Smith's foundations, the Merchant Seamen's Orphan Asylum. A few indications of the scale of the work are given, the society's school in Wapping being commended for its aid to 'the numerous and destitute children of Seamen and Rivermen' with 180 boys and 90 girls in attendance. The Floating Chapel, also at Wapping, reported two services every Sunday with a monthly Communion service, yielding an annual attendance of 17,585 at services, 9,014 of these being seamen; there were 135 seamen attendances at Communion.[2]

If these developments were not enough, it was at this time that the next important foundation took place, the Mariners' Church Society. At various times, there were several societies using this name. This one, of either 1825 or 1827, merged with the British and Foreign Seamen's and Soldiers' Friend Society and Bethel Union in January 1846 to form the Seamen's and Soldiers' Evangelical Friend Society, becoming in 1848 the Seamen's Christian Friend Society, a markedly protestant organisation, and particularly given to tract dissemination.[3] This original Mariners' Church Society can be traced to Smith.[4]

1. *Missionary Register*, 1826, 233.
2. *Missionary Register*, 1828, 227.
3. C.H. Milsom, *Guide to the Merchant Navy*, 132.
4. Kverndal, *Seamen's Missions*, 266ff. Stephen Friend, *The Rise and Development of Christian Missions amongst British Fishing Communities during the Nineteenth Century*, (hereafter, *Fishermen's Missions*) 85, suggests that this was intended to be an auxiliary of the BFSFSBU, that the relationship was soon fraught, Smith being forced to resign in 1826 when he was in the process of founding a third seamen's mission in London. I have rather dodged the complicated issue of Smith's many foundations and fallings-out but the message is clear enough.

It was based in the old and disused Danish church in Wellclose Square, London, perhaps to be associated with the Home opened there at No.19 by George Gambier and Captain R. Elliott, who financed the venture from November 1827, appointing a mate to issue relief, and allowing Smith to use it as an operational base. On 1 January, 1828, a warehouse was opened offering straw beds (straw-filled mattresses) for sailors, the 'donkey's breakfast' of the sailor's bunk; then, when the Brunswick Theatre collapsed on 28 February, 1828, its site was obtained, to be replaced with a Home in 1829. At this point, Smith resigned, perhaps to initiate other work; opinion is divided on whether the parting was amicable. Gambier withdrew at the same time, Elliott remaining, together with an unnamed Captain RN, identified only as a supporter. Elliott at this time was involved with the Church of England, starting in January 1828, a Home in Dock Street under its auspices.

The Wellclose Square Mariners' Church Society assumed in 1827 the title of British and Foreign Seamen's Friend Society and Bethel Union, which had been discarded by the earlier British and Foreign Seamen's and Soldiers' Friend Society and Bethel Union on its amalgamation with the Port of London Society. This Mariners' Church Society had a monthly magazine called the *Steam Packet*, renamed the *New Sailor's Magazine*, which resembled very closely the *Sailors' Magazine* of the old British and Foreign Seamen's and Soldiers' Friend Society and Bethel Union.[1] To add to the confusion, its first Annual Meeting was held under the name of the British and Foreign Seamen's and Soldiers' Friendly Society, but the contemporary *Missionary Register* makes it clear that this was indeed the Mariners' Church Society renamed. This meeting was well attended (requiring a second room), not least by Anglicans, some involved with the Episcopal Floating Church. The Report for this Mariners' Church Society in 1829 is further confused in the *Missionary Register* by being indexed under 'Episcopal Floating Church Society', and claiming among its achievements, 'The Sailors' Home' or Royal Brunswick Maritime Establishment, with its Receiving and Shipping Depot, Distressed Sailors' Refuge and a Sea Boys' Rendezvous; The Sea and River Tract Society and Thames Mission; and The Sailors' Orphan House Establishment for 50 boys and 50 girls.[2]

---

1. *Missionary Register*, 1827, 236. Names are sufficiently similar to be very confusing.
2. *Missionary Register*, 1829, 212, 216. There were a number of foundations for orphaned or destitute children of seamen around this time. The Port of Hull Society for the Religious Instruction of Seamen, founded 1821, initially opened a floating chapel, followed by a school to teach men to read, then in 1837, by its Sailors' Orphan Institution (Milsom, *Guide to the Merchant Navy*, 166f). On the Thames was the Sailors' Orphan Girls Episcopal School and Asylum, of 1829, among its patrons, Captain R.J. Elliott. The children were 'ministered to by the Rev. C.B. Gribble, Chaplain of the newly erected Church for Seamen'. Children to be admitted were required to show evidence of baptism and vaccination and to attend the Established Church twice on Sundays. On leaving, each received a copy of the *Book of Common Prayer*. These details survive in its 20th Annual Report (1848). Miller, *From Shore to Shore*, 48-49.

There is much confusion here with a number of the works overlapping. Apparently Smith, Gambier and Elliott remained on good terms, despite Elliott's move towards the Established Church. Indeed, Elliott seems to have moved to ease pressure on Smith's existing work, going at Smith's suggestion to found the Dock Street Home. Little has been said of rivalry and disagreement, but much of the confusion between these early Protestant societies derived from the character of Smith. *The New Sailor's Magazine* of 1829 reveals that Smith's relations with the committee of his original Bethel foundation had reached a stage where one committee member, named only as 'Philo-veritas', took it upon himself to precede Smith's preachments about the country with letters to people of influence accusing Smith of dishonesty in his direction of the society's funds.[1] Despite the Port Society's disclaimer of Philo-veritas it advertised a meeting to examine the state of the trust, proposing that all monies coming through Smith or the Seamen's Friend Society might be returned to donors. Smith fulminated in print, likening himself to the apostle John on Patmos, reminding readers what his labours of 20 years had achieved among seamen, and drawing attention to the circulation of his *New Sailor's Magazine* (the foundation of the magazine surely confirmation of earlier troubles) which was triple that of the magazine of which he had been deprived. His new 'Sailors' Guardian Society' would be firmly allied to the British and Foreign Seamen's and Soldiers' Friend Society, 'lashed, yard-arm and yard-arm'. Smith convened a meeting of ministers to arbitrate. According to Kverndal, these accusations were found to be unfounded and Smith received a public apology from his calumniator. Since more accusations and fallings-out followed, Smith was either trampling on egos, cutting corners, or over-working.[2] It is hard not to think of ruffled feathers and broken egg shells. The original slander seems to have originated with an assistant secretary of the British Reformation Society, whose name was coupled with that of Lieutenant Brown, Secretary of the Episcopal Floating Church Society, these two bodies having separate offices under a shared roof.

A comprehensive unravelling of Smith's foundations appears in Kverndal's *Seamen's Missions*. Once the confusion has been acknowledged, the reader grasps with relief the bits which can be understood relatively easily. For example, in London the straw bed asylum, which replaced 19 Wellclose Square, was a warehouse in Dock Street. The Royal Brunswick Theatre was replaced by a Sailors' Home in London's Well Street, now Ensign Street. The Royal Brunswick Maritime Establishment, to allay suspicions of heterodoxy, was placed under the auspices of the Bishop of London in 1831, though continuing its association with Smith's work, and its Chaplain, Mr Gribble, the incumbent of St Paul's Church, Dock Street. Perhaps in 1829, certainly before 1835, Elliott set up his own 'crewing office' to try to avoid some of the evils of the crimping system by which seamen were drugged, got drunk, or otherwise recruited against their will

---

1. *New Sailor's Magazine*, 1829, 384ff, 406ff, 464ff.
2. Kverndal, *Seamen's Missions*, 275f.

for ships needing crews; often the first a sailor knew of his recruitment was on waking, groggy, on board a ship at sea.[1] The Home was extended with the support of the dowager Queen Adelaide, widow of William IV, in 1848, and enlarged in 1865, retaining its royal patronage. This refuge for destitute seamen became a model for other, albeit smaller, institutions serving sailors around the globe. By 1890, it included the adjacent St Paul's Church for Seamen, had a staff of more than 40 people, and provided 4 meals a day, hot baths, a tailor's shop, over 500 beds in individual cabins, a savings bank, a barber, a daily visit from a surgeon, reading and smoking rooms, a library, and more, plus a Navigation School.[2] This concern for the welfare of the sailor contrasts with Ashley's almost total silence on the subject of welfare. He cannot have been unaware of the material needs of sailors, but such things do not appear in newspaper accounts of his public speaking. That said, in fairness one should remember that his ministry was largely to outward-bound crews already on board their ships.

The confusion of the many titles and organisations of the first half of the nineteenth century, of which Kverndal lists a great deal more, hides a firm foundation being laid for a style of sea apostolate by which the Church went to the seafarer. Smith, virtually alone, had woken the denominations, even the Church of England, from somnolence. His was the first sailors' home of modern times, and his the hand which lay behind so many groups working among seafarers around the world. At another time, this might not have been so but London's position at the centre of a growing merchant fleet made a better time hard to find; most modern missionary activity on behalf of the seafarer in the churches can be traced directly or indirectly to Smith, an achievement undiminished by his imprisonment for debt in 1836, and on three subsequent occasions.[3] The fissiparous nature of his foundations reflects something of the character of the man. In the second half of the century, these societies would begin to coalesce, most of the undenominational societies into what became the British Sailors' Society, and the Anglican ventures into The Missions to Seamen. It was John Ashley's lot, working in the period of the earliest mergers, to initiate a mission which took the Gospel to the seafarer afloat, a step obvious in hindsight, but a novelty in its day.

And what of Bristol?

In a paper on the work of the Bristol churches among seamen in this busy port,[4] Martin Crossley Evans claimed that the 'most influential and long-established

1. Kingsford, *W.H.G. Kingston*, 125ff. See also the Annual Reports for these years.
2. Alston Kennerley, *British Seamen's Missions and Sailors' Homes . . .* , *passim*. Alston Kennerley, Joseph Conrad at the London Sailors' Home, 70-102.
3. Friend's *Fishermen's Missions . . .* , offers more detail of these difficulties. It seems Mrs Smith left home at some point. Kverndal, *George Charles Smith of Penzance*, 104.
4. In Joseph Bettey (ed), *Historic Churches and Church Life in Bristol*, Bristol & Gloucestershire Archaeological Society, 2001, 162ff.

society dedicated to the conversion of seamen in Bristol during the nineteenth
century' was the Seamen's Friend Society and Bethel Union, a title which
immediately connects it to G.C. Smith.[1] There is some evidence that Smith
had considered starting something in Bristol as early as 1816 or 1817.[2] In 1820,
he visited Bristol, *Felix Farley's Bristol Journal* (5 August) reporting at length a
speech made by him before a large assembly in the city. It was followed by a
long letter over the initials G.C.S., asking:

> what efforts have been made by this country to promote the morals and
> establish the piety of her seamen? . . . The Naval and Military Bible
> Society has particularly supplied the navy and revenue service with the
> Scriptures; the Merchant Seamen's Bible Society has been very generous
> in diffusing its various publications; and the Port of London Society has
> nobly exerted itself and established a Floating Chapel on the Thames
> for the use of seamen. . . .

The letter added that 'the Bethel Seamen's Union, British and Foreign', a
variant title of an organisation already considered, had been newly launched
in London, in connection with which, a footnote to the letter informed
readers:

> It is in contemplation of some *decided and respectable friends in episcopacy*,
> to provide a ship, for the use of seamen, in which the Church Liturgy
> shall be read, and the Gospel preached to them every Lord's Day;
> the same ship to be moored in the Thames, off the Tower of London
> [original emphasis].

The reference to episcopacy, the Church Liturgy and the floating church in
London might suggest that behind this move lay the influence of the London
Episcopal Floating Church Society, though that society only claimed foundation
from 1825. That the London floating church in existence at the time of Smith's
writing was nondenominationally protestant makes his footnote something of a
curiosity.[3] He was not unwilling to work with members of the Church of England,
but to this extent is unexpected. The explanation may lie in the requirement that
nonconformists of the day were required to register a place of worship with the
local bishop. A floating chapel using the formularies of the Established Church
needed no such registration.[4]

1. Kennerley, 'British Seamen's Missions in the Nineteenth Century', Lewis R. Fischer
   et al (eds), *The North Sea*, Stavanger, 1992, 83. Kennerley reproduces the regulations
   of the Bristol Seamen's Friend Society on page 92.
2. Kverndal, *Seamen's Missions*, 171, 224-6.
3. Kverndal, *Seamen's Missions*, 182ff for details of HMS *Speedy*, the first such floating
   church in London obtained in 1818. For an illustration, see 187.
4. Kverndal, *Seamen's Missions*, 628 reproduces the text of the original 'Application for
   Registration of Sanctuary' made to the Bishop of London by the Port of London
   Society, dated 18 April 1818. Smith's name is not among the signatories.

The *Bristol Journal*, a week later, reported a meeting to start a Bristol Seamen's Friend Society, at which proposals were made for obtaining a 'convenient place for divine worship' and the establishment of a Marine School 'where sailors and sea boys should be instructed in the Holy Scriptures'. The principal speaker was Smith. 'A large blue flag, "The Bethel Union", floated behind the chair.' The successful outcome of Smith's appeal is succinctly revealed in the *Bristol Mercury*'s report of the funeral of Lieut. Kemball RN in its issue of 3 December, 1853.

> To [Kemball] is due the honour of raising the necessary funds for the purchase and equipment of HM's ship *Etna*,[1] for the services of the Seamen's Floating Chapel, and year after year keeping up the interest and order of regular worship there. . . . [A] mark of respect paid by the Committee of the 'Seamen's Friend Society'. . . . The existence of a Sailors' Home in the city of Bristol is, moreover, to be traced to the assiduity and undaunted energy of this true seamen's friend. For some years he had cherished the hope of seeing such an institution which his own philanthropy had given birth to. . . . He, however, lived to see his desires fulfilled. His have been the labours, others will enter and reap the fruit thereof.

Mathews's Bristol Directory in the 1820s lists a Bristol Merchant Seamen's Bible Association conducted by a committee of 24 gentlemen. By 1830, it also listed the Marine School Society, School House, Queen Square (very close to the docks) 'for the instruction of the Sons of Seamen and other boys designed for the Marine Service'. From 1831, *Mathews's* listed under 'Dissenting Places of Worship': *'Seamen's Floating Chapel, or Ark, at the Grove* – Sundays, half past 10 forenoon, 6 evening; Thursdays 7 evening'. Whether Ashley was influenced by knowledge of these local efforts of which, given their regular appearance in the Bristol Press over many years, he can hardly have been unaware, cannot be said with certainty, but the period in which they were founded, and the local concern for the education of sons of seamen, is suggestive. The Bristol Sailors' Society floating chapel 'List of Arrangements of the Public Worship Sub Committee' for the period 1825 to 1835 survives, giving names of preachers and numbers of seamen attending. The name of John Ashley does not appear in it; that of Kemball is prominent throughout. The eventual interlinking of work in Bristol was illustrated by the Trustees of the Bristol Seamen's Institute at 33 Queens Square, in their welcome, in 1887 of The Missions to Seamen chaplain as chaplain of their institute.[2]

---

1. Kverndal, *Seamen's Missions*, 168 names the vessel *Aristomenes*.
2. Bristol's *List of Arrangements* . . . (DMS/2/2) and the Trustees' *Minutes* (DMS/2/1) which survive can be found in the Hull History Centre.

The London Episcopal Floating Church Society

The work of the undenominational societies among seamen, especially in London, had stirred members of the Church of England into action, beginning with the formation of the London Episcopal Floating Church Society (LEFCS). If there was an element of competition, there was certainly the view that undenominational work lacked the episcopally-ordained ministry and sound teaching considered essential by the Established Church. Even supposing space could be found for a church to be built in a dock area, construction was not cheap. Hulks and former naval vessels had long been moored on the Thames for use as prisons, for coal storage, sea schools, and other purposes, but to use one as a church had novelty. Smith had shown the economy to be derived from the acquisition of an old naval ship for conversion to a floating church, invariably moored alongside. There was sometimes the thought that sailors would feel more at home worshipping on board a ship; the thought perhaps more in the minds of those ashore than of serving sailors. The provision of a floating church would allow the Established Church a facility near the sailors intended as its congregation at a price that could reasonably be afforded.

The LEFCS held its first meeting on 20 July, 1825, at the City of London Tavern, with the Lord Mayor in the chair. Among those present were Lord Bexley,[1] Mr Alderman and Sheriff Brown, Lord Calthorpe, Robert H. Marten Esq.,[2] Admiral Sir Richard Keates,[3] the Hon. Captain Waldegrave RN,[4] Zachary Macaulay Esq.,[5] W.H. Locker Esq.,[6] John Pynder Esq., The Rev. W.A. Evanson, the Earl of Clarendon, W.T. Money Esq., and The Rev. T. Webster, a list that illustrates the kind of people the Church of England was able to draw upon, some of whom have already been encountered and others yet to be met, members all of Evangelical and Establishment networks.

The meeting resolved that

> the instruction of British seamen, on principles which shall introduce
> them to an acquaintance with the Doctrines and Precepts of the

---

1. Nicholas Vansittart, sometime Chancellor of the Exchequer, a Director of the Greenwich Seamen's Hospital, whose father had been lost at sea.
2. Despite being the man of influence here Robert Humphrey Marten was a Congregational deacon. Kverndal, *Seamen's Missions*, 177.
3. Sometime Governor of Greenwich Hospital.
4. From a distinguished naval family. Later Earl Waldegrave.
5. Governor of Sierra Leone and one of the Clapham Sect. Kverndal, *Seamen's Missions*, 31.
6. William Hawke Locker, civilian layman, a 'staunch supporter of the new piety in the navy' (R. Blake, *Evangelicals in the Royal Navy 1775-1815*, 182 n12) former secretary to Admiral Sir Edward Pellew.

Christian Religion, to be a duty of solemn national obligation, and eminently entitled to the support of as many as would desire to combine the universal diffusion of true Christianity, with the moral exaltation and commercial prosperity of the British Empire.

[L]ong experience having proved the general ignorance of Seamen on the subject of Religion, and their disinclination to join in the Worship of a Congregation on Shore, to be insuperable difficulties in the way of their deriving advantage from the existing Parochial Churches . . . that the establishment of Floating Chapels, in connection with the Church of England, offers the only practicable form in which the benefit of her Worship may be generally extended to the seafaring part of the community.

[A]n Institution now be formed . . . The Episcopal Floating Church Society, for promoting the diffusion of Religion among the Seamen of the Empire, agreeably to . . . the Church of England.

[B]y aiding in the institution of Floating Churches and Schools, for the Religious and Professional Improvement of Apprentices; . . . the establishment of Depositories for the Scriptures, Prayer Books, Homilies, and Tracts, and the provision of Circulating Libraries. . . .[1]

The use of the plural throughout suggests ambitious plans. Only some of the resolutions were achieved; others were soon overtaken by the rise of the PBHS, the difference between them that the PBHS had no intention of providing churches and the other settled arrangements here proposed.

The LEFCS established itself at 32 Sackville Street, Picadilly, the London House of the Religious and Charitable Societies, a facility apparently founded in 1822 under the trusteeship of the Earls of Roden and Rocksavage, Viscount Lorton, and Lords Calthorpe, Farnham, Barham, and Bexley.[2] The treasurer of the house was Henry Drummond, its secretary a Mr Lamprey.[3] Each society using this address had its own rooms but shared such facilities as waiting and committee rooms. The principal work of the LEFCS was its floating church, moored off the Tower in the Pool of London, like most of the floating churches obtained from the Admiralty, in this instance the erstwhile HMS *Brazen*. Its position was ideal as, at this time, all merchandise had to enter London via the legal quays, situated on the north side of the Pool of London; only later were London's large, enclosed docks built to ease the pressure caused by increasing trade and bigger ships. A former Naval lieutenant, The Rev. Horatio Montague, was appointed to visit ships from London Bridge to the Pool.[4] The *Brazen*'s first service was held on Good Friday, 1826, with Divine Service held regularly

---

1. *Missionary Register*, 1825, 309f.
2. *Missionary Register*, 1823, 517.
3. *Missionary Register*, 1825, 220.
4. M.R. Kingsford, *Life of W.H.G. Kingston*, 125.

thereafter until 1845, when the work had declined to the extent of being no longer practicable, that is that the *Brazen* had capsized in 1831 and had continued to deteriorate thereafter.

The Liverpool Mariners' Church Society

Contemporary with the LEFCS was the Liverpool Mariners' Church Society, formed in 1825 when a group of local people approached The Rev. Dr William Scoresby with a plan for a floating chapel, perhaps stimulated by the Nonconformists' two decker, the *William*, moored in Liverpool's King's Dock since 1820. The Admiralty made HM frigate *Tees* available.[1] The *Tees* was moored in a corner of the George's Dock, and managed by the Liverpool Mariners' Church Society, formally founded in 1826, with the Bishop of Chester as patron. It had seating for some thousand people. Scoresby had been a whaling ship captain and Arctic scientist. After a conversion experience in 1817, he began to hold religious services on his ship. A move to Liverpool in 1819 had led him in 1821 to join G.C. Smith and others in founding the Liverpool Seamen's Friend Society and Bethel Union.[2] In 1823, he sought ordination in the Church of England, being ordained in 1825 to an assistant curacy at Bridlington. He came to the Mariners' Church in May 1827. Scoresby served as its Chaplain until 1832, when his wife's declining health determined their departure. His successor died in office, 45 years later, in 1875. The large congregations attracted by the novelty had soon begun to dwindle. When W.H.G. Kingston visited it in 1856, he found few seamen in a congregation mostly drawn from the shore-side population. There were two Sunday services, taken by duly licensed clergymen. By the time the Trustees handed the vessel over to the Mersey Mission to Seamen in 1879, it had been moved to Birkenhead, probably following its sinking in the George's Dock in 1872, a familiar story in the history of floating churches.

---

1. The converted *Tees* is shown in Kennerley, 'British Seamen's Missions in the Nineteenth Century', 80, 82 where are also reproduced illustrations from Smith's *New Sailors' Magazine*, (1828) insert.
2. Kverndal, *Seamen's Missions*, 287ff.

Conclusion

What has been achieved?

Andrew Huckett's challenge was to produce an accurate account of Ashley's life, beginning with the received story of his son prompting his sea apostolate. The evidence in this book confirms Huckett in his view of this need, adding details previously little known of Ashley's domestic life, his religious faith, and his temperament.

In the process, several of Huckett's very helpful details have been amended or supplemented. Ashley's correct date of birth (29 December 1800) is revealed in his father's sworn testimony before Ashley's diaconal ordination. Those confusing entries in *Crockford* regarding Ashley's academic career have been replaced with accurately dated details, giving the summer of 1823 for his graduation and 1832 for his higher degrees, in each case from Trinity College, Dublin. The dates and dioceses of his ordinations (deacon, Advent 1823 and priest, 6 April 1828) have been provided from contemporary diocesan documents. The site of his grave has been securely identified, no novelty but something largely forgotten, for the incumbent of East Finchley, himself a former Missions to Seamen chaplain, indicated he had earlier brought it to the Society's attention.

To these have been added the identity of Ashley's school (Winchester), his title parish (Sutton Veny) and succeeding assistant curacies (Downton and Croscombe), an explanation for his presence in Gosfield (an interregnum), and his dates in Somersham as Curate in Charge. Newspaper reports of Ashley in his parish work have been helpful. Details of his court cases and his harness patent, previously omitted from accounts of his life, have been resurrected. A little light has been shed on the later years of his first marriage, and some on his second, allowing a glimpse of each Mrs Ashley. A little more can be discovered about his second wife. When he was questioned by counsel in Court he claimed to have lodged in Kilburn with a 'woman named Treadwell', but named her in his Will, at much the same time, as 'my dear wife'. The frivolous behaviour of her young guests ('friends') in Somersham, of whose behaviour she claimed in the same Court to think 'nothing', may say something of the former Miss Treadwell. Of Ashley's own character, more will be said below.

John Ashley's faith

A factor that helps explain Ashley's place in the history of the maritime apostolate was the Evangelical Revival in the nineteenth-century Church of England. The narrowness of his views is evident in his 1870s tracts. Though Ashley was more protestant than evangelical, in his day a distinction seldom made, the influence of this revival cannot be dismissed. His first thirty or so years coincided with a growth in the number of evangelicals campaigning for the abolition of slavery, some members of the so-called Clapham Sect, William Wilberforce and his circle among them. More would be known about his type of evangelicalism if any mention of his attitude to the Abolition question had survived in reports of any of his speeches. Although Ashley built the *Eirene* when the post Abolition compensation was flowing freely, it would press the evidence too far to suggest that it was seen in any sense as a laundering of what many today would see as 'tainted' money, though it is likely that the bulk of the money, which facilitated the schooner's building, came from this source. William Heaven's purchase of Lundy Island was made possible by this compensation.[1] Many clergy were connected with Jamaican estates and some, one of the better known Exeter's Bishop Henry Philpotts, received very large sums from the same source.

The passage of time has led perception of Ashley's role in the sea apostolate to become a victim of selective memory. Almost forgotten is his lack of judgement that almost destroyed the Bristol Channel Mission; instead he continues to be seen, partly through the dependence of successive authors on his own account, more so in Mary Walrond's book, mostly through ignorance, as the father of Anglican work among seafarers. Other Anglicans with a concern for the merchant seafarer in other ways, had preceded Ashley but these were almost certainly unknown to him. Corporate loss of memory is not peculiar to the Ashley story. It can be observed in the reputation of other heroes of the sea apostolate. The building that houses the Royal National Mission to Deep Sea Fishermen is named Mather House, despite the unfortunate sequence of events that prompted its founder's departure; Mather's reputation today is principally derived from his own version of events. For the same reason, the turbulence in the life of G.C. Smith, a pioneer in the field of modern maritime mission, attracted little negative comment from his biographer, Roald Kverndal. The same phenomenon can be witnessed in the place assigned by the Catholic Church to the role of Peter Anson in its mission to seafarers. Popular versions of history are not easily displaced by facts. So it is with Ashley's place in the popular history of The Missions to Seamen, in which the legend of his little

---

1. Lundy's owner, Bristol-born William Hudson Heaven (1800-83), contemporary of Ashley, also of British/Irish stock, heir to 6 Jamaican estates of various sizes, purchased Lundy in 1834 for 9,400 guineas using his compensation. It is likely that the two men were long acquainted.

boy's question is unlikely to disappear and perception of Ashley's role in the history of the Mission to Seafarers to be revised in any significant way. The present state of his gravestone, at the time of writing in need of refreshing, may indicate the real, rather than the apparent, level of interest of those Anglicans who today continue Christian work among seafarers in the name of the man whose grave it marks.

Whether Ashley left the Church of England, a departure trumpeted in his 1870s pamphlets, is not certain; there is neither formal means of recording such a departure nor an obvious record of his having arrived in another denomination. His threat to leave was made while Curate in Charge of Somersham, effectively his only public employment in the Church of England since 1828. That he left this only on the appointment of a new incumbent suggests that his desire to leave the Established Church was less than overwhelming. After his departure from Somersham, his clerical title (The Reverend) is seldom in evidence, but use of his doctorate continued. His funeral adds nothing to our knowledge; a funeral conducted under the auspices of the Church of England is no indicator of denominational allegiance. It hints only at a continuing friendship with at least one among the Church of England clergy. His description as 'clerk' on his death certificate and the reappearance of his ministerial title on his grave stone suggest that there were those, among them his widow, who considered him still a *bona fide* member of the church of his baptism, a view I share.

The Contradictions

It is difficult to assemble the various periods of Ashley's life in such a way that a satisfactory picture can be obtained. Confusion most obviously arises when evidence given at his case against Haward is compared with what is known about his earlier decades. Among the contradictions are his description of his domestic circumstances, the number of his children, his early claims of being a keen horse-and-carriage man here denied under oath, as also those widely published occasions of incapacity by illness or accident in his *Eirene* days claimed never previously to have been suffered in either respect. Readers will have spotted other examples.

Impulsive and unpleasant outbursts occur with some frequency across the years: his newspaper response to the Caldy 'Visitor', the battle with his Bristol Channel Mission Committee in the 1840s, his disagreement in the 1860s with the toll gate official, the speedy demand for justice from the magistrate following his cook's alleged transgression, and, most egregiously in the 1870s, the decision to prosecute his neighbour for assault and trespass.

It is difficult to discover the truth of his relationship with his first wife. She appears very seldom in his story, principally as the person who bears his children. It was suggested to him in Court that it was he who had evicted her from the marital home. He claimed that she had transferred her affections to another and had left of her own accord. It seems that, when she moved to her final address in Bath, she went with the encouragement of their children, who then disappear completely from their father's story. Ashley's claim that his wife had made him live like a widower for 25 years (a figure not too precise if the date of birth of their last child is considered), if it contains even a grain of truth, and her decision to move, could equally be understood as an attempt to avoid his attentions, which might have become increasingly unwelcome in her later years, particularly if the causes of death given on her death certificate were today identified as bowel cancer and stroke – uncertain but not impossible.

While it is easy to be negative about Ashley, it is possible to make a case for his being a generous man, particularly if he was the principal source of finance for the *Eirene*. The evidence for this is limited, but gains credence from the jibe, to which he took such exception, that the cutter was Ashley's pleasure yacht. Thereafter it seems he was willing to use his private income, so long as it remained substantial, to subsidise his ministry to seamen, to whom, in the few years logged, he devoted many hours of hard labour in appalling conditions. What that income might have been is difficult to guess, nor is it known what his inheritance might have been. Some details about Ashley senior's estate in Jamaica are available but not what Ashley senior might have bequeathed to his numerous children, without access to his Will. Ashley junior's changes of abode and the contents of his Will hint at a certain straightening of circumstances but not actual poverty. The claimed 1840s' reduction in his fortune connected with the import of Cuban sugar may have been a reality, but equally it could have been used to mask his increasing alienation from his committee.

Dependence on newspaper reports for most of the evidence which survives about Ashley means that little is known about the man as opposed to his work. He seems to have been an eloquent speaker. Repeated mention of the length of his speeches is probably only what might have been expected by audiences of the period. Occasional references in newspapers give the impression that he had a certain regard for dogs and horses, which would commend him to his fellow Englishmen. His small son's supposed role in the beginning of his work among seafarers would have been very well-received by Victorian audiences but no evidence of its ever having been mentioned survives, though a reference to a holiday walk with his children, when the glinting windows on the Holms were spotted, seems to have been included in some of his accounts of his work. Socially, he appears to have enjoyed the respect and in some instances the friendship of evangelical clergy of a certain hue, something more certain if his move to Kilburn was viewed as one evangelical rallying to support another. [1]

Ashley's ministry, as that of others, was assisted by the arrival of cheap printing, which allowed him to distribute Bibles and tracts in large quantities;

---

1. The attempt of the Protestant Truth Society's founder in 1890, four years after Ashley's death, to become a warden at St Augustine's church illustrates very well the kind of battlefield ecclesiastical Kilburn had become.

also for his work to be made more widely known as newspapers became increasingly accessible. Nor can it have been hindered by the slow but steady rise in literacy levels nationally and among seafarers, in part a product of the early Sunday School movement. Where the century had begun with a measure of shore-side provision by Christians for seafarers, now Ashley's ministry was almost certainly the first (if voyage chaplains are excepted) serious attempt to take the Gospel to men afloat.

The Church, afloat and ashore, evolves and develops as it seeks to bring the Christian Gospel to the world. The large fleets of wind-bound vessels to which Ashley ministered in the Bristol Channel, like those in the Solent visited by Childs, would disappear as steam replaced sail. Later the same would be true of the Mission to Deep Sea Fishermen's ministry to the fishing fleets of the North Sea. Another ministry of the Church, which has disappeared due to changes in the shipping pattern, in the latter half of the twentieth century, was the large dockside ministry which was displaced by the rise of vessels too large to be accommodated in the old dock areas, their need for a quick turn-around and the ability of ship owners to fly in relief crews quickly making the hostels redundant. The Bristol Channel Mission was a product of its time.

The inscription on Ashley's gravestone that he was the founder of missions (plural) to seamen is true only in the general sense that his early work in the Bristol Channel Mission prompted others to found, for example, the Thames Church Mission (Appendix One) and, less directly, the St Andrew's Waterside Mission (Appendix Two). It would not be true if the inscription was understood to mean he was the founder of The Missions to Seamen, despite his connection via Childs to Kingston. The Bristol society joined The Missions to Seamen only after the latter's foundation and joined largely through the force of circumstance. Kingston's choice of the plural (Missions) to name his amalgamation of societies was prompted by his vision of other societies joining, something lost in today's title, Mission to Seafarers; a loss begun when the names of the other societies in the amalgamation ceased to be included, despite the original agreements, under The Missions to Seamen masthead.[1] The change of 'Seamen' to the non-gender-specific 'Seafarers' is less contentious and reflects the increasing number of women at sea, though it was clear from the *Eirene*'s logs that Ashley included in his ministry all whom he found afloat, women included, without distinction.

Among the questions that remain to be answered, those about the ownership and subsequent history of the *Eirene* stand out. Though the vessel played such a significant part in Ashley's ministry, I have found no satisfactory answer about the fate of the vessel, its ownership, or if there was a second, perhaps concurrent, *Eirene*, something implicit in a few ambiguous press reports; a puzzle which someone else may be prompted to solve.

---

1. I can remember seeing these on Missions to Seamen letterheads in the mid-1960s.

There is plenty of evidence to confirm M.R. Kingsford's opinion about the story of Ashley's son, that 'it is unlikely that . . . the Missions to Seamen will ever sacrifice to accuracy . . . Dr Ashley's little son.'[1] The following displays, still very public in January 2016 make no mention of the boy (except in a Wikipedia account). Despite the present book's more accurate version of who Ashley was and what he did, the popular version will surely continue to run.

A visitor to the head office of The Mission to Seafarers, now in the church of St Michael Paternoster Royal in the City of London, will find in the vestibule a board bearing a text in gold upper case letters, dating from 1970:

IN 1835 THE REV. JOHN ASHLEY LOOKING AT A FLEET OF VESSELS LYING IN PENARTH ROADS HEARD A CALL TO UNDERTAKE A MISSION TO THE CREWS ON BOARD. ON THIS FOUNDATION WAS BUILT IN 1837 THE BRISTOL CHANNEL MISSION WHICH IN 1845 WAS REORGANISED & NAMED THE BRISTOL CHANNEL SEAMEN'S MISSION. IN 1855 UNDER THE NEW NAME OF THE BRISTOL MISSION TO SEAMEN IT EXTENDED ITS WORK TO THE ENGLISH CHANNEL. A NATIONAL ORGANISATION HAVING BEEN FORMED IN 1856 TO PROMOTE MISSIONS TO SEAMEN THE BRISTOL MISSION WAS UNITED TO IT IN 1858 UNDER THE NAME OF THE MISSIONS TO SEAMEN & THE FLAG OF THE FLYING ANGEL WAS ADOPTED. IN 1904 THE THAMES CHURCH MISSION FOUNDED IN 1844 WAS INCORPORATED WITH THE MISSIONS TO SEAMEN & IN 1939 THE ST ANDREW'S WATERSIDE MISSION FOR SAILORS FOUNDED IN 1864 WAS ALSO INCORPORATED.

One hundred miles to the west, in Poole (Dorset), on the town Quay, the excellent Oriel café displays in its entrance a mural of a rather flamboyant angel and the claim:

IN 1835 THE REVEREND JOHN ASHLEY
BEGAN THE VOLUNTARY MINISTRY
'MISSIONS TO SEAMEN', SOMETIMES
KNOWN AS THE 'FLYING ANGEL'
(FROM THE EMBLEM ON ITS FLAG)
THIS BUILDING WAS THE
POOLE BRANCH FROM 1860-1954

A note on the menu adds that the upper room was used as the seamen's chapel.

Wikipedia (5 December 2015) rewarded a search for 'John Ashley' with a brief paragraph, beginning: 'In 1835 he was on the shore at Clevedon with his son who asked him how the people of Flat Holm could go to church'. Following his three-month ministry to the island population, 'he recognised the needs of the seafarers on the four hundred vessels in the Bristol Channel and created the Bristol Channel Mission. . . . This became the Missions to Seamen'.

1. M.R. Kingsford, *The Mersey Mission to Seamen*, 1957, 139.

Appendix One

John Ashley: An Inspiration

The Thames Church Mission

At several of John Ashley's public meetings, mention was made of another society arranging for a vessel to serve on the River Thames to emulate the work of the Bristol Channel Mission.[1] Ashley's new board of Directors, in 1850, in an early circular, wrote of the Thames Church Mission that 'they [the TCM] are the more encouraged to commence this important work by the success which has attended The Rev. Dr Ashley's efforts in the Bristol Channel'. The primary founders of the TCM were disquieted by the moribund state of the London Episcopal Floating Church Society (LEFCS). Ships, and therefore sailors, were moving away from the Pool of London and the LEFCS's floating church, HMS *Brazen*, moored off the Tower of London, the effectiveness of which can hardly have been helped by its capsizing in 1831.[2] The Bristol Channel Mission and Ashley's work seemed to offer a way forward.

The TCM was inaugurated at a meeting in London's King William Street on 23 February, 1844. Captain The Hon. W. Waldegrave, who had been present at the founding of the LEFCS, took the Chair. With him were several others present, who had served on the committee of the LEFCS, among them Captain Henry Hope CB, Captain R.J. Elliott RN,[3] and four from Trinity House (Captains Rees, Frederick Madan, Stephenson Ellarby, William E. Farrer). According to the Minutes, 'At 2 p.m., the above Gentlemen assembled at the office of the Seamen's Hospital, 74 King William Street, to promote the formation of a Society, to afford Pastoral Superintendence to the Colliers, and other Shipping on the Thames.'[4] Some of the Elder Brethren of Trinity House on routine inspections of lights in the Bristol Channel had seen in Ashley's

---

1. See e.g., *Gloucester Journal*, 5 February 1853, for one example among many.
2. TCM Minute books and other papers, inherited by The Missions to Seamen, now in the Hull History Centre, provide much of the information which follows.
3. Robert James Elliott, nephew of the Earl of Minto. For the origins of Elliott's faith see M.R. Kingsford, *Life of W.H.G. Kingston*, 126.
4. TCM *Minutes* (Hull History Centre DMS/2/9).

work something which might be possible on the River Thames.[1] Others, unable to attend, included Lord Henry Cholmondley, pleading illness, and The Hon. Captain Maude RN,[2] prevented by distance.

A number of Resolutions were passed, among them that the new Society should be called 'The Thames Church Mission Society'. Its Committee, which had the power to co-opt members (by Rule 4, limited to 24 members, 4 retiring by annual rotation, but eligible for re-election), was to consist of those already named, together with Henry Blanchard Esq., Captain Vernon Harcourt RN, Lord Henry Cholmondley, Captain Alfred Chapman, Thomas Chapman Esq., The Hon. Captain Francis Maude RN, and The Rev. C.A.J. Smith (unrelated to G.C. Smith). Captain Farrer was to act as Secretary. Captain Madan was appointed Treasurer. Captain Elliott, from this point, became one of the most active of the Committee members. Previously a promoter of the Wells Street Sailors' Home, his first task here was to investigate statistics for vessels on the Thames. Plans were made to draw up a prospectus and the Subcommittee, which would do this, met at 32 Sackville Street, the home of the LEFCS.

A Deputation, which had been appointed to wait upon the Bishop of London for his 'Sanction and Patronage', was sufficiently well received by the Bishop for him to offer to write to the Archbishop of Canterbury seeking the latter's agreement to become Patron. To this, the Archbishop graciously agreed, his appointment a sign of respectability and an assurance that the TCM was within the fold of the Established Church, something not true of those bodies whose line of succession derived from G.C. Smith. The Lord Mayor of London, as Conservator of the River Thames, agreed to be a Vice President, together with the Bishops of Rochester and Winchester.

The first of the Rules and Regulations established the title of the Society, the second stated that the Object of the TCM was to serve shipping between the Pool of London and Gravesend. The third covered the appointment of a chaplain to conduct services on Sundays and visit ships on weekdays. Rule seven required the chaplain to be a member of the Established Church, nominated by the committee and approved by the Bishop of London. Other rules related to the conduct of meetings. The rules were approved on 10 May, 1844.

Two weeks later, the Admiralty transferred the *Swan*, a redundant 144-ton cutter from the years of the Napoleonic war, to the TCM. Captain Elliott, who had been instrumental in obtaining the vessel from the Admiralty, reported that the *Swan* was in a very poor condition but that the Admiralty was willing to make the vessel sound, by painting and caulking the hull. Painting and rigging the *Swan* was to be attended to by Trinity House. The *Swan* arrived at Blackwall jury rigged, to be fitted out by Messrs Wigrams at cost. Made seaworthy, and rendered capable of accommodating a congregation of 120, the *Swan* was officially opened on 21 April, 1845. This was to be the TCM's *Eirene*.[3]

1. Kverndal, *Seamen's Missions* 396.
2. Erstwhile NMBS secretary.
3. Kverndal, *Seamen's Missions* 396.

Advertisements were placed for the Society in the London papers, the *Standard*, *Times*, *Record*, *Herald* and *Morning Post*. Money began to come in at a satisfactory rate, allowing J.W. Hancock, ex-coxswain of HMS *St Vincent*, to be appointed as Master of the *Swan*, his salary was four pounds a month with rations. After 4 months, the TCM was able to report that vessel, master, committee, eminent Patrons, were all in place and £381 in the bank. Even so, the new master of the *Swan* prudently enquired into 'the Permanency of the Institution' before accepting his appointment.

The TCM adopted the flag and pennant of the Bristol Channel Mission, omitting from the flag the word 'EIRENE'. These, and copies of the Bristol Channel Mission's signal flags, were obtained for use on the *Swan*. The Admiralty granted two boats for the *Swan*. Still outstanding was the appointment of a chaplain, which seems to have been left largely in the hands of Captain Elliott. In September 1844, he rejected a well-recommended curate, formerly an officer of the East India Company, for he 'felt himself conscientiously bound to say, that on the score of Power in his Preaching, and the Entire Absence of Energy in his manner, the Minister he went to hear, would not be likely to sufficiently interest the seamen'. The search for the right man continued.

The *Swan*, during this time, was allowed to winter, free of all charges, in the East India Dock, where fitting out continued, the chapel being provided as in churches ashore with seats, pulpit, communion table, and boards displaying creed, commandments and Lord's prayer. Eventually, a chaplain, The Rev. Thomas Morton of Plymouth was appointed to start on 25 March, 1845, to use all these furbishments. Until that date, the TCM had an offer to conduct services from another clergyman, the Bishop being agreeable but the Rector of Poplar, in whose parish the East India Dock was situated, as was his right, refused to countenance any services, creating an insurmountable obstacle, behind which almost certainly lay the question of churchmanship. As an enquiry revealed that the entire dock lay within his parish boundaries; no way could be found around the impasse.

Funds were raised mainly by subscription: to encourage subscribers, small subscription, books were to 'be laid on the Bankers' tables, Lloyd's Coffee House, the Jerusalem Coffee House, &c., &c.', a system with which underwriters would be familiar in their daily business. The appointment of a Collector, who would receive ten per cent of all the new subscriptions and donations that he could obtain, and five per cent on such other monies that he was able to collect, reveals how societies set about raising money at this time. Tracts for use on the vessel were supplied by the Religious Tract Society and the Prayer Book and Homily Society (PBHS), the Secretary of the latter expressing a willingness to co-operate with the TCM.

The inaugural service on the *Swan*, now at Trinity Moorings in the Thames off Blackwall, took place on the afternoon of Monday 21 April, 1845, with almost everyone from the Trinity Yard attending. The chaplain was in residence on board and ready to begin visiting ships. Aft, with Admiralty permission, flew the White Ensign, surmounted by the adapted Bristol Channel Mission flag. Hopes were high that Mr Morton would earn his £300 per year. He was in sole command of the *Swan*, subject to the TCM committee and its detailed bye-laws to govern chaplain and master. One Bye-Law for the chaplain was headed 'Immorality':

> He will reprove and check every immoral act which he may have the pain to witness, remembering never to speak to a Drunken Person, during the time of his intoxication, but carefully to avoid him, seizing the first opportunity when the offender is sober, quietly to point out the wickedness of the act.

Twenty days later, the committee heard of the *Swan*'s first accident: whilst on the buoys, it had been run into by the *Duke of Portland*, then in tow and attempting to avoid another vessel. Despite the bustle of the Thames, accidents involving the *Swan* were not to be frequent.

The next year proved a poor one for the Society. The chaplain left, despite being expected to serve for three years, on his appointment to a living by the Simeon Trustees, a markedly Low Church patronage society. He was allowed to read himself into his new parish, appointing an assistant curate to look after it while he remained with the TCM until a successor was appointed.[1] A sharp decline in income prompted economies: the crew was reduced in number and the salary of the new chaplain, The Rev. W. Holderness from Lancaster, appointed in July, was set at £200 per year. Holderness seems to have been a man of enthusiasm, undaunted by warnings about the TCM's finances, taking up his appointment in a flurry of activity, which included the purchase of a small organ for the *Swan*, and the arrangement for the words 'THAMES CHURCH' to be painted on the ship's side in large letters. For its part, the TCM applied without success to the Church Pastoral Aid Society (an organisation not dissimilar to the Simeon Trustees in churchmanship) for a grant. Holderness was able to report some healthy statistics at the end of his first quarter's work:

Services held	61
Ships visited	956
Tracts disseminated	3,049
Bibles sold	63
Testaments sold	184
Prayer Books sold	71
Congregations	about 2,646

On his own initiative, he had done some preaching on the TCM's behalf, for example, in Hull.

---

1. An incumbent took hold of his benefice by reading publicly the Thirty-nine Articles, assenting to the Prayer Book and *Book of Homilies*, and taking the Oath of Allegiance to the Sovereign; only then could he enjoy its fruits.

The TCM committee expressed satisfaction with Holderness' work through the award of a bonus. Others were less pleased. Although the MSABS had offered him Bibles, he usually obtained them from the NMBS and sold them at the latter's rate. The MSABS complained that it was being undercut, the TCM selling Bibles for 8d. whereas 10d. was the MSABS's rate. Reference to the NMBS allowed the matter to be resolved; a slight matter which allows insight into life on a church ship and the relations between evangelical societies. The SPCK provided books for the *Swan*, making a lending library possible. Under the chaplain's instruction, 3 crew members became Scripture Readers, and the captain was appointed a sub-agent of the PBHS. Generally, Mr Holderness had brought improvement. Funds were sufficient to permit investment of a modest surplus. By the end of 1848, it could be said that the TCM was fulfilling the vision of the founders.

New work was initiated. At the request of the Marine Society, 50 of the society's boys were allowed to attend Divine Service on Sundays in the chapel of the *Swan*. The attendance of these boys preparing for a sea-going profession would have been welcome. An essay competition was started at the end of 1848, evidence of the TCM's willingness to extend outreach. The first essay, 'A Life of St Paul', was sufficiently successful for another, on 'The Sailor's Sabbath', to be advertised, open to 'sailors, the crews of steamboats, barges, canal-boats, fishermen and watermen, in all cases to be "men before the mast" or apprentices',[1] with a prize for the winner. The response is not known.

The TCM began to cast its net more widely. Although the Rules were not altered to include a ministry to visit 'Emigrants, Convicts, Passengers' until 1851, all variously to be found on board ships or hulks in the Thames. in emulation of Ashley's work in the Bristol Channel, the Society began to work among these groups, which could be found waiting on the river. Specifically, in 1849, the TCM received a grant of £50 from the British Ladies Female Emigration Society towards the stipend of a lay assistant for the visitation of emigrants. A letter to the TCM from the secretary of the PBHS, which warned that he saw here a potential clash of interests between his Society and the TCM, was ignored and no action was taken to avoid a clash, though the visitation of emigrants fell into abeyance in 1851, to be renewed at the end of the year, perhaps with an eye on a further grant from the British Ladies Female Emigration Society. This proved too much for the PBHS, which demanded the appointment of two subcommittees, one from each society, to resolve matters. This was achieved in early 1852 by the agreement of 4 rules: prior invitation would give the invited society precedence on board; such invitations would be communicated between societies; in cases for which there had been no invitation, precedence would go to the first society to board; failing these rulings, agents were to remember

---

1. i.e., not officers.

that the good of the emigrant was the deciding factor. These rules prompted the British Ladies Female Emigration Society, for no obvious reason, in disapproval to withdraw its grant in 1853. The Rules did, however, bring peace between the PBHS and the TCM, perhaps united by their opposition to the Government Emigration Agent's objection to the TCM Scripture Reader addressing emigrants. Meanwhile, the TCM chaplain went about his work: on 28 February, 1855, he noted that, 'In consequence of the River having been covered with large masses of Ice, for the last fortnight, the Chaplain has been prevented from visiting the Ships.'

W.H.G. Kingston addressed the TCM Committee Meeting of 7 March, 1856, on the possibility of the TCM joining his proposed amalgamation, here described as 'The Central Society for Missions to British Seamen Afloat and Ashore . . . through forming part of *One Great Scheme* without losing in any way its individual character [original emphasis]'. The committee declined his offer, turning instead to domestic matters, such as complaints from the master of the *Swan*.

The TCM continued its work on the Thames. Acting as the agent for the NMBS until that society stopped supplying merchant seamen at the end of 1857, the TCM turned instead to the BFBS,[1] which was, at the beginning of 1858, looking for a society to relieve the BFBS of its two colporteurs on the Thames. These, the Thames Mission offered to undertake but, as it involved hiring another man and a boat, on condition that the BFBS should be willing to pay the £135 necessary for the first year of operation. The BFBS declined, preferring to continue its work with the 'New Metropolitan Agency about to be called into Existence', which was probably, but not certainly, The Missions to Seamen. At the same time, the TCM was having further problems with the PBHS, which objected to the failure of the TCM chaplain to use the 'Ritual of the Church of England', conducting instead extempore services on board ship, an indication of the party within the Church of England with which the TCM continued to identify itself.

In August, 1862, The Missions to Seamen's Secretary, Walrond,[2] wrote to Captain Maude:

> Will you kindly give attentive consideration to the following subject of which I have been thinking frequently. It is the advisability and practicability of establishing a connection link between the Thames Church Mission and ourselves.

---

1. The NMBS gave way to the BFBS and its Merchant Seamen's Auxiliary Bible Society.
2. Secretary Walrond was the father of Mary Walrond, author of, *Launching out into the Deep*. According to Kingsford, *W.H.G. Kingston*, 134 n50, Walrond had been curate of 'Langton Budville', near Wellington in Somerset. There is a Langford Budville near Wellington, and on the River Tone, which may be reflected in the name which Kingsford gave the parish.

1. Advisability. The work carried on by the two societies is identical in style. . . .

2. . . . As long as we approve of the Chaplain and have an account of his work, and your accounts pass through ours we should [think?] that a sufficient union was effected. . . . Thus retaining almost in toto your present independence of action – call yourselves Missions to Seamen Thames Church Mission Branch.

A further point suggested that The Missions to Seamen should 'make good' any cash deficiencies and that the Thames Mission should hand over any surpluses. Walrond would not have been able to write this, however, if he had not had the approval of his committee. The response to his offer is not recorded.[1]

In April 1865, the TCM received another letter from Walrond, couched in similar terms, something implying that discussion of the matter had not entirely ceased. A subcommittee was appointed to consider this. By May, however, it was clear that the TCM was unhappy with the idea of a merger. Nevertheless, a public meeting on 1 June, 1865, came out in favour, suggesting points which might allow union to be achieved:

- that the society be designated the Thames Church Mission in union with The Missions to Seamen;
- 'that the present arrangements, appointments and management of the [Thames Church] Mission remain as before';
- that any extension of work on the Thames be considered jointly;
- the future appointment of a chaplain to the *Swan* to be in the hands of the Thames Church Mission committee;
- the Thames Church Mission to report quarterly to The Missions to Seamen, its report to be printed in The Missions to Seamen journal, *The Word on the Waters*;
- The Missions to Seamen committee to guarantee £680 *per annum* to the Thames Church Mission and the Thames Church Mission to hand over surplus collections, etc., to The Missions to Seamen;
- such surplus to be devoted to Thames Church Mission work;
- the Thames Church Mission to incur no extra expenses without sanction from The Missions to Seamen;
- The Missions to Seamen Secretary to be an *ex officio* member of the Thames Church Mission committee;
- the Thames Church Mission accounts to be audited and sent to The Missions to Seamen annually.

The Thames Mission committee was informed on 16 June that Walrond had made a river trip on the *Swan*, and had found great alterations to be necessary to the structure of the ministry. It is difficult to establish quite what the required alterations were, but it seems fairly clear that one was

---

1.   Hull History Centre DMS 1/37. Missions to Seamen Letter Book from 1858.

concerned with the rather blurred relation of the TCM to the Church of England in some of its practices. A subcommittee was formed to examine changes in the shipping pattern to see how they affected the work of the TCM. By December, total amalgamation or reversion to the original position was the choice to be faced. Two motions regarding salaries and committees were passed by the TCM, which, if rejected by The Missions to Seamen, would be followed by the *status quo ante*, and the TCM forced to draw on its contingency fund. Though this implied that shortage of funds lay behind the TCM's willingness to talk to The Missions to Seamen, the TCM committee felt able to ignore Walrond's call for immediate and total amalgamation. On failing to achieve satisfaction from The Missions to Seamen, a General Meeting of the TCM was called for 22 February, 1866. This dissolved the 'union' and was followed by a committee meeting to consider the situation: the TCM reverted to independence, perhaps as a gesture of defiance extending its work by appointing an additional two workers, and obtaining an office and a secretary. It is possible that this revision to its structure reflected some of the alterations suggested by Walrond.

Reconstituted and newly invigorated, the TCM made good progress in the short term, receiving help from the Evangelization Society, the Pure Literature Society, and the Dock Street Sailors' Home, where The Rev. Dan Greatorex, a TCM committee member, was chaplain. In 1868, there was some question about the *Swan* chaplain using the surplice and the Litany at weeknight services, to the annoyance of nonconformist captains and others; a matter resolved by directing the chaplain to use short extempore services, with the Litany at his discretion, and without the surplice, a garment seen here more as a red rag than the white over-garment of actuality. In 1864, partly in reaction to the TCM's churchmanship (as evidenced by those extempore prayers, dislike of the surplice, and disregard of local incumbents), the St Andrew's Waterside Church Mission (SAWCM) began to work at Gravesend, where shortly a dispute arose with the TCM over the ship-board baptism of the child of an emigrant, technically within the bounds of the parish of Gravesend. The TCM chaplain informed his committee that he had seen the Vicar of Gravesend, Robinson, who had been co-operative over the matter of registering the baptism, adding that Robinson 'seemed disposed to leave to [the TCM] the undisputed control of the highway of the River', which proved to be a disposition of short duration.

Little did they know the Vicar of Gravesend. In February, 1867, Mr Robinson, apparently a man with a puckish sense of humour, protested that he, as incumbent, had not been informed, as courtesy would require, of a TCM meeting to be held in his parish. He enclosed details of his society, the SAWCM, to show that it was not antipathetic to the TCM's aims, and suggested – perhaps mischievously – an amalgamation of the TCM and the SAWCM; a suggestion the TCM committee declined. Robinson's next ploy was to deplore the overlapping of the work of the two societies and suggest that the TCM should make a grant to the SAWCM to do its work at Gravesend or hand that work over to SAWCM in the entirety. This too was declined.

The TCM also clashed briefly with The Missions to Seamen in the mid-1870s, when the latter appointed a lay reader to visit ships on the Thames. Since the lay reader's work was limited to a portion of the Thames which was included in the parish of The Rev. Dan Greatorex, presumably with his approval, the TCM could only protest. The work of the TCM on the rest of the Thames remained unaltered. The TCM struggled on, despite a worsening financial situation, in 1875-6 sub-letting part of its office to the National Truss Society, before moving to new offices at 31 New Bridge Street, Blackfriars.[1] In 1877, Captain Maude's influence with the Admiralty on behalf of the TCM proved to be enough to stop the Admiralty acceding to a SAWCM request for a launch.

In 1878, pressure from the committee that produced for the Church of England's Convocation a report on Church of England work for seamen produced a slight thaw in relations with The Missions to Seamen.[2] It was agreed that The Missions to Seamen could appoint chaplains and readers to Thames-side parishes as funds allowed, something to which the TCM could hardly object. Despite the TCM's staff problems, otherwise good relations continuing to operate at those points where the societies overlapped, though it was not until July 1903 that another serious meeting between the two societies to reconsider the possibility of amalgamation took place; a special meeting was arranged for this purpose to take place in September 1903. The TCM's ministry to people who were not seamen was one obstacle. Other points considered were: the relation to the Church of England of its staff of chaplain and eight laymen; the maintenance of the TCM's river work; an examination of its four halls run at Tilbury, Radcliffe, Leigh and Erith; the state of the TCM finances; and the retention of its name. It was agreed to retain the TCM staff, replacing them gradually with members of the Church of England. The relationship between the TCM halls and the parishes in which they lay being considered as tenuous at best, it was agreed that maintenance of them would continue for the time being, provided their use would be for seamen only.

Little could be done about the TCM's finances; in 1902, there had been a working deficit of £1,239 and investments, mainly its pension fund, of £4,781. The Bishops, by October 1903, had expressed themselves in favour of an amalgamation; this was agreed subject to use of the *Book of Common Prayer*, emphasis on use by seamen of the TCM halls, continued employment of TCM staff, and the incorporation of the TCM name in The Missions to Seamen title. Financial and episcopal pressure

---

1. The prevalence of hernias among seamen has been noted in connection with St Artemios (Miller, *One Firm Anchor*, 32). It is not clear if these industrial injuries explain the Thames Church Mission's connection with the National Truss Society.
2. Miller, *One Firm Anchor*, 144ff.

combined to ensure the acceptance of these terms by the TCM on 3 November, 1903. Subscribers had been informed that the terms were to take effect from 31 March, 1904. For many years, though long since discontinued, the name of the TCM did, indeed, appear beneath the official title of The Missions to Seamen. In this way, The Missions to Seamen could now be said to include work begun in 1825 by the Episcopal Floating Church Society.

The TCM, in the 1880s, had spawned what is now the Royal National Mission to Deep Sea Fishermen.[1] The Thames Mission's then Secretary, Ebenezer Joseph Mather, had become aware of the North Sea fishing fleets and persuaded his committee to allow him to obtain a trawler to initiate work among this neglected class of seafarer. Mather was to prove a colourful figure. A member of the Plymouth Brethren at the time of his appointment, he switched to the Church of England when supporters pointed out that the TCM was supposedly a Church of England society. When it became obvious that the North Sea work was a 'step too far' for the TCM, Mather left the Thames society to become Secretary of the Mission to Deep Sea Fishermen; he was to pioneer an important ministry, fighting a well-publicised battle against the copers who peddled alcohol, luxury goods and pornographic literature to the fishermen. The TCM *Minutes* of 1886 show that Mather's resignation was not straightforward. That of 18 February, 1886, recorded his retirement as Honorary Secretary 'in consequence of the appointment of the Rev. H. Bloomer as paid Secretary'. On 18 June, Mather resigned from the Finance Committee, 'promising £25 towards the amount required for establishing a Superannuation Fund'. On 12 December, the committee agreed to ask Mather to return the society's address books (listing supporters) 'without delay' as these were the Thames society's property, having been 'written at a period antecedent to the "Division"'. On 17 December, it was recorded that Mather had agreed to resign from the General Committee, something requested because of his failure to attend meetings and 'the confusion that had arisen in the minds of contributors to it and the Mission to Deep Sea Fishermen'. His going, a prolonged process, was accompanied by 'misunderstandings'. It is, therefore, not a surprise to discover years later that Mather's time with the Mission to Deep Sea Fishermen ended when he was sacked for mistakes made on his claim for expenses.[2]

The North Sea fishing fleets have long gone, as have the wind-bound vessels of the Bristol Channel, both overtaken by the advance of steam. There is no evidence to suggest that Ashley's ministry to the wind-bound sailors in the Bristol Channel prompted Mather's interest in the fleets of the North Sea, despite the similarities in their ministries, but Ashley's role as the inspiration of the TCM allows him to be placed in the ancestry of the Royal National Mission to Deep Sea Fishermen. The TCM *Minutes* of 1886, which record Mather's departure also note the death of one of the founders, a lifelong supporter, Captain the Hon. Francis Maude. Ashley's death in the same year went unremarked.

Through the Thames Church Mission and the Mission to Deep Sea Fishermen, a link can be claimed between Ashley and the *Œuvres de Mer*, a Catholic work

1. Miller, *One Firm Anchor*, 225ff.
2. Thames Church Mission records are kept in the Hull History Centre: DMS/2/25.

initiated in the 1890s to bring the Gospel and much-needed succour to the French fishing fleets working off Newfoundland and Iceland.[1] The key figure in the foundation of the *Œuvres de Mer* was M. Bernard Bailly whose knowledge both of the work of the Mission to Deep Sea Fishermen and of the Church of England's Order of St Paul as well as the work of the latter with the men of the Merchant Navy, resulted in the *Œuvres de Mer*. Its work among the French fishing fleets, at least at sea, had effectively ceased by 1930, another consequence of the forward march of technology. The structure of the *Œuvres de Mer* in turn provided the template used in 1930 to form the world-wide Catholic work among seafarers, the Apostleship of the Sea.[2] It can only be guessed what Ashley would have thought had he been allowed to foresee his contribution to this ministry of the Catholic Church.

---

1. Miller, *One Firm Anchor*, 264ff.
2. Miller, *One Firm Anchor*, 332.

Appendix Two

Dr Ashley: An Indirect Inspiration

The St Andrew's Waterside Church Mission (SAWCM), the full title not always used (its name taken from the dedication of a Gravesend waterside chapel fronting the River Thames), was founded in 1864 by The Rev. C.E. Robinson, incumbent of the parish of Holy Trinity, Milton-next-Gravesend. According to Kverndal, Robinson, when Vicar of St James' Ryde, on the Isle of Wight, 'had watched with deep interest the ministry of Chaplain Childs on the Channel Coast' in 1857. It will be recalled that Childs had been appointed to this chaplaincy by the resurrected Bristol Channel Mission, thus providing a link with Ashley. In the English Channel, according to Kverndal, who had sourced his information from the *New Sailors' Magazine* of G.C. Smith, Childs had fitted out a cutter and named her *Eirene* after her Bristol Channel predecessor.[1]

It may be wondered why, with so many societies working on the River Thames, another was thought necessary. Though the amount of shipping on the river at this time, when London lay at the heart of an expanding Empire, meant that there was always more work to be done, it was mainly the factional nature of the Established Church which led to the foundation of the St Andrew's Mission. The evangelical stance of the TCM and The Missions to Seamen was inimical to Tractarians and their Anglo-Catholic successors, in their emphasis on Church order, the parochial system of which was intended to ensure pastoral care for all, seamen included.

At first, the SAWCM's work was limited to Gravesend. From its inception, the Mission was subject to financial problems. It seems to have enjoyed the favour of the Bishop of Rochester, in whose diocese Gravesend was situated. The Bishop advised that it should continue for a further year, despite the financial uncertainty, advice apparently justified, for the SAWCM reported an improvement in 1868, though the income was never to match either that of the TCM or The Missions to Seamen.

Bibles and Prayer Books were distributed, as were vast quantities of books and

---

1. Kverndal, *Seamen's Missions*, 387, 394. Whether this should be understood as the original *Eirene* refitted or as a vessel functioning like the *Eirene* is nowhere clear.

magazines, the latter donated by the public and freighted free of charge by the local railway company. The 1868 *Report* quoted *The Monthly Packet* of October 1868, describing the 'Waterside Mission' as housed in Gravesend's former Spread Eagle Tavern, facing the river and with its own quay, its lower floor converted into a chapel, and, above, a Mission House with reading room, library and night school. The clergy worked on the principle that if sailors came not to them, to the sailors they must go. Their ministry from the beginning, in January 1864, included the crews of passenger and cargo vessels, plus anyone connected with these, and local fishermen. Outward bound steamers coaled at Gravesend from twelve coal hulks; on board each hulk was a family, which the SAWCM staff visited. Gravesend was also the place where ships changed pilots. Following the opening of the Suez Canal, a marked increase in the number of ships pausing at Gravesend occupied the attention of the SAWCM. Ashore, a Mothers' Meeting was begun for the many families of seamen in Gravesend. These families provided much work for the SAWCM. Its pastoral care apparently surprised the recipients for whom such attention was a novelty, at the same time illustrating the strengths of a well-run parochially-based ministry.

The improvement in SAWCM's income was maintained in 1869, with some £100 cash in hand, a deposit account of £200, and a further £200 put aside towards the purchase of a Mission House, presumably to make that described in *The Monthly Packet* a permanency. Money was raised mainly through deputations (parish preachments), with income increasing as the work became more widely known. Office expenses were absorbed by the parish. A donation of £1,000 in 1870 to the chapel fund allowed the laying of a foundation stone on St Peter's Day, 1870, and consecration on St Andrew's Day, 1871. The local yacht club offered the use of a steam yacht to facilitate ship-visiting, a Ladies' Committee supported the work, and small grants for books were received from the SPCK. All of which was timely. The building of a Sailors' Home, although contemplated, was never achieved.

In 1872, the SAWCM could boast a staff of 2 chaplains, 2 honorary chaplains, 1 Reverend Treasurer, and a lay reader; effectively the Gravesend parish staff. The Archbishop of Canterbury agreed to become Patron. An organist was appointed for the newly-acquired chapel organ. Chapel windows were installed, which with the organ represented a significant advance in any Victorian church building programme. A day school was started for fishermen's children. A new boat was presented the following year. Improved finances allowed the opening of a branch to serve London's Victoria Dock, in St Mark's (later, on the division of the parish, St Matthew's) parish, where ship-visiting was begun, 130 libraries were issued, and an anonymous donation was received towards the cost of a missionary curate, that is, a curate licensed to the parish but appointed specifically to work in the docks.[1] At Gravesend, for ship-board

1. The Victoria, first of the Royal Docks, opened in 1855, followed by the adjoining Albert Dock in the 1880s.

services, a portable Holy Table and linen were acquired. The Society for the Propagation of the Gospel gave £25 towards the visitation of emigrants and £10 was received from the Pure Literature Society, small-sounding sums in today's terms but then something useful.[1]

In 1874, the SAWCM *Report* mentioned a first contact with The Missions to Seamen, following the receipt of 'some gifts' (unspecified but, at a guess, hymn books). The SAWCM's work in London's expanding dockland was extended by making a grant to the Vicar of St Luke's, Millwall towards the stipend of a missionary curate to visit ships in the Millwall and West India Docks, while in the Victoria Dock, the Victoria Docks Company provided a permanent church for seamen. Appeals for help were beginning to come from abroad. An Honorary SAWCM chaplain had been appointed at Corfu, and the SAWCM was arranging to supply him with a safe boat from Malta. Parcels of books, presumably to be dispensed by local honorary chaplains, were being sent to Yokohama, Naples and Algiers for visiting seamen, to Jamaica for the seamen's hospital, and to Odessa for the Sailors' Home. At this time, Odessa was being visited by some 7,000 British sailors annually, prompting the SAWCM to appeal for £200 per year for room rental, and an additional £25 for furnishings.

Most requests for assistance to the SAWCM were repetitious (books, boats and missionary curates), but they give an idea of how the society was growing and its method being copied. In 1875, its Secretary visited Rotterdam, Hamburg, Copenhagen and Gothenburg to investigate possibilities. It was aware that the Bishop of Gibraltar was doing similar work in his diocese and opened a fund to assist him.[2] An appeal from Naples had born fruit to the extent of establishing a flourishing Sailors' Home. At Grimsby, the SAWCM was committed to providing half the stipend of a missionary curate.

There were plans to place a curate at Tilbury, just across the river from Gravesend, TCM territory, where the railway company was developing docks; the St Andrew's Mission perhaps prompted by the TCM's incursion to begin some sort of outreach work among the navvies extending those docks. The incumbent of Chadwell St Mary, in whose parish the Tilbury Docks were situated, wrote to the Archbishop of Canterbury in March, 1883, that he was not prepared to work with the TCM, because he was already doing Church work among the Tilbury navvies, with support from the SAWCM. His principal objection was that the General Secretary of the TCM, Mather, was 'an avowed Plymouth Brother and that their tenets largely if not exclusively prevail in the Thames Church Mission Society'.[3] Whether Dr Friend's opinion that it was this that prompted the TCM's General Secretary and his wife to join the Church

---

1. *Classified Digest of the Records of the SPG in Foreign Parts, 1701-1892,* 1893, 819. SPG support for the St Andrew's Waterside Mission continued until 1882.
2. Miller, *One Firm Anchor,* 179ff.
3. Miller, *One Firm Anchor,* 225.

of England shortly after, is correct or not, the Chadwell incumbent's objection supports the view that issues of Churchmanship lay behind the differences between the two societies. The possibility of the TCM losing the patronage of the Archbishop of Canterbury would add weight to Friend's explanation of the Mathers' change of denominational allegiance.[1]

Readers would have begun to feel a certain familiarity in each year's report. Further gifts were received from the SPCK (£150), the Society for the Propagation of the Gospel (£25), and The Missions to Seamen (hymn books). Appended to the annual report were impressive numbers of ports receiving books, with honorary chaplains appointed. Although the 1876 *Report* to Convocation showed the SAWCM income for the year as no more than £600, this increasing presence in the ports makes it possible to see why Canon Scarth, who had succeeded Mr Robinson at Gravesend, was able to speak with confidence at the annual Church Congresses. A small but interesting detail in the 1876 report indicated that ships wishing to exchange libraries could fly the code flag for M from the mizzen, while those holding a service on board were encouraged to fly the same flag from below the ensign. That this system, though differing from that devised by John Ashley, could operate with the expectation of being understood suggests that the SAWCM was beginning to make an impression among seafarers.

Perhaps with the Convocation *Report* in mind, in June 1876 the SAWCM's Constitution was confirmed at a General Meeting. Essentially, it was:

1. '[T]o advance the influence and teaching of the Church of England among Sailors, Fishermen, and Emigrants, on board ships and elsewhere, through the agency of the parochial clergy at home, and the responsible clergy abroad'.
2. '[G]overned by a Council consisting of 25 Members, and the Presidents and the Vice-Presidents of Local Committees who shall be ex-officio Members of the Council. The Council shall appoint the Chairman, Secretary and Treasurer, and fill up vacancies in the three Trustees, if need be. . . .'
3. 'The Council shall meet annually. . . .'
4. Any station may have a local committee.
5. The Annual General Meeting to be held in London.
6. Those entitled to vote at an AGM are Council Members, donors of £5 or more, all clergy and churchwardens who have given offertory collections in the last 12 months, all local committee members.
7. A Standing Committee shall meet at least quarterly.
8. Officers of the Society are the Honorary Treasurer and Secretary.
9. Any supporting parish may have a Local Association.
10. (This item is taken up with Accounts.)
11. 'There shall be a commemoration service on the day of the AGM. All meetings are to begin with prayer.'

---

1. A copy of the letter forms Appendix ii, in Friend's MPhil thesis, *Rise and Development. . . .*

12. 'A Quarterly Paper relating to the affairs of the Mission shall be prepared and published'.
13. 'The Standing Committee and Local Committees shall have power to make bye-laws to be approved by the Council at the next Annual Meeting'.

This Report shows how the SAWCM went about its work in these early years. There were its Corresponding Members, that is, usually chaplains who had little, in many instances, to do with the SAWCM, beyond sending it an annual account of their work, but liked to feel that they were associated with it in some way. Sometimes, they received a SAWCM grant towards their work. Meanwhile in Gravesend, with its unequalled and increasing amount of shipping, the parish mission continued to show what an ambitious and imaginative parish could do. It had depots for the reception of books at Gravesend and London, the latter providing also waiting rooms for captains and officers wishing to attend to correspondence or receive guests, a facility illustrating rather well the differing needs of those who served amidships from those in the fo'c'stle. A small but helpful innovation was the production for distribution of maps of dock areas in Gravesend, London, Genoa, Naples and Bordeaux marked with places of importance to the seafarer, among them the places of worship provided by the Church of England.

In 1877, the SAWCM took over the emigrant work in Liverpool of the Society for the Propagation of the Gospel and the SPCK in return for financial aid from both societies. In London, the attention of the SAWCM seems to have turned to lightship crews. At Gravesend, the report noted that the combination of salt and freshwater men (i.e., deep sea and local men) both using the reading room was not making for harmony.

In 1878, a major society, not named but probably The Missions to Seamen, launched an appeal for £5,000 for work in London's dockland, which the SAWCM saw as an invasion of territory. Indeed, the Honorary Secretary worked so hard in his attempt to remedy the damage this appeal caused to the SAWCM's funds that he required a Mediterranean holiday for his health. The campaign for a Bishop of the Seas added to his troubles; the SAWCM, committed to working through existing parochial structures, argued that such an appointment would diminish even the little attention work among seamen was receiving from territorial bishops and parish clergy.[1] Meanwhile, the SAWCM was beginning to work among troops at Gravesend, Dartmouth and Madeira, presumably on troopships, if the interest of SAWCM in the presence of troops in seaports is to be explained.

To view a society from its annual reports is not sufficient. Another picture comes from the appendix to the 1878 *Chronicle of Convocation*, which described the SAWCM as 'excellent but smaller' than The Missions to Seamen, the office address 36 City Chambers, Railway Place, Fenchurch Street, London EC; in the heart of the city, and near the railway station, which was the

---

1. Miller, *One Firm Anchor*, 145ff.

terminus of its supportive railway company and probably too the address of its waiting rooms for officers. It mentioned Canon Scarth's succession as Secretary, his extension of the SAWCM work generally, and confirmed the primacy of the society's work at Gravesend where two curates assisted in 'the arduous and important duty of visiting the numerous . . . ships passing in ceaseless succession'. The SAWCM provided the stipends of 3 other curates for the Port of London. It dispensed some 25,000 books to seafarers annually. Mentioned too were the society's many correspondents, together with the North Sea work, which seems to have consisted in supporting with grants the North Sea Church Mission.[1] This North Sea Mission was run very much on SAWCM lines by the Vicar of Gorleston, using a fishing smack rigged out as a church ship to visit the fleets in the name of the Established Church. A small grant towards the provision of a curate for this work was obtained from the Additional Curates Society.

Increasing commitments stretched the SAWCM's budget. A Minute of 12 August, 1881, authorised the Treasurer to discharge liabilities as cash came in, a 'hand to mouth' existence. The recruitment of more clergy, even a bishop or two, to make appeals on behalf of SAWCM, particularly at St Andrew's tide, helped and support continued to come from other sources, now lost to the historian, if not to the archivist of dusty reports, such as the £10 received from the 'Canterbury Mission Society for promoting Missions to Seafaring and Waterside Populations, upon closing that Society, which now leaves the field open for contributions to this Mission'. The charitably inclined Baroness Burdett-Coutts, builder of better housing for the poor and provider of endowments for significant Anglican Sees in the Colonies, was moved in 1879 to send the St Andrew's Mission an abundance of copies of 'A Service for Use at Sea' as used 'on board her ladyship's steam yacht, *Walrus*'.

In 1881, the SAWCM opened its first major foreign work. An unnamed lady offered the Mission £100 for its funds if Canon Scarth would go out to organise a permanent chaplaincy in Port Said.[2] Scarth, at this time, was taking a holiday abroad for his health through temporary chaplaincy work. Providence favoured the SAWCM, for in a very short time, the shipping company P & O had offered Scarth a free return passage; at the recommendation of *M*. de Lesseps, President of the Suez Canal Company, the Administrators of the Canal made a grant of some sixty square yards of land (then worth about £3,000) to the SAWCM. The Canal Company had promised all possible assistance. An English Church, Hospital, and Sailors' Home were planned, subject to the permission of His Royal Highness the Khedive. The Rev. F.W. Strange left chaplaincy work at London's Victoria Dock to become the Port Said chaplain.

1. Miller, *One Firm Anchor*, 154, 174.
2. For the context see Freda Harcourt, 'The High Road to India . . .', *IJMH* XXII (2), Dec 2010.

The SAWCM at this time was fostering work among Lascar crews in the Port of London. Indeed, the whole of its London enterprise was prospering. Then in 1882 an anonymous, Liverpool-sourced, donation of £1,000 allowed the SAWCM to extend considerably its work in Liverpool. By 1885 'Grants for the Year' were being made:

to the Port of London	£1,050
Other Home Ports and the North Sea Fleet	395
Port Said	100
Genoa	50
Constantinople, Hong Kong, Rangoon New Brunswick, Hastings £25 each	125
Other small grants	445
	£2,165

The Hastings grant is of interest; once a Missions to Seamen port, it was then to be run on parochial lines following the resignation of The Missions to Seamen chaplain, perhaps a result of the small scale activity of the port. Some of the shipping companies were helpful to the SAWCM: British India, P & O, Allan, and Orient Lines carried its parcels of books and associated goods free of charge. In 1886, the SPCK donated books worth a total of £250 and continued to make similar grants annually.

The SAWCM was beginning to extend its ministry to the fishing industry beyond assistance to the North Sea Church Mission. In 1886, Brixham fishermen asked the SAWCM to help their curate to accompany them in a mission ship, to which end they subscribed £60, no mean sum. The SAWCM had so far maintained that it worked ashore whilst The Missions to Seamen worked afloat, a distinction not recognised here and one further eroded in 1889, when the SAWCM was given three vessels to facilitate its work afloat. These were the small steamer *Kestrel* for use at Gravesend, the RTS yacht *Sapper* to be a church ship, and the *Water Kelpie* (54 tons) for use as a floating church (i.e., alongside). Hopes that one of these might serve the Dover-Lydd-Rye area came to nothing. In 1891, however, a petition, perhaps circulated to all the societies because it noted gratefully the work of The Missions to Seamen ashore and afloat, was received from 36 East Coast clergy, asking for a church ship in the North Sea to serve the fishing fleet. These clergy envisaged a ship 'perhaps partly paying her own expenses by working as a trawler with the fishing fleets, when not otherwise engaged', a model favoured by the TCM and the Mission to Deep Sea Fishermen, but with a chaplain on board. The relationship to the North Sea Church Mission of those appealing is unclear, which may indicate shortage of income in the North Sea Church Mission or possibly an issue of churchmanship.

The 1894 Report makes it clear that the lack of funds had prevented the *Sapper* from being sent to sea. Instead, the *Goshawk*, lent by J.R. West Esq. RYS, after fitting out as a church ship, made a trip among the fishing fleets under the society's flag of St Andrew.[1] The inaugural service on board took place at Gosport on 3 July, 1893. It was crewed mainly by Brixham fisherman, and carried a surgeon and chaplain, its first trip not to the North Sea but to the Shambles lightship, Dartmouth, Brixham, Torquay, Milford Haven, Cardigan Bay lightship, Ramsey (IoM), Oban and Aberdeen. A second trip was made in 1896. It proved too expensive to run, though, when the Vicar of Gorleston set about raising the money to purchase a vessel locally (which implies that the original fishing smack had ceased to be of service) it seems that the SAWCM was shamed into running it again among the North Sea fleets.

The following year, the society decided to change its name to the more general 'Saint Andrew's Church of England Mission to Sailors, Emigrants and Fishermen'. The society recognised that the old name would die hard, as proved to be the case. Other societies might have preferred a change of attitude. In 1888, there was a spat between the SAWCM and the Thames Church Mission following a TCM advertisement in the *Guardian* and other national papers, which Canon Scarth maintained misrepresented the SAWCM's work among sailors in the Port of London; perhaps the TCM's response to the SAWCM's placing the *Kestrel* on the Thames. The TCM's advertisement quoted the Bishop of London. Canon Scarth, wanting to protest against this apparent episcopal sanctioning of TCM claims, had a Statement drawn up, signed by all London incumbents in receipt of SAWCM aid, to be laid before the Bishop by the Archdeacons of Essex and Rochester. The Archdeacons, unhappy with this, suggested instead that the Bishop be asked to chair the next SAWCM Annual General Meeting, when his attention might be drawn to the Statement. How the matter was resolved does not appear; things rumbled on for a year or two, the 1892 and 1893 Reports strongly refuting an unspecified claim that seamen in the Port of London lacked Church provision. Despite this, the 1893 Report, giving thanks for the improvements since the foundation of the SAWCM in the lot and behaviour of the merchant seaman, yet coupled the SAWCM's efforts with those of the TCM, The Missions to Seamen, and the British and Foreign Sailors Society, perhaps intending an olive branch, but adding:

> The distinction between these and the St Andrew's Waterside Church Mission is, that the latter works purely on Church principles, acting simply as a helper of the Church, passing all her grants through parochial and responsible Clergy, without regard to any special views.

Church principles were sufficiently elastic for the 1894 Report to reveal that the SAWCM had begun to distribute literature which had been produced by Miss Weston for her nondenominational work among men of the Royal Navy.[2]

---

1. A picture can be found in the 1894 Report, 55. Stephen Friend, in his thesis, says that *Sapper* was used in the North Sea, Holland and France in 1890 but was unsuitable for North Sea work. *Water Kelpie* was lent to the Grimsby mission in 1891 but, proving unsuitable, was moored in Grimsby fish docks as a reading room, with occasional Church services on board, attracting local and visiting fishermen.

2. Miller, *One Firm Anchor*, 150, 174. Agnes Weston, *My Life Among the Blue Jackets*, 1909.

In 1896, the society was incorporated, its income rose and it was able to initiate a number of works. One was among seal fishers in the Pacific, through the agency of the Victoria (British Columbia) Harbour Mission; another, the provision of a Mission House for the pearl fishers, almost exclusively Japanese, off Thursday Island, North Queensland. Naval work in the Mediterranean was increasing, which may explain the SAWCM's distribution of Miss Weston's tracts. By 1898, income had risen to £4,227, plus £1,000 allotted to the society by the Bishop of London for work in the Port of London, but then began to fall, as charitable donations generally were affected by the South African War, a famine in India, and a fire in Ottawa. By the turn of the century, the SAWCM claimed correspondents in:

America (including the West Indies and Canada)	12
China (including the Bishop of Corea [*sic*])	5
Japan (the Bishop of Osaka)	1
India (including the Bishop of Rangoon)	4
Persian Gulf	2
Australia	4
New Zealand	4
New Guinea	2

The financial effects of the South African War persisted for some years beyond its conclusion (1902), but the SAWCM's expansion continued. In 1905, the society supported the first of the Annual Seafarers' Services in St Paul's Cathedral. In 1906, SAWCM accepted responsibility for chaplaincy work on the Thames training ship *Warspite*. By 1907, SAWCM was providing grants to some 50 stations: 9 in the Port of London, 20 on the British Coast, and 21 abroad. In 1909, the society absorbed the work of the North Sea Church Mission at Gorleston, off the Norfolk coast, with which the society had been associated since 1895. In 1903, the *Kestrel* was replaced with the *St Andrew*, which seems to be identical with or intended as a successor to the *St Andrew the Fisherman* (YH 1018), built in 1885. The name, the St Andrew's flag on its bows,[1] and the Gorleston church dedication to St Andrew, imply that the association between the North Sea Church Mission and the SAWCM had long been a close one, which might suggest the North Sea Church Mission had been a rather ambitious SAWCM Local Committee. In Grimsby, north of Gorleston, a missionary curate visited the local lightship, served a fishermen's church and mission room near the parish church, and, from 1898, an orphanage for the daughters of fishermen and sailors. It is not always clear in the records which of the fishing ports the SAWCM vessels were serving. The general picture suffices; those who want more detail can find it elsewhere.[2]

---

1. I am indebted to Mr L. Hawkins of Norwich, author of 'The Mission Boats', *Sea Breezes*, January 1973, for this information, based on a photograph in his possession, conveyed in a private letter.
2. Stephen Friend, *Fishermen's Missions, passim*.

Before the 1914-18 war, the SAWCM aided the North and Central European Sailors' Mission, about which little is known. For Church of England purposes, North and Central Europe came under the Bishop of London, his ministry usually exercised through one of his suffragan bishops. The 1913 Report describes the North and Central European Sailors' Mission as one of the 'two important Continental Missions for sailors', the other being the Gibraltar Mission. The North and Central European Sailors' Mission seems to have consisted of some sort of work in the ports of Libau and Neufahrwasser; work that ceased on the outbreak of war.

War usually prompts a rise in the income of seamen's missionary societies, the public responding generously to appeals for work among sailors in a time of increased danger. Grants were received from the British Sailors' Relief Fund of Canada and the King George's Fund for Sailors. The outbreak of war coincided with the SAWCM's Jubilee year. The society's continued work among fishermen, many of whom assumed the uniform of the Royal Navy to serve on mine sweepers in the North Sea, may lie behind reports of 'parade services, work amongst soldiers as well as sailors, hospital visitation of both'. Port chaplaincy work, however, decreased, as an increasing number of clergy volunteered to serve with the armed forces, and many docks were made secure areas. In June 1917, the SAWCM's London office was bombed in an early Zeppelin raid; no SAWCM staff member was injured.

The War's end coincided with a number of retirements of long-serving office staff, making change inevitable. Finances were returning to their pre-War state; by 1920, despite the recruitment by a new Clerical Organising Secretary of a further 30 local associations, income had barely increased. The SAWCM's general decline may date from this period. Apart from the work in London and Liverpool, attention of the SAWCM was still drawn to fishermen around the British Coast but the 1920s saw many fishing boats laid up. Small initiatives continued, for example, the provision of libraries to all Trinity House lighthouses and ships. In 1922, a Ladies' Committee was formed to encourage fundraising on a national scale, its target £400 a year. The 'Ladies' had a sale of disused jewelry in 1923. There was an appeal for 'a million magazines' and 'nearly as many novels' for the despatch of which, on receipt of a postcard, the SAWCM would send sack, label and packing needle. These things were but whistling in the dark: SAWCM finances continued to flounder, Reports became shorter, and by 1927, when a service of thanksgiving for 50 years' work on the Thames was announced, a deficit was carried forward for the first time. Grants were reduced to 6 for the London, Tilbury and Gravesend area, 15 to other home ports (Liverpool receiving only one), and 16 for overseas work.

A BBC appeal by the Bishop of Chelmsford and grants from Trinity House and Lloyd's failed to improve the situation, which was exacerbated by the nationwide depression. In 1932, money had to be transferred from the legacy account to the current account. Most missionary societies, their cash flow irregular, have to juggle accounts, balancing them at the year's end after

Christmas generosity; here the juggling emphasised the continuing trend. The 1935 Report literally <u>underlined</u> the bad financial situation. Grants were further reduced: 5 to London, 12 to other home ports, 8 sent overseas. A welcome donation came from Cunard-White Star from the proceeds of a public viewing of the newly-launched *Queen Mary*.

In 1937, an augmented Ladies' Committee under a new President organised a special matinee 'shared with another well-known Sailors' Organisation' (unspecified) which netted the SAWCM over £800. The SAWCM Minutes tell a darker tale. Debts had risen from £500 to £2,000 in the decade to 1937, offset in October 1937 by sale of stock to the value of £1,700. The appointment of a new Organising Secretary in April 1938 brought no improvement. The SAWCM's Chairman, the Bishop of Exeter, in the next annual Report, announced by letter:

> It was Resolved that the Offer of The Missions to Seamen as set out in their Offer dated 29th April, 1939, to take over and continue the work of St Andrew's Waterside Church Mission for Sailors be and is hereby accepted AND that the Executive Committee be and is hereby authorised to notify The Missions to Seamen accordingly. . . .
>
> As Chairman of the SAWCM since 1928, I am convinced that this step is a wise one. The proposal was first made to the Executive Committee on my initiative. . . .

This was accompanied by a letter from the Archbishop of Canterbury commending the Bishop's action, perhaps to deflect any suggestion that Jonah was being swallowed by the whale, and to emphasise his responsibility for all decisions made.

Hindsight reveals the SAWCM's financial position had long been insecure, while speeches at Church Congress and elsewhere encouraging the societies to work more closely give the steps which led to this amalgamation a longer history than at first seems obvious. In 1922, a letter dated 22 November had arrived from Lambeth Palace addressed to The Rev. B.S. Mercer, then Organising Secretary, Archbishop Randall Davidson writing,

> Dear Mr Mercer,
>
> . . . I am not quite clear as to what I ought to do with regard to your request that I should send a message of encouragement in order to give a new stimulus to the work of S.A.W.M. I have, as perhaps you know, been for a long time wondering, and sometimes enquiring, whether it would not be possible for the work of the Mission to be incorporated with that of the Missions to Seamen. I know the value of the work of the SAWM during these many years, but it does not seem to me that it now differs in any marked way from the work of the Missions to Seamen, and I should like to know whether the subject is under consideration of a possible amalgamation of the two agencies. The idea of amalgamation is not due to any thought of deficiency or inadequacy on the part of either. . . .

Mercer had replied to this on 30 November, St Andrew's Day:[1]

> Yr Grace,
>
> . . . I am replying unofficially because this will enable me to write more freely. The 3 outstanding reasons why we do not become absorbed in the Missions to Seamen are these:
>
> 1. We do different work
> 2. We tap a different source of income
> 3. We feel that the advantages of amalgamation are less than the disadvantage of losing our identity.
>
> I regret all three reasons; and that not as a novice.... But the reasons remain intact. – I understand that the Missions to Seamen set up an independent organisation in whatever parish or port where they work ([crossed out:] some keen [illegible] Incumbents resent the erection of a local Bethel) whereas we work exclusively on parochial lines, making grants to Incumbents. . . . Not a few Incumbents and Chaplains gladly welcome our form of assistance whereas they would resent independent ministrations and the erection of an independent Bethel. Your Grace will understand this is no adverse criticism of the Missions to Seamen for which I have the greatest respect. In my vagabond life of preaching, from Lancashire to Kent and from Yorkshire to Devon I found not a few churches which welcome us but which would not welcome the Missions to Seamen and vice versa. We are reputed Catholic, and they are reputed Protestant.[2] The distinction is unreal, but the opinion still survives. And what influences certain churches also influences certain donors. Your Grace will probably know about the meeting held this month of *representatives of societies* doing home work. . . . The spirit of the meeting was acutely in favour of friendliness and acutely inimical to [illegible] amalgamations . . . and the same was urged re the Missions to Seamen and ourselves.

A Minute of 10 February, 1926, reveals no progress:

> The unauthorised correspondence that had passed between the Rev. B.S. Mercer, former Organising Secretary of the Mission and the Archbishop of Canterbury was considered and after full discussion it was Proposed . . . that the correspondence be allowed to remain on the table, as it was felt no good purpose could be attained by the re-opening of the matter – carried unanimously.

---

1. The text of is taken from Mercer's copy on the back of the Archbishop's letter.
2. Various St Andrew's Mission Reports show pictures (Sharpness being a good example) of churches displaying all the signs of advanced Churchmanship, whereas The Missions to Seamen *Word on the Waters* from this period does nothing to dispel the impression of Low Churchmanship.

The Missions to Seamen and the SAWCM continued as uneasy bed fellows, but now without the public invective of early Church Congresses, hinted at in Mercer's letter. A Minute of 16 October, 1930, records a Conference convened by The Missions to Seamen, attended by representatives of sailors' societies working in London, the SAWCM among them, which agreed to continue to meet quarterly. Despite this positive sign, when later in the same year The Missions to Seamen asked the SAWCM to match funding for a chaplain in Freemantle (SAWCM £100, Missions to Seamen £100, SPCK £125), the SAWCM declined 'as it would be against the principle of the working of the Mission, in addition to no funds being available'.[1]

In 1931, the SAWCM refused to sign a 'Resolution of the United Seamen's Missions and Sailors' Homes', a resolution intended to avoid overlapping of members' work, because its committee had no jurisdiction over parishes and could not in any way bind the clergy in their work on behalf of sailors, a matter in which it was, technically, correct.[2] In 1932, the SAWCM refused a grant to Townsville *because* it was a Missions to Seamen port.[3] Yet, the pressure for a thaw was increasing, though this minute of 31 October 1934, raising hope of an early Spring, was followed by no recorded action:

> Careful consideration was given to the position of the Mission and the Representative Council of Seamen's Missions and Sailors' Homes. The Memorandum submitted by the Missions to Seamen to the Representative Council was reviewed . . . the Chairman should communicate with the Archdeacon of London with a view to co-operative action between the Missions to Seamen and S. Andrew's in future.

However, meetings were taking place, though unrecorded in the SAWCM Minutes. The first intimation came on 9 February, 1939, when a Special Subcommittee's Report was presented, confirming that there had been deliberations in the months preceding:

> In the absence of the Secretaries, the Executive Committee discussed the recommendation contained in the Sub-committee's Report that Mr G.N. Croucher, the General secretary, be retired on a pension of £200 per annum. The Committee then proceeded to discuss the suggestion of the Chairman that the time had arisen for further negotiations with the Missions to Seamen. It was then decided to appoint the Rev. W.C. Brown and the Rev. G.C. Moore, to open talks with the Representatives of the Missions to Seamen, and to report back. . . .

---

1. SAWCM Minute, 11 Dec 1930.
2. SAWCM Minute 24 March 1931; see also 16 July 1931.
3. SAWCM Minute 18 Feb 1932.

A week later, following the report of these two gentlemen, it was noted that The Missions to Seamen 'seemed anxious to re-open discussions', with peaceful talks following the strained relations of the past, confirming that The Missions to Seamen was prepared to consider amalgamation with a society as stretched financially as the SAWCM; a circumstance differing from that of 1856, when a similar shortage of money in Bristol had prevented The Missions to Seamen agreeing to amalgamate with the rump of the Bristol Channel Mission.

On 16 March, 1939, the Bishop of Exeter chaired a meeting of the two societies at the office of The Missions to Seamen. Here the SAWCM conditions for a merger were laid out:

All grants to be maintained while present incumbents remained in grant-aided parishes.

The Book Department to remain whilst there is a need for it.

If possible, grants to parishes to be maintained on change of incumbents, and in the spirit of SAWCM.

All monies to be used in the spirit of SAWCM.

Incumbents of grantee parishes shall, as before, be free in their work save for sending an annual report of their work.

The Missions to Seamen shall have the right, in consultation with the Bishop of the Diocese, to discontinue grants where they are no longer required or the work is not being done.

Pension rights of SAWCM General Secretary.

Employment of the Assistant Secretary.

Hope was expressed for the continued employment of the SAWCM Book Packer.

SAWCM Representatives to be on The Missions to Seamen Committee.

A supplementary memorandum explaining these conditions was added. It emphasised the desire for continued employment for former SAWCM staff. It agreed to grants to parishes being subject to annual review, with the caveat that grants should not be withdrawn on grounds of grantee's churchmanship. It was hoped that the SAWCM's aid to seaside parishes, considered a 'good work', if not always connected with the seafarer, might continue. The desire was expressed that the amalgamation would be a true amalgamation rather than the continuation of two societies under one roof, the evidence for which would be the appearance of the SAWCM name on all publications of The Missions to Seamen in the same way as 'The Thames Mission', that is, beneath that of The Missions to Seamen.[1] The desire to unite, it said, comes 'in the interest of true religion and in the face of the increasing secularisation of the appeal for Sailors', revealing that the merger had come about with a surprising degree of skill and charity.

---

1. This has not been honoured for many years.

From the historian's point of view, if not that of the merging SAWCM, this was the end of a society the inspiration for which could be traced beyond the impression made upon The Rev. C.E. Robinson's by the work of the Rev. T.C. Childs, off Ryde, sufficiently to start something similar at Gravesend, to the work of the original Bristol Channel Mission, and John Ashley himself.

Appendix Three

Dr Ashley's Siblings

Among the pieces of information generously provided by Andrew Huckett is this list of Ashley's siblings, which he credits to the work his brother David. The only family contact that I found in the preparation of this book was a newspaper paragraph referring to Ashley's presiding at the marriage of his youngest sister, Ellen, also noted here. Andrew refers to an oil painting on the *Eirene* as the work of one of Ashley's brothers. Beyond that, his siblings seem to have impinged little upon his life as it can be traced today.

John Ashley

Abt. 1775	Born
16 September 1799	Married Elizabeth Busteed in Bristol
	1841 census – residence: Milford, Hampshire
21 February 1850	Died at Manor House, Little Marlow, Buckinghamshire (Notice)

❊ ❊ ❊

Elizabeth Busteed

Abt. 1779	Born at Dublin, Ireland
	1841 census – residence: Milford, Hampshire
	1851 census – residence: Little Marlow, Buckinghamshire (Mother-in-Law)
April 1854	Died at Eton, Buckinghamshire

❊ ❊ ❊

1.   **Son: John Ashley**
      Appendix Four

2.   Daughter: Elizabeth Martha

1803   Born at Vere, Jamaica

25 October 1808   Baptised Vere, Jamaica

3.   Son: Jephson Busteed

1805   Born at Vere, Jamaica

25 October 1808   Baptised Vere, Jamaica

4.   Daughter: Martha Mary

Abt. 1806   Born at Clifton, Gloucestershire

            1851 census – residence: Little Marlow, Buckinghamshire

            1861/1871 census – residence: 2 Park Villas, Datchet, Buckinghamshire (Head)

27 July 1871 Died at 2 Park Villas, Datchet, Buckinghamshire (Probate)

5.   Daughter: Olive

1808   Born at Vere, Jamaica

25 October 1808   Baptised Vere, Jamaica

6.   Son: Francis Busteed

9 March 1811   Born at Clifton, Gloucestershire

27 July 1826   Baptised Clifton, Gloucestershire

    Married Mary Ann (born abt. 1818 Bellary, Madras, India) in India (?)

Children: Eliza B (1832-, born Linzapore, India), Mary Ann (1836-), Olive (1841-), Ellen (1845-1917), Frederick Morewood (1846-), Sophia Charlotte (1848-1914), Caroline (1850-1915) and Frances Kate (1852-1935)

1841 census – residence: Kirkby Lonsdale, Westmorland

            1851/1871/1881 census – residence: Wooburn, Buckinghamshire

            1861 census – residence: Clerkenwell, Middlesex (Visitor)

            1891 census – residence: St. Mary Magdalene, Sussex

23 October 1897   Died at 5 East Ascent, St. Leonards on Sea, East Sussex (Probate)

Ellen Ashley

5 July 1845   Born at Holme, Westmorland

Sept 1845   Baptised Holme, Westmorland

1851 census – residence: Wooburn, Buckinghamshire

1871 census – residence: Reigate, Surrey (Governess)

1881 census – Paddington, London (Servant)

1891 census – St Mary Magdalene, Sussex (Daughter)

1901 census – St Mary Magdalene, Sussex (Head)

1911 census – Hastings, East Sussex (Head)

17 May 1917   Died at 67 London Road, St Leonards-on-Sea, East Sussex (Probate)

❀ ❀ ❀

7.   Son: Ambrose Humphrey

4 August 1812   Born at Clifton, Gloucestershire

25 August 1812 Baptised Clifton, Gloucestershire

8.   Son: Joseph Biscoe

1813   Born at Clifton, Gloucestershire

20 August 1813 Baptised Clifton, Gloucestershire

15 May 1837   Died at Gloucester (Probate)

9.   Son: Ambrose Humphreys

1815   Born at Clifton, Gloucestershire

8 June 1815   Baptised Clifton, Gloucestershire

19 August 1859 Married Sarah Ball (born abt. 1830) at St Olave's, Bermondsey (Register)

Children: Louisa (1852-), Arthur (1856-) and Ellen (1857-)

3 September 1902   Died at 3 Sion Hill, Clifton, Bristol (Probate)

10.   Daughter: Ellen Swete

1819   Born at Clifton, Gloucestershire

17 September 1819 Baptised St. Andrew's. Clifton, Gloucestershire

13 August 1845 Married William Frederick Snell (1808-) at Clifton, Bristol

[Bristol Mercury (16 August 1845): "August 13, at Clifton church, by the Rev. John Ashley LLD, Lieut-Col Snell, late of Scots Fusilier Guards, to Ellen Swete, youngest daughter of John Ashley Esq, York Crescent, Clifton, and of Ashley Hall, Jamaica."]

Children: William Frederick (1850-), Emily F. (1851-) and Jessie (1857-)

28 June 1904   Died at "Curraghmore", Bournemouth, Dorset (Probte)

Appendix Four

Dr Ashley, his Wife and Children

Andrew Huckett's summary of John Ashley's life, produced with the help of his brother David, proved a very valuable resource. A few details need slight adjustment (date of birth, attendance at Trinity College Cambridge, date of diaconate, place of burial).

1801   Born Ashley Hall, Clarendon, Jamaica
       Eldest son of John and Elizabeth Ashley

23 March 01 [John Ashley] Baptised at Vere, Jamaica (Register: 1801 JA-bapt)

1821 [John Ashley] Graduated from Trinity College, Cambridge as LLD – recorded in *Crockford* but no record at Trinity College

1824 [John Ashley] Made a deacon

3 August 1824   [John Ashley] Married Catherine Ward at All Saints' Church, Millbrook (Register)[1]
       Residence given as 'All Saints in the Town & County of Southampton'.

Notice in '*The Annual Register* Volume 66' by Edmund Brake – 'At Millbrook, near Southampton, the Rev. John Ashley, eldest son of John Ashley, esq., of Ashley-hall, Jamaica, and Clifton, Gloucestershire, to Catherine, third daughter of the late Charles Ward, esq., of Merrion-square, Dublin, and Holly-mount, Queen's country, Ireland.' (Notice: 1824-marr)

⊠ ⊠ ⊠

Catherine Ward

c.1802   Born Dublin, Ireland
       1841 census – Westbury Upon Trym, Gloucestershire
       1851 census– Easton in Gordano, Somerset
       1861 census – Walcot, Somerset
13 October 1867   Died at 28 Gay Street, Bath, Somerset (Probate)

1. *Hampshire Chronicle*, 16 August 1824. The marriage register is on microfilm in the Hampshire Record Office.

❊ ❊ ❊

1.   Daughter: Catherine

3 June 1825   Born at Downton, Wiltshire
                        (*Salisbury and Winchester Journal*, Monday 20 June 1825)
15 July 1825   Baptised St Laurence, Downton, Wiltshire, diocese of Salisbury
           1841/1851/1861 Census – residence as family

2.   Daughter: Ellen

12 May 1828   Born at Croscombe, Somerset
10 July 1828   Baptised Clifton, Gloucestershire
           1841/1851 census – residence as family
           1861 census – Weston, Somerset (visitor)
25 November 1867   Died at 28 Gay Street, Bath, Somerset (Probate)

1828   [Ashley] Ordained as a priest

3.   Son: John

17 April 1833   Born at Sion Row, Clifton, Gloucestershire
                        (*Bath Chronicle and Weekly Gazette*, Thursday 2 May 1833)
20 June 1833   Baptised, Clifton, Gloucestershire
           1841 census – residence as family
           1851 census – School at Westbury on Trym, Bristol (pupil)

4.   Daughter: Jane

1835   Born at Banwell, Somerset
24 November 1835   Baptised St John's Church, Weston
           1841/1851/1861 census – residence as family
           1871 Census – Walcot Trinity, Somerset (lodger)
13 November 1873   Died at 7 Weymouth Road, Frome, Somerset (Probate)

5.   Daughter: Elizabeth

13 June 1836   Born at Woodhill, Portishead, Somerset
                        (*Bath Chronicle and Weekly Gazette*, Thursday, 7 July 1836)
17 September 1836 Baptised at Portishead, Somerset
           1841/1851/1861 census – residence as family
           1871 census – Datchet, Buckinghamshire (niece)
           22 March 1883 Died at Russell House, York Road, Montpelier, Bristol
(Probate)

6.   **Daughter: Olive**

1837   Born at Portishead, Somerset
4 October 1837   Baptised Portishead, Somerset

1841 census [John Ashley] Clergyman Partis College, Weston, Somerset
                    (Newbridge Hill, Bath)[1]
1841 census Catherine and five children resident in
                    Westbury upon Trym, Bristol

7.   **Daughter: Mary**

1844   Born at Shirehampton, Gloucestershire
30 October 1844   Baptised St Mary's Church, Shirehampton,
                           Gloucestershire
         1851/1861 census – residence as family
         1871 census – Walcot Trinity, Somerset (lodger)
         1881 census – Walcot, Somerset
         1891 census – Bath, Somerset (Head)
28 March 1903 Died at 16 New King Street, Bath (Probate)

1851 [John Ashley] Residence Easton in Gordano, Somerset

1861 census [John Ashley] Residence Walcot, Somerset

13 October 1867 Wife Catherine died at 28 Gay Street, Bath, Somerset
(*Western Daily Press*, Friday, 18 October 1867).

15 September 1868 [John Ashley] married Elizabeth Treadwell at St
Marylebone, London (Register).

⊗ ⊗ ⊗

Elizabeth Treadwell

December 1838   Born Bristol

1851 census Brislington, Somerset (visitor)
1861 census St Mary Redcliffe, Bristol (visitor)
1871 census Gosfield, Essex
1881 census Lewisham, London
1891 census Bournemouth, Hampshire (Head)
1911 census Croydon, Surrey (lodger)

June 1917   Died in Croydon, Surrey

---

1. Ashley was staying at the time of the census with the Partis College Chaplain, the
    treasurer for the Bath Auxiliary of the Bristol Channel Mission, and subsequently a
    Director of its successor, the Bristol Channel Missions to Seamen.

❈ ❈ ❈

1871 Census [John Ashley] Residence, Gosfield, Essex

Date unknown, between 1871 and 1881   [John Ashley] Somersham, Rectory, Suffolk

1881 census   [John Ashley] Residence Lewisham, London

30 March 1886   [John Ashley] died at 6 The Grove, Clapham Common,
                          Surrey (*London Standard*, Monday, 5 April 1886) (Probate)

3 April 1886   [John Ashley] Buried Holy Trinity, Hampstead (Register)

Bibliography

Books and Pamphlets

Publication in London unless stated otherwise.

Books

Adams, H.C., *A History of Winchester College and Commoners*, 1878.

Anson, P.F., *The Call of the Cloister*, 1964.

Ashley, John, *Bristol Channel Mission Society: Correspondence between the Committee*, Bristol, 1845.

A Wykehamist (Ashley, John) *The Church of the Period*, privately published, 1871.

——, *The Church of the Period; . . . also Sequel to 'Church of the Period' with the Author's Reasons or Leaving the Church of England*, 1874, and Brisbane, Australia 1879.

Blackheath, Lee, Lewisham and Greenwich Directory, 1886.

Blake, Richard, *Evangelicals in the Royal Navy 1775-1815*, Woodbridge 2008.

Book of Homilies.

Book of Select Homilies.

Bullock, F.W.B., *Voluntary Religious Societies 1520-1799*, 1963.

Burtchaell, G.D. & Sadleir, T.U. (eds), *Alumni Dublinensis*, Dublin 1935.

Canton, W, *The History of the BFBS*, vol. ii, 1904.

Catalogue of Graduates who have proceeded to Degrees etc., Dublin 1869.

Clergy List, The, 1841.

Clerical Guide or Ecclesiastical Directory, 1829 and 1836.

Cook, Godron C., *Disease in the Merchant Navy*, Oxford 2007.

Crockford's Clerical Directory.

Down, Bill, *On Course Together*, 1989.

Gollock, G.A., *At the Sign of the Flying Angel*, 1930.

Higman, B.W., *Jamaica Surveyed* etc., University of the West Indies Press, 2001.

Jacob, Michael, *The Flying Angel Story*, 1973.

Kelly's London Suburban Directory (Southern Suburbs), 1872.

Kingsford, M.R., *The Work and Influence of William Henry Giles Kingston*, Toronto 1947.

——, 'A Cruise on the Mersey', appendix in *The Work and Influence of William Henry Giles Kingston*, Toronto 1947.

Kingston, W.H.G., *The Mersey Mission to Seamen*, Abingdon 1957.

——, *A System of General Emigration* etc., 1848.

Kverndal Roald, *Seamen's Missions: their origin and early growth*, Pasadena (CA), 1986.

———, *George Charles Smith of Penzance*, Pasadena (CA), 2012.

Lubbock, Basil, *Round the Horn before the Mast*, John Murray, 1903.

Mathews's Bristol Directory, Bristol 1839.

Miller, R.W.H., *From Shore to Shore*, Nailsworth, 1989.

———, *Priest in Deep Water*, The Lutterworth Press, Cambridge 2010.

———, *One Firm Anchor*, The Lutterworth Press, Cambridge 2012.

Milsom, C.H., *Guide to the Merchant Navy*, Glasgow, 1968.

Moody, Robert, *Mr Benett of Wiltshire*, Salisbury 2005.

Post Office London Street Directory, 1869.

Post Office London Suburban Directory, 1876.

Report of the BCM Society with list of Donors and Subscribers, Bristol 1842.

Smith, G.C., *Bethel or The Flag Unfurled*, 1819.

Strong, L.A.G., *Flying Angel: The Story of The Missions to Seamen*, 1966.

Tucker, H.W. (ed), *Classified Digest of the Records of the SPG, 1701-1892*, 1893.

Vann OP, Gerald, *The Divine Pity*, 1949.

Walrond, Mary, *Launching out into the Deep*, 1904.

Weston, Agnes, *My Life Among the Blue Jackets*, 1909.

Articles

Boon, Andrew and Webb, Julian, 'Legal Education and Training in England and Wales: Back to the Future', *Journal of Legal Education*, March 2008.

Crossley Evans, Martin, 'Nonconformist Missionary Work Among the Seamen of Bristol', in Joseph Bettey (ed.), *Historic Churches and Church Life in Bristol*, Bristol & Gloucestershire Archaeological Society, 2001.

Harcourt, Freda, 'The High Road to India', *IJMH*, Dec 2010.

Hawkins, L, 'The Mission Boats', *Sea Breezes*, January 1973.

Kennerley, Alston, 'British Seamen's Missions in the Nineteenth Century', in Lewis R. Fischer *et al.*, *The North Sea*, Stavanger 1992.

Kennerley, Alston, 'Joseph Conrad at the London Sailors' Home', *The Conradian*, vol. 33 (i), Spring 2008.

Wilcox, Martin, '"These Peaceable Times are the Devil": Royal Naval officers in the post war slump, 1815-1825', *IJMH*, August 2014.

Newspapers and Magazines

Bath Chronicle

Bristol Mercury

Essex Newsman

Exeter Flying Post

Felix Farley's Bristol Journal

Freeman's Journal (Dublin)

Gloucester Journal

Hampshire Advertiser

Ipswich Journal

London Standard

Missionary Register

New Sailors' Magazine

North Devon Journal
Salisbury & Winchester Journal
Soldiers and Sailors Magazine
Steam Packet
Taunton Courier
The Word on the Waters
Western Daily Press

Unpublished Theses

Friend, Stephen, *The Rise and Development of Christian Missions Among British Fishing Communities during the 19th Century*, MPhil, University of Leeds, 1994.
Kennerley, Alston, *British Seamen's Missions and Sailors' Homes 1815-1970*, PhD CNAA, 1989.

Websites

Legacies of British Slavery: www.ucl.ac.uk/lbs
Jamaican Family Search website: www.jamaicanfamilysearch.com

Index

Ashley, Catherine
  parents 6.
  marriage 6.
  death 7, 76.
Ashley, John
  parents 1ff, 64.
  Jamaica 1, 44.
  birth/ baptism 1.
  education
    Winchester 2f.
    Middle Temple 4f.
    Dublin university 6, 7, 14ff, 76.
  first marriage 138.
    Southampton 6.
    children 7, 14, 65, 137f.
    separation 76.
  deacon 1, 7f.
  priest 8ff.
  carriage driving 13, 37.
  assistant curacies
    Sutton Veny 9, 76.
    Downton 9f.
    Croscombe 10-12.
  founds BCM
    visits fleets 18.
    visits islanders 17f.
    severe illness 44f.
    accident on Eirene 43ff, 64.
    Letter to Press 32.
    resigns BCM 32ff, 55, 64.
  Vice President Missions to
    Seamen 58, 61.
  moves to Bath 59, 64ff.
  horse harness patent 13, 65, 73.

  prosecutes cook 66.
  prosecuted for toll fee 66.
  death of first wife 65, 67.
  moves to Kilburn 67, 76.
  second marriage 7, 67f.
  Gosfield interregnum 59, 69, 73.
  Somersham curate i/c 59, 72f.
    Ashley v. Howard 74ff.
    retirement 79ff.
  death 82.
  grave 81.
  Will 67, 83.

Bristol Board of Merchants 2, 35, 37f, 39.
Bristol Channel Mission 19, 29ff, 51, 55, 57, 59-62, 120.
Bristol Channel Seamen's Mission 19f, 43ff, 53ff.
  merges with MtS 56ff.
Bristol Merchant Seamen's Bible Association 99.
Bristol Seamen's Friend Society 99.
British & Foreign Bible Society 25, 84, 88, 114.
British & Foreign Sailors Society etc 86, 93, 95, 97.
British & International SS 94.
British Ladies Female Emigration Society 113f.
British Sailors Society 94, 127.

Caldy (Caldey) Island 18, 33f.
Canterbury, Archbishop of 19, 50f, 57, 63, 110, 121, 123, 130.

Childs, The Rev T.C.
at Devonport St Mary 49f.
recruits W.H.G.Kingston 49.
at Ryde 49, 56, 134.
resigns from MtS 50, 57, 61.
Nympton St George 57.
Collier, The Rev. Henry N. 68, 82.
Colonization Society 51.

Dublin
Ashley's inheritance 14, 65.

Eirene
building 20ff, 46.
  bye laws 22, 27f.
chapel 23.
crewing problems 28, 30f.
collision 43ff.
laying up 38f, 46, 57.
refitting 45, 50, 64.
final status 60.
Elliott, Capt. R.J. 95f, 109ff.
Evangelization Society 116.

**Flags (BCM, TCM, SAWCM,
Bethel)** 22, 24f, 33, 86, 93, 99,
111, 123, 127.
Flat Holm 17.
Franklin, Sir John 48.

Gibraltar Mission to Seamen 129.
Gosfield interregnum 59, 69, 72.

Homilies, Books of 94f.
Haward, Frederick,
Ashley v. 74f.
Haward, mother 77.

Kemball, Lieut RN 99.
Kennion, The Rev Mr 68f.
Kilburn
23 Greville Road 67.
St Augustine's Church 12, 68.
St Mary's 68.

Kingston, W.H.G. 49, 114.

Liverpool
Mariner's Church Society 100, 102.
Seamen's Friend Society etc 101f.
**London Episcopal Floating
Church Society** 19, 93, 96,
100ff, 109f.
Lunday (Lundy) **Island** 18, 104.

Maginn, William 15.
Mariners' Church Society 94f.
Marine School Society 99.
Marine Society 113.
Marten, Robert H. 93, 100.
Marylebone Parish Church 68, 82f.
Maude, The Hon Captain
Mather, E.J. 118, 122.
Merchant Seamen's Orphan Asylum
94.
**Merchant Seamen's Auxiliary Bible
Society** 25, 85, 88ff, 93, 98, 113.
Mersey Mission to Seamen 102.
Mission to Deep Sea Fishermen
118.
Mission to Seamen (Bristol) 50, 53,
64.
Missions to Seamen 49, 51ff, 58ff,
97, 114ff, 122, 124, 126, 130ff.

National Bible Society of America
89.
Naval Awakening 84f.
Naval & Military Bible Society 85,
87, 98, 113f.
Naval Correspondence Mission 85,
92.
**North & Central European Sailors'
Mission** 129.
North Sea Church Mission 123f,
128.

Prayer Book & Homily Society 85,
90, 101, 111.

Port of London Society 85f, 92, 94, 98.

Pure Literature Society 116, 122.

Religious Tract Society 85, 87, 111.
Robinson, The Rev. C.E.R. 49, 120f.
Rogers, Zebedee 85.

St Andrew's Waterside Mission 49, 52, 116f, 120-134.
School on board 22, 23, 47.
Scoresby, The Rev. William 102.
Seamen's Christian Friend Society 94, 98.
Shipwrecked & Distressed Sailors Family Fund 94.
Slaves 1.
Smith, G.C. 5, 24f, 85, 92ff.
Society for the Promotion of Christian Knowledge 85f, 113, 124.

Society for the Propagation of the Gospel 51, 86, 122, 124.
Somersham 59, 72ff.
Steep Holm 17.
Stubbin, The Rev. Newman J. 72.
Sugar 44.
Swan 110ff, 115.

Thames Church Mission 33, 48, 58, 61, 110-118, 127.
Thames revival 84f.
Treadwell, Elizabeth 67ff, 76, 81f.
Trinity College Dublin 6, 7, 14ff.
Trinity House 17f, 29, 33, 89, 109f, 129.

Visitor to Caldy 34f.

Victoria Harbour Mission 128.
Watermen's Friend Society 94.

Also Available from The Lutterworth Press

By R.W.H. Miller

Priest in Deep Water

Charles Plomer Hopkins (1861–1922), a Victorian church organist, was called by circumstance to a seamen's chaplaincy on the Indian sub-continent, and eventually achieved an unlikely apotheosis in his announcement and leadership of the first, and so far only, international seamen's strike in 1911.

Priest in Deep Water restores Hopkins to his rightful place in the public consciousness for his major contribution to the welfare of merchant seamen, to the development of the maritime apostolate in the Anglican and Roman Catholic Churches, and to the restoration of the religious life to the Church of England. At one level, this is a gripping and eventful story featuring accusations of sexual impropriety, murder, financial malpractice and other alarms, set against a backdrop of the British Empire, the Raj, and the Catholic revival in the nineteenth century Church of England. At another level, *Priest in Deep Water* is a well-researched and detailed narrative that will also be of value to maritime historians.

> In the rather unlikely event that readers . . . eagerly anticipate titillation
> and skullduggery they will be disappointed. The "regular" reader on
> the other hand will be fascinated and hopefully seize an opportunity
> to encourage internationally situated, comparative studies of church,
> chapel and seafarers. This recommendation comes from an atheist.
> **Prof Tony Lane**, Cardiff University
> (Review in *International Journal of Maritime History, vol.* XX111(1), 386f)

*Available now with more excellent titles in Paperback, Hardback,
PDF and ePub formats from* **The Lutterworth Press**

www.lutterworth.com

Also Available from The Lutterworth Press
By R.W.H. Miller

One Firm Anchor

One Firm Anchor uncovers nineteen centuries of contact between the churches and the seafarer. Until now, much has been written of the sea, but little about the relationship of the seafarer to Christianity.

R.W.H. Miller adeptly sets out the origins of seafaring mission in the Early Church, the medieval era and considers the early modern period. A detailed exploration follows of the developments in the nineteenth century which saw the foundation of The Missions to Seamen, the British Sailors' Society, the Apostleship of the Sea and the Mission to Deep Sea Fishermen. Particular attention is given to the work of the Catholic Church during the nineteenth and twentieth centuries. Miller reveals the role of key figures, such as G.C. Smith, John Ashley, Francis Goldie SJ and Peter Anson, whose determination and vision instigated real change.

One Firm Anchor is both a triumph of scholarship and a lively narrative of heroic ministry and (occasionally) erring clergy, and will appeal to historian, academic, and student alike.

> Robert Miller has, with his new book, given a great and lasting service to maritime mission studies.
>
> **Dr Roald Kverndal**, author of *Seamen's Missions*
> (Review in *The Mariner's Mirror*, vol. 99:2, 252f)

> Miller . . . begins to reveal the extent to which maritime ministry has been a product and, perhaps, facilitator of sweeping historical forces such as empire and globalization. . . .
>
> The effect is that readers gain a better sense of the Church's position within the maritime world, and the ways in which that position was shaped by factors unique to the seafarer's lifestyle.
>
> **Johnathan Thayer**, Seamen's Church Institute of New York
> (Review in *International Journal of Maritime History*, vol. XXV(1), 404f)

Available now with more excellent titles in Paperback, Hardback,
PDF and ePub formats from **The Lutterworth Press**

www.lutterworth.com